T0305477

Festival Encounters

Festivals and events are of enormous significance to many communities around the world. They can have historic, religious, cultural and traditional significance, and they are also important parts of community building.

This book focuses on these small-scale, non-metropolitan events (i.e. rural, regional and peri-urban) to explore the complex relationships between place, community and identity and the ways in which festival events bring these into being. By drawing on the notion of 'encounter', this book examines how festivals and events can be seen primarily as spaces where different people meet. This notion of encounter helps us to understand how conviviality and social relations are developed, and what this then means in terms of social cohesion and social justice. It also draws on current theoretical and methodological approaches that can tell us about the role of festivals in contemporary life, and it includes the sensual approach, the geographies of affect and emotion, the notion of the right to the city and non-representation theory.

The book brings together these perspectives and examines their relevance in the community events context, identifying and discussing theoretical frameworks drawn from (including but not limited to) human geography, sociology, anthropology, leisure studies and urban planning, as well as tourism and event studies. For these reasons, *Festival Encounters* will be a valuable read for students and academics working on a wide range of disciplines.

Michelle Duffy is an Associate Professor in Human Geography in the School of Environmental and Life Sciences, University of Newcastle, Australia. In broad terms, her research explores how interactions between people and place contribute to notions of community and identity, and hence the processes of belonging and alienation. Her work includes a critical examination of community resilience, well-being, and sustainability; the significance of emotion and affect in creating notions of belonging and exclusion; the role of art practice – specifically that of sound, music and performance – in creating and/or challenging notions of identity and belonging in public spaces and public events; and an exploration of the body as a means of embodied, emotional and affective communication.

Judith Mair is a Senior Lecturer in Event Management in the Tourism Cluster of the UQ Business School, University of Queensland, Australia. Her research interests include the impacts of events on community and society; consumer behaviour in events and tourism; the relationship between events and climate change; and business and major events. Judith is working on a number of projects including researching the links between events and social capital; understanding the benefits for attendees of attending conferences and conventions; and assessing the potential impacts of climate change on the tourism and events sector. She is the author of *Conferences and Conventions: A Research Perspective* and *Events and Sustainability*, both published by Routledge in 2015, as well as more than 35 academic papers in internationally recognised journals. http://researchers.uq.edu.au/researcher/10389

Routledge Advances in Event Research

Edited by Warwick Frost and Jennifer Laing
Department of Marketing, Tourism and Hospitality,
La Trobe University, Australia

For a full list of titles in this series, please visit www.routledge.com/tourism/
series/RAERS.

Festival Encounters

Theoretical Perspectives on
Festival Events

Michelle Duffy and Judith Mair

Routledge
Taylor & Francis Group

LONDON AND NEW YORK

First published 2018
by Routledge
2 Park Square, Milton Park, Abingdon, Oxon OX14 4RN

and by Routledge
605 Third Avenue, New York, NY 10017

First issued in paperback 2021

Routledge is an imprint of the Taylor & Francis Group, an informa business

© 2018 Michelle Duffy and Judith Mair

Publisher's Note
The publisher has gone to great lengths to ensure the quality of this reprint but
points out that some imperfections in the original copies may be apparent.

British Library Cataloguing-in-Publication Data
A catalogue record for this book is available from the British Library

Library of Congress Cataloging-in-Publication Data
A catalog record for this book has been requested

ISBN 13: 978-1-03-224214-9 (pbk)
ISBN 13: 978-1-138-18602-6 (hbk)

DOI: 10.4324/9781315644097

Typeset in Times New Roman
by Apex CoVantage, LLC

Michelle: To my mum, Denise
Judith: To my boys, Stewart and Scott

Contents

Figures

1 Introduction

This book will consider the interrelationship between festivals and communities on a number of levels. It will look at how festivals have traditionally been celebrations of various notions or definitions of community, and it will also consider how the modern world is changing this. The book will also examine how festivals have become an instrument of policy, particularly at the local authority level, staged and funded with the aim of achieving particular policy goals, often around economic and community development.

In order to position our book, we will start by considering how we are defining some of the concepts that we will be using, starting with the concepts of 'festival' and 'community'.

Definitions of festivals

The structure and role of festivals in the contemporary world have their origins in religious celebrations and public cultural practices. Many festivals retain links to specific traditions (Ahmed 1992; Diaz-Barriga 2003; Nolan and Nolan 1992; Ruback et al. 2008). Religious pilgrimages, the feast days of saints, and carnival are events that purposely separate the time and space of the festival from that of everyday life. Activities such as rituals and associated symbolic practices are used as a means to identify group members. They also help reinforce Durkheim's (1915/1976) notions of binding people together through the festive play and rhythm of special events, which then encourages opportunities for enacting a collective consciousness (Eade and Sallnow 2000; Falassi 1987; Handelman 1990; Sepp 2014).

Festivals have been defined in various ways over the years, and the disciplinary background, as well as the paradigm of authors, has influenced these definitions. For example, Falassi (1987: 2), coming from an anthropological tradition, defines festivals as 'a sacred or profane time of celebration, marked by special observances'. Falassi (1987) also points to the display, consumption and competitive rites that form part of a festival. Culture is also an important part of festivals for geographers. Gibson and Connell (2011: 4) define a festival as an 'irregular, one-off, annual or bi-annual event with an emphasis on celebrating, promoting or exploring some aspect of local culture'. Getz (2005: 21), on the other hand, coming from a business perspective, opts for a much broader definition of festivals as 'themed, public celebrations'. Festivals can be considered to be different from other types of planned events because of their celebratory or thanksgiving focus (Getz et al. 2010; Sharpe 2008) and the fact that they incorporate many 'cultural and social dimensions of ritual and symbolism' (Getz et al. 2010: 31). The most common typology for events is that proposed initially by Jago and Shaw (1998) which divides events into mega, major, hallmark and local (or minor). Festivals may be considered in this typology in relation to their size, rather than any other specific characteristics. Arguably, there is no agreed typology for describing and categorising festivals.

Getz (2010) undertook a review with the aim of defining and delimiting festival studies. Drawing from the tourism, hospitality and events literature, he identified three major discourses from this review – a classical discourse, concerning the roles, meanings and impacts of festivals in society and culture; an instrumentalist discourse, where festivals are viewed as tools to be used in economic development, particularly in relation to tourism and place marketing; and an event management discourse, which focused on the production and marketing of festivals and the management of festival organizations (Getz 2010). His first conclusion was that the classical discourse was under-acknowledged in extant festival studies and that more connections should be made between festival studies and other disciplines such as sociology and anthropology. Additionally, Getz (2010) noted that there was an over-emphasis on consumer motivations and economic impacts, with a corresponding lack of emphasis on comparative and cross-cultural studies. He concluded that a triple bottom line approach was lacking in much of the research included in his review (Getz 2010). However, as this review focused on studies published in the areas of tourism, hospitality and events, there is a possibility that these conclusions may apply only in those contexts.

Other reviews of festivals have also been limited by a focus on papers published in journals associated with only one discipline or field of study. For example, Cudny (2014) took a geographical perspective and identified that much of the existing work could be categorized under a few key themes including culture, a social perspective, economic impacts, political and historical issues and time-space analyses – research focusing on the spatial distribution of different types of festivals and their evolution in time. Cudny (2014) called for more theoretical research to underpin the future development of festival studies.

In anthropology and sociology, festivals are often conceptualised as events set apart from the everyday (Durkheim 1915/1976). Engagement through rituals enables participants to enter another state, one of in-between-ness or ambiguity, defined by anthropologists as a 'state of liminality.' The liminal period temporarily suspends conventional social rules, thus opening up a space in which existing tensions may be resolved or where change may be facilitated (Gluckman 1955; Schechner 2003; Turner 1957, 1969). Liminal events are understood to offer some contact with the sacred or divine. Hence, they support the individual's transformation into a full participant of the community or group, exemplified in anthropological literature by ceremonies of initiation (Lewis and Dowsey-Magog 1993).

Frost (2015) reviewed anthropological studies of festivals, which broadly position festivals as sites of cultural practice and experience. Frost (2015) contends that festivals have been studied over a long period of time from an anthropological standpoint and, therefore, any contention that festivals and events are a new area of study should be rejected. Nonetheless, it is argued (Getz 2010) that the ethnographic approach that commonly informs anthropological studies can go only so far in terms of understanding and conceptualizing a range of business, management and tourism issues related to festivals.

Discussion of community

Community is most often understood as being those people, usually of a specific locale (be that real or virtual), who share a set of values and social relations characterised by personal connections. Yet many commentators have noted that in Western communities generally there has been a loss of a sense of community. Sennett (1970) has argued that the new global economy has led to increased anxiety and a much more fragmented sense of identity. This new global economy is embedded within processes of globalisation in which the turbulence and uncertainty generated by the rapid circulation of people and ideas, and the sorts of strategies created in response to social change, has led to feelings of social disintegration and disconnection (Sernau 2012). This, in turn, has led to questions over who has the right to belong, a contestation that is played out in the public spaces of cities and towns (Harvey 2003; Lefebvre 1996; Purcell 2002). In a more nuanced reading of public space, Butler (2015) points out that debates about who has freedom of assembly – that is, who can rightly claim to be of 'the people' – is part of an inherent tension in democratic theory. As she explains,

> when bodies assemble on the street, in the square, or in other forms of public space (including virtual ones) they are exercising a plural and performative right to appear, one that asserts and instates the body in the midst of the political field, and which, in its expressive and signifying function, delivers a bodily demand for a more liveable set of economic, social, and political conditions no longer afflicted by induced forms of precarity.
>
> (Butler 2015: 11)[1]

Public spaces are important sites for social relations, because it is here that different types and forms of relational networks overlap and meet. However, tensions can arise because of perceived or real fears about crime, violence and terrorism; racial intolerance; uncertainty; and insecurity, such that some groups feel uncomfortable and excluded from public space – and, as Butler (2015) suggests, such exclusion is deliberate. Hence the once common idea that public space is a shared space for social interaction comes under question. As Brown (2012: 801) notes, 'the capacity to share public space has been identified as a crux contemporary issue, especially where claims to space are being made through increasingly diverse subjectivities.' How individuals and groups respond to diversity is itself varied: some people celebrate these everyday spaces as a representation of a cosmopolitan sense of shared connectedness; others may feel uncomfortable, excluded or alienated; still others will use public space as a means to challenge normative processes of place making. Nonetheless, there is a strong argument for the openness of public space, because it is here that we can encounter and engage with the 'vital mix of uses critical to urban life' (Vidler 2001 online), the 'common ground where civility and our collective sense of what may be called "publicness" are developed and expressed (Francis 1989: 149; see also Iveson 2007). We therefore need to carefully consider the ways in which power is embedded within public space; that is, how difference is defined within the public sphere and the ways in which otherness and hence 'not belonging' are constructed.

One popular form of creating and/or re-affirming a sense of community has been to generate festival events that serve to create a sense of shared identity and belonging (Gibson and Connell 2005; Quinn 2003). What underpins such festivals is the desire to promote social cohesion through discourses of an official 'imagined' community (Anderson 1991), even as others suggest that tension and debate – perhaps better conceptualised as *agonism* (Mouffe 1996) – plays an important role in acknowledging the heterogeneity of contemporary life and thus retains the potential to transform democratic politics. Therefore, festival events are much more than simply a source of financial gain; rather, the processes of festivals enable notions of place, community, identity and belonging to be created, questioned and experienced. Festivals are significant to a politics of belonging because of the ways in which they are utilised as a common framework for community celebration and for reinvigorating notions of a shared community (Jepson and Clarke 2015). In this framework, these community-oriented events are most often actively constructed by local government, organisations and audiences as being about local communities situated in a particular place and celebrating a local communal identity (De Bres and Davis 2001; Duffy 2000; Getz 2007; Jaeger and Mykletun 2013; van Winkle et al. 2013) or generating new forms of identification (Auerbach 1991; Lavenda 1992; Lewis and Dowsey-Magog 1993; Picard 2015). This focus on a celebration of 'community' constructed within a festival framework is particularly evident in places of cultural and ethnic diversity, where organisers as well as participants view social cohesion as the goal of the event (Auerbach 1991; Permezel and Duffy 2007). Festivals are viewed as a means to contribute to processes that facilitate new forms of belonging and enabling active public engagement, as well as incorporating activities that foster social harmony and integration (Derrett 2003; Duffy 2003, 2005; Duffy et al. 2007; Gibson and Connell 2005; Kong and Yeoh 1997; Leal 2015; Lee et al. 2012a; McClinchey 2015; Österlund-Pötzsch 2004; Permezel and Duffy 2007; Quinn 2003; Shukla 1997; White 2015). A focus on enabling active public engagement is understood as especially important for promoting ongoing dialogue and negotiation between members of diverse communities, such as migrant, diasporic and transnational groups (Permezel and Duffy 2007). Festivals have a powerful and intoxicating effect that is significant to sustaining and transforming social life. Festivals, then, not only recreate and celebrate a feeling of connection to place and people, but also are sites in which notions of community and who belongs can be playfully questioned and at times more rigorously challenged.

What is also important in this focus on the festival as a site of community identity and notions of belonging is that the festival event is considered congruent with its geographical and social context. Increasingly the focus in some fields of festival research is for a better understanding of the influences and effects of the festival event as it spills out beyond its temporal and spatial boundaries, a process called *festivalisation* (Roche 2011; Yardimci 2007). Festivalisation processes draw on collective understandings and practices of space, time and agency that are then deployed so as to shape communal notions of identity and belonging (Roche 2011). Moreover, these events are interpolated into a community's calendar of "memorable and narratable pasts, with the sociocultural rhythm of life in the present, and with anticipated futures" (Roche 2011: 127–128; see also Duffy et al. 2011). Festivals, rather than transcending the everyday, are now examined for the ways they are intimately embedded within the public sphere as normative and at times transformative processes (Giorgi and Sassatelli 2011). As such these events are recognised as political mechanisms that help constitute individual feelings of acceptance and belonging within an imagined, collective sense of community.

Yet the notion of belonging that underpins the festival event is complex and problematic. Defined in terms of a politics of belonging, these feelings of attachment create a sense of connection in particular ways or to particular collective identities, and these attachments and identities are embedded within the narratives that people tell about themselves as a community. We can belong in many different ways and to many different objects, people and places. Such senses of belonging and connection range from an abstract feeling about what we think of as 'our' place or community to a much more concrete notion of belonging in which we participate in activities that display our allegiances, such as dance and other cultural performances, the wearing of certain costumes, and the availability of specific foods that are viewed as representative of certain communal identities. These processes and activities, and the feelings they produce, are dynamic things, arising in and out of certain moments of generating community. In an increasingly globalised world – where cultural difference, in its broadest sense, is the norm in everyday life, particularly in urban but increasingly in regional locations – local communities become places through which issues of difference, and the dynamics of coexistence, isolation, inclusion and racism, are played out. Festivals have been proliferating in response to a range of social and planning policies that encourage participation by all so as to increase opportunities for interaction, thereby minimising social isolation and facilitating greater understanding of difference. However, there remains a need to critically engage with such ideas and practices.

There is an assumption in much of the policy research that festivals generate social benefits. Indeed, as Fincher and Iveson (2008: 176, 177) point out, festivals 'have become an established part of the repertoire of contemporary urban planning' in the hope that 'festivals will promote greater tolerance and understanding.' This is a reiterated in the work of Dunn et al. (2001: 1577) in their survey of multiculturalism in Australia, which finds that policies that attempt to foster positive intercommunal relations 'are largely designed either to mitigate tensions or to celebrate cultural diversity.' Although this may be one successful approach to the challenges of diversity, multicultural policies nevertheless pathologise difference. For example, Hage (1998) suggests that Australian multiculturalism and its promotion of the tolerance of difference are strategies aimed at reproducing and disguising relationships of white power, a 'form of symbolic violence in which a mode of domination is presented as a form of egalitarianism' (1998: 87). Furthermore, he argues that multiculturalism operates within an illusory space in which the '[w]hite fantasy of the multicultural collection are imagined as dead cultures that cannot have a life of their own except through the "peaceful coexistence" that regulates the collection' (1998: 163). The festival is not about inclusivity, he argues, but rather about containment and the subsequent enrichment of Anglo-Australia through a managed Anglo-Celtic appropriation of this diversity (Hage 1998; see also Valentine and Sadgrove 2012; Valentine 2007). This means, then, that the festival is a paradoxical thing; festival events function as a form of social integration and cohesion, while simultaneously they are sites of subversion and protest. It is precisely this paradoxical nature that creates the festival's socio-spatial and political significance (Duffy and Waitt 2011).

Critiques such as Hage's are important in determining social policy in the contemporary world, where issues of diversity and difference, especially in terms of race and ethnicity, are part of attempts to 'manage public space in ways that build sociality and civic engagement out of the encounter between strangers' (Amin 2008: 6). As Fincher and Iveson (2008: 3) argue, planning efforts, particularly at the local level, need a 'set of "social logics"' that respond to different kinds of diversity such that opportunities are provided for increased sociality. Yet, the challenge in festival research lies in understanding, identifying and measuring the impacts of events on the local community in ways that capture their intangible benefits – such as civic pride, community cohesion, community identity and a sense of belonging – and addressing issues of social justice in ways that acknowledge the complex, fragmentary, difficult and even agonistic social relations that operate in public spaces. Such partial and fragmentary relations that unfold during and around the festival event are significant to the formation and transformation of what community means for that particular time and place. This, in turn, has implications for the social and spatial organisations of neighbourhoods, towns and cities and how issues of social capital, cohesion and justice are valued. For Fincher and Iveson (2008: 3), planning and policy needs to do more than celebrate, embrace or accommodate difference and diversity; it is 'a matter of disentangling the different kinds of diversity which characterise city life and distinguishing between those forms of diversity which are just and those that are unjust.' They provide a set of social logics – redistribution, recognition and encounter – as a means to respond to different kinds of diversity. It is the third social logic, the encounter, which offers a means to explore in greater detail the assumed beneficial processes and outcomes of the festival.

This book is structured in such a way as to allow the reader to consider some of the fundamental concepts and theories that are important and relevant to understanding festivals and the encounter. Following this Introduction, Chapter 2 will review some of the existing research on festivals and events that helps to situate the book within the existing body of knowledge in this area. In particular, Chapter 2 will consider some of the key overarching themes in festival research to date around festivals and people, space and emotions, and it will also look at how festivals and tourism are interrelated.

The book then moves on to consider the conceptual framework of our approach to understanding the encounter. Chapter 3, *Encounter as our underpinning theory*, examines how public spaces are constituted through encounter and examines the social logic of encounter. Chapter 4, *Rituals of community: encounters of cohesion and subversion,* considers key aspects of festivals themselves, such as the rites and rituals associated with festivals, notions of *communitas* and liminality, the carnivalesque and the process and results of festivalisation. Chapter 5, *Mobilities and the shaping of encounter*, seeks to view festivals through the lens of mobilities and the new mobilities paradigm. Chapter 6, *Festivals, non-representation theory and encounter,* considers festival bodies, affect and emotion, and the notion of affective political terrains.

This book also looks at a number of different ways in which the encounter is activated, particularly in relation to the community and social objectives and outcomes sought by local authorities and festival funding bodies. Chapter 7, *Festivals and social justice,* considers festivals in relation to social justice, examining how social justice is understood in different parts of the world and considering how local authorities are looking to festivals to achieve social justice aims. Chapter 8, *Social inclusion, social exclusion and encounter,* looks at notions of social inclusion and social exclusion, with discussion of the social policy debates around inclusion and exclusions, as well as some investigation of how festivals may contribute to social inclusion aims, or, conversely, how they may act as spaces of exclusion. Chapter 9, *Festivals and social capital,* studies the links between festivals and social capital, with particular reference to the ideas of bridging, bonding and linking social capital and how these can be related to festivals.

Finally, the book considers some case studies that exemplify and illustrate some of the conceptual ideas and theoretical perspectives that we have discussed in the book. Chapter 10, which focuses on the Yakkerboo Festival, examines this in relation to historical notions of the idealised community and compares these notions with the current, transitioning, community. Chapter 11 concerns Experience!, a multicultural festival set up by a local authority with the specific objective of acknowledging the diversity within the community and trying to increase tolerance and understanding of that diversity. Chapter 12 takes the case of the Clunes Book Festival and considers the impact of in-migration on rural locations and how the festival model is used both to activate opportunities for economic development or regeneration and to enhance social connectedness through cultural activities. Finally, Chapter 13 examines the Noosa Jazz Festival and takes a sensual geographies perspective, considering how the embodiment of participants and spectators contributes to feelings of community.

Chapter 14 will provide some conclusions and closing thoughts about festivals and the encounter.

Conclusion

Festivals are very much about celebrating a sense of community, be that one connected to a community's shared history, one connected to a need to re-establish a sense of identity or one arising out of shared interests or values. Much work has been done on the ways in which festivals can be used to construct particular ideas about identity and notions of belonging (Derrett 2003; Duffy et al. 2007; Duffy and Waitt 2011; Gibson and Connell 2005; Kong and Yeoh 1997; Quinn 2003). The festival is most often understood as an occasion characterised by the festival's location and the community involved, be that a community with a long-established connection to a particular place, one that has had a more recent migration and settlement, or one that differs in some way from the dominant group. However, as Fincher and Iveson (2008: 146) suggest, the festival also offers a means to facilitate an exploration and experimentation in the design of our communities, and this can mean 'planning for disorder.' What this means, they argue, is that city and town planners need to pay attention to the 'importance of small-scale, casual and unpredictable encounters' (Fincher and Iveson 2008: 146), because it is through fostering encounters with difference and diversity that we can start to address injustice and inequality. This book presents a set of theoretical approaches and case studies that help uncover how the festival provides opportunities for such unpredictable encounters and what these may mean for thinking about ways to enhance social connectedness and inclusion.

Note

1 Although, as Fincher and Iveson (2008: 2) suggest, 'some forms of homogeneity might not be a bad thing, and [. . .] some forms of diversity are not necessarily desirable.'

References

Ahmed, Z. U. (1992). Islamic pilgrimage (Hajj) to Ka'aba in Makkah (Saudi Arabia): An important international tourism activity. *Journal of Tourism Studies*, 3(1), pp. 35–43.

Amin, A. (2002). Ethnicity and the multicultural city: Living with diversity. *Environment and Planning A*, 34(6), pp. 959–980.

Amin, A. (2008). Collective culture and urban public space. *City*, 12(1), pp. 5–24.

Anderson, B. (1991). *Imagined Communities: Reflections on the Origin and Spread of Nationalism*. London, New York: Verso.

Auerbach, S. (1991). The brokering of ethnic folklore: Issues of selection and presentation at a multicultural festival. In Stern, S. and Cicala, J. A. (Eds.) *Creative Ethnicity: Symbols and Strategies of Contemporary Ethnic Life*. Logan: Utah State University Press, pp. 223–238.

Brown, K. (2012). Sharing public space across difference: Attunement and the contested burdens of choreographing encounter. *Social and Cultural Geography*, 13(7), pp. 801–820.

Butler, J. (2015). *Notes Towards a Performative Theory of Assembly*. Cambridge, MA: Harvard University Press.

Cudny, W. (2014). Festivals as a subject for geographical research. *Geografisk Tidsskrift-Danish Journal of Geography*, 114(2), pp. 132–142.

De Bres, K. and Davis, J. (2001). Celebrating group and place identity: A case study of a new regional festival. *Tourism Geographies*, 3(3), pp. 326–337.

Derrett, R. (2003). Making sense of how festivals demonstrate a community's sense of place. *Event Management*, 8(1), pp. 49–58.

Díaz-Barriga, M. (2003). Materialism and sensuality: Visualizing the devil in the festival of our lady of Urkupiña. *Visual Anthropology*, 16(2–3), pp. 245–261.

Duffy, M. (2000). Lines of drift: Festival participation and performing a sense of place. *Popular Music*, 19(1), pp. 51–64.

Duffy, M. (2003). We find ourselves again? Recreating identity through performance in the community music festival. *Australasian Music Research*, 7, pp. 103–112.

Duffy, M. (2005). Performing identity within a multicultural framework. *Social and Cultural Geography*, 6(5), pp. 677–692.

Duffy, M. and Waitt, G. (2011). Rural festivals and processes of belonging. In: Gibson, C. and Connell, J. (Eds.) *Festival Places: Revitalising Rural Australia*. Clevedon, UK: Channel View Press, pp. 44–59.

Duffy, M., Waitt, G. R. and Gibson, C. R. (2007). Get into the groove: The role of sound in generating a sense of belonging in street parades. *Altitude: A Journal of Emerging Humanities Work*, 8, pp. 1–32.

Dunn, K., Thompson, S., Hanna, B., Murphy, P. and Burnley, I. (2001). Multicultural policy within local government in Australia. *Urban Studies*, 38(13), pp. 2477–2494.

Durkheim, E. (1915/1976). *Elementary Forms of Religious Life*. Trans. J.W. Swain. Second edition. London: Allen & Unwin

Eade, J. and Sallnow, M. J. (2000). *Contesting the Sacred: The Anthropology of Christian Pilgrimage*. Urbana, Chicago: University of Illinois.

Falassi, A. (1987). *Time Out of Time: Essays on the Festival*. Albuquerque: University of New Mexico Press.

Fincher, R. and Iveson, K. (2008). *Planning and Diversity in the City: Redistribution, Recognition and Encounter*. Hampshire, UK: Palgrave Macmillan.

Francis, M. (1989). Control as a dimension of public space quality. In: M Sorkin (Ed.) *Variations on a Theme Park*. New York: Hill and Wang, pp. 147–172.

Frost, N. (2015). Anthropology and festivals: Festival ecologies. *Ethnos: Journal of Anthropology*, 81(4), pp. 569–583.

Getz, D. (2005). *Event Management and Event Tourism* (2nd ed). Putnam Valley, NY: Cognizant Communications.

Getz, D. (2007). *Event Studies: Theory, Research and Policy for Planned Events*. Oxford: Butterworth-Heinemann.

Getz, D. (2010). The nature and scope of festival studies. *International Journal of Event Management Research*, 5(1), pp. 1–47.

Getz, D., Andersson, T. and Carlsen, J. (2010). Festival management studies: Developing a framework and priorities for comparative and cross-cultural research. *International Journal of Event and Festival Management*, 1(1), pp. 29–59.

Gibson, C. and Connell, J. (2005). *Music and Tourism: On the Road Again*. Clevedon: Channel View Publications.

Gibson, C. and Connell, J. (2011). *Festival Places: Revitalising Rural Places*. Bristol, Buffalo, Toronto: Channel View Publications.

Gibson, C., Connell, J., Waitt, G. and Walmsley, J. (2009). *Reinventing Rural Places: The Extent and Impact of Festivals in Rural and Regional Australia*. Wollongong, NSW: University of Wollongong.

Giorgi, L. and Sassatelli, M. (2011). Introduction. In: Delanty, G. (Ed.) *Festivals and the Cultural Public Sphere*. London and New York:Routledge, pp. 1–11.

Gluckman, M. (1955). *Custom and Conflict in Africa*. London: Blackwell.

Hage, G. (1998). *White Nation: Fantasies of White Supremacy in a Multicultural Society*. Annandale, NSW: Pluto Press.

Handelman, D. (1990). *Models and Mirrors: Towards an Anthropology of Public Events*. Cambridge: Cambridge University Press.

Harvey, D. (2003). The right to the city. *International Journal of Urban and Regional Research*, 27(4), pp. 939–941.

Iveson, K. (2007). *Publics and the City*. Oxford: Blackwell.

Jaeger, K. and Mykletun, R. J. (2013). Festivals, identities, and belonging. *Event Management*, 17(3), pp. 213–226.

Jago, L. K. and Shaw, R. N. (1998). Special events: A conceptual and definitional framework. *Festival Management and Event Tourism*, 5(1), pp. 21–32.

Jepson, A. and Clarke, A. (Eds.). (2015). *Exploring Community Festivals and Events*. Abingdon: Routledge.

Kong, L. and Yeoh, B. S. (1997). The construction of national identity through the production of ritual and spectacle: An analysis of National Day parades in Singapore. *Political Geography*, 16(3), pp. 213–239.

Lavenda, R. H. (1992). Festivals and the creation of public culture: Whose voice(s)? In: Karp, I., Mullen Kreamer, C. and Lavine, S. (Eds.) *Museums and Communities: The Politics of Public Culture*. Washington, DC: Smithsonian Institute Press, pp. 76–104.

Leal, J. (2015). Festivals, group making, remaking and unmaking. *Ethnos: Journal of Anthropology*, 81(4), pp. 584–599.

Lee, I. S., Arcodia, C. and Lee, T. J. (2012). Key characteristics of multicultural festivals: A critical review of the literature. *Event Management*, 16(1), pp. 93–101.

Lefebvre, H. (1996). *Writing on Cities*. Oxford: Blackwell.

Lewis, L. and Dowsey-Magog, P. (1993). The Maleny 'Fire Event': Rehearsals toward neo-liminality'. *The Australian Journal of Anthropology*, 4(3), pp. 198–219.

McClinchey, K. A. (2008). Urban ethnic festivals, neighbourhoods, and the multiple realities of marketing place. *Journal of Travel and Tourism Marketing*, 25(3), pp. 251–264.

McClinchey, K. (2015). 'Something greater than the sum of its parts': Narratives of sense of place at a community multicultural festival. In: Jepson, A. and Clarke, A. (Eds.) *Exploring Community Festivals and Events*, Routledge, Oxon and New York, pp. 137–156.

Mouffe, C. (1996). On the itineraries of democracy: An interview with Chantal Mouffe. *Studies in Political Economy*, 49, pp. 131–148.

Nolan, M. L. and Nolan, S. (1992). Religious sites as tourism attractions in Europe. *Annals of Tourism Research*, 19(1), pp. 68–78.

Österlund-Pötzsch, S. (2004). Communicating ethnic heritage: Swedish-speaking Finn descendants in North America. In: Kockel, U. and Craith, M. N. (Eds.) *Communicating Cultures*. Munster: Li, pp. 14–41.

Permezel, M. and Duffy, M. (2007). Negotiating cultural difference in local communities: The role of the body, dialogues and performative practices in local communities. *Geographical Research*, 45(4), pp. 358–375.

Picard, D. (2015). The festive frame: Festivals as mediators for social change. *Ethnos: Journal of Anthropology*, 81(4), pp. 600–616.

Purcell, M. (2002). Excavating Lefebvre: The right to the city and its urban politics of the inhabitant. *GeoJournal*, 58, pp. 99–108.

Quinn, B. (2003). Symbols, practices and myth-making: Cultural perspectives on the Wexford Festival Opera, *Tourism Geographies*, 5(3), pp. 329–349.

Roche, M. (2011). Festivalisation, cosmopolitanism and European culture: On the sociocultural significance of mage-events. In: Giorgi, L., Sassatelli, M. and Delanty, G. (Eds.) *Festivals and the Cultural Public Sphere*. London and New York: Routledge, pp. 124–141.

Ruback, R. B., Pandey, J. and Kohli, N. (2008). Evaluations of a sacred place: Role and religious belief at the Magh Mela. *Journal of Environmental Psychology*, 28(2), pp. 174–184.

Schechner, R. (2003). *Performance Theory*. London: Routledge.

Sennett, R. (1970). *The Uses of Disorder: Personal Identity and City Life*. New York: Knopf.

Sepp, T. (2014). Pilgrimage and pilgrim hierarchies in vernacular discourse: Comparative notes from the Camino de Santiago and Glastonbury. *Journal of Ethnology and Folkloristics*, 8(1), pp. 23–52.

Sernau, S. (2012). *Global Problems: The Search for Equity, Peace, and Sustainability*. Boston: Pearson.

Sharpe, E. K. (2008). Festivals and social change: Intersections of pleasure and politics at a community music festival. *Leisure Sciences*, 30(2), pp. 217–234.

Shukla, S. (1997). Building diaspora and nation: The 1991 'Cultural Festival of India'. *Cultural Studies*, 11(2), 296–315.

Turner, V. (1957). *Schism and Continuity in an African Society: A Study of Ndembu Village Life*. Manchester: Manchester University Press.

Turner, V. (1969). *The Ritual Process: Structure and Anti-Structure*. Chicago: Aldine Press.

Valentine, G. (2007). Theorising and researching intersectionality: A challenge for feminist geography. *The Professional Geographer*, 59, pp. 10–21.

Valentine, G. and Sadgrove, J. (2012). Lived difference: A narrative account of spatiotemporal processes of social differentiation. *Environment and Planning A*, 44(9), pp. 2049–2063.

Van Winkle, C., Woosnam, K. and Mohammed, A. (2013). Sense of community and festival attendance. *Event Management*, 17(2), pp. 155–163.

Vidler, A. (2001). Aftermath: A city transformed: Designing 'Defensible Space'. *New York Times*, September 23 [online]. Available at: www.nytimes.com/2001/09/23/weekinreview/aftermath-a-city-transformed-designing-defensible-space.html?scp=1andsq=september%2023,%202001,%20vidlerandst=cse [Accessed 31 March 2017].

White, L. (2015). Swiss and Italian identities: Exploring heritage, culture and community in regional Australia. In: Jepson, A. and Clarke, A. (Eds.) *Exploring Community Festivals and Events*. Abingdon, New York: Routledge, pp. 197–211.

Yardimci, S. (2007). *Festivalising Difference: Privatisation of Culture and Symbolic Exclusion*. Florence: European University Institute.

2 Approaches to festival research

Introduction

The structure and role of festivals in the contemporary world have their origins in religious celebrations and public cultural practices. Many festivals retain links to specific traditions (Ahmed 1992; Diaz-Barriga 2003; Nolan and Nolan 1992; Ruback et al. 2008). Religious pilgrimages, the feast days of saints, and carnival are events that purposely separate the time and space of the festival from that of everyday life. Activities such as rituals and associated symbolic practices are used as a means to identify group members. They also help reinforce Durkheim's (1915/1976) notions of binding people together through the festive play and rhythm of special events, which then encourages opportunities for enacting a collective consciousness (Eade and Sallnow 2000; Falassi 1987; Handelman 1990; Sepp 2014).

This book intends to propose a new lens through which to examine festivals – that of the encounter. This will be discussed more in Chapter 3. Initially, in order to explore how festivals have been researched, and the various theoretical, disciplinary and conceptual frameworks that have been used, the chapter will provide a thorough review of the existing body of knowledge, which can be used to underpin the remainder of the book.

Festival research methods

The majority of research in the area of festival studies has taken a quantitative approach. Our review found that in some areas of festival literature (notably festival management and marketing), over two-thirds of all papers used quantitative methods, primarily factor analysis and structural equation modelling of survey data collected during festivals. Quantitative approaches, including surveys and attendance data, are most often used in the fields of economic geography, tourism and event management in order to measure the economic impacts of festivals (e.g. Saayman and Roussow 2010; Boo and Busser 2005; Chhabra et al. 2003; Frey 1994; Peterson and Crayton 1995; Kim et al. 1998; Tohmo 2005), but these approaches have also been deployed in order to determine a range of impacts and benefits generated by hosting festivals. These include attendance motivation

(Crompton and McKay 1997; Formica and Uysal 1996; Mair and Laing 2012; Nicholson and Pearce 2000; Yuan and Jang 2008), research that attempts to capture the broader perceptions held by attendees on social and cultural factors, such as community identity and civic pride, social benefits such as job creation and place regeneration (Allen and Shaw 2000; Arcodia and Whitford 2006; Brennan-Horley et al. 2007; Small et al. 2005), as well as a more recent focus on issues of sustainability and environmental impact (Mair and Jago 2009).

Qualitative research was slightly more common in other areas of festival studies, including in relation to community festivals and arts festivals. Qualitative studies have focused more on accessing the social and cultural aspects of festivals, such as the ways that festivals function as sites of identity formation or contestation (Cornish 2015; Duffy and Waitt 2011; Jackson 1988; Lavenda 1992; Leal 2015; Permezel and Duffy 2007) and how the festival event itself can generate positive community outcomes including development of culture and the arts, urban regeneration, education and tourism (Bowdin et al. 2011; Fincher and Iveson 2008; Wood et al. 2005). Studies within the anthropological literature, with a greater emphasis on an ethnographic mode of analysis, have addressed the festival as the site of identity construction by interrogating cultural performance as a series of social relations (Lewis and Dowsey-Magog 1993; Nebasifu 2013; see also Mackellar 2013). Holloway et al. (2010) go as far as to title their work 'Meaning not measurement: using ethnography to bring a deeper understanding to the participant experience of festivals and events'. Recent work, particularly in cultural geography, has sought to examine the experiential and sensory elements of festivals as a means to capture the significance of emotions, affect and bodily experiences of festival participation (Waitt and Duffy 2010; Wood et al. 2007). However, even in the areas of community and arts festivals, quantitative approaches predominate. There have been a number of studies using case study methods, as well as some literature reviews and analyses of secondary data. Some authors have published conceptual papers (e.g. Arcodia and Whitford 2006; Esu 2015; Jago and Shaw 1998; Picard and Robinson 2006), although it is difficult to say whether these conceptual papers actually contribute to building theory in the festival studies area, as few of them have been subsequently empirically tested. Overall, the field appears to have been explored in great detail by those favouring a quantitative approach. It may be speculated that the focus on quantitative research methods may be due to the positioning of festivals and events studies in business schools rather than within arts or social sciences, where qualitative research is more commonly accepted (Dredge and Whitford 2010).

Research on festivals and people

Festivals are understood as inherently about 'people celebrating themselves and their community in an "authentic" and traditional way, or at least emerging spontaneously from their homes for a community-wide expression of fellowship' (Lavenda 1992: 76). Many studies in sociology, anthropology and human geography have explored ways in which festivals help to create and express ideas about the identity of a community or place through distinctive cultural artefacts and activities, such as music, costume, dance and food (Cudny, 2014; Derrett 2003; Duffy et al. 2007; Duffy and Waitt 2011; Gibson and Connell 2003; 2005; McClinchey 2008; Quinn 2003). Often festivals are a means to preserve traditions and group identity, particularly in spaces of contestation and transition (Auerbach 1991; Brennan-Horley et al. 2007; Costa 2002; Fortier 1999; Matheson 2005). They are ways to reconnect to specific traditions and community identities (Fortier 1999; Kong and Yeoh 1997; Duffy and Mair 2014). Hence, multicultural festivals are especially important for minority groups seeking to maintain cultural traditions (Lentz 2001; Rokam 2005). Thus, festival organisers often promote these festivals in terms of 'authentic' cultural practices.

Festivals can also contribute to processes that facilitate new forms of belonging, especially for migrant, diasporic and transnational groups (Duffy 2003, 2005; Leal 2015; Permezel and Duffy 2007; McClinchey 2015; Shukla 1997; White 2015). Multicultural festivals are often promoted as sites for ongoing dialogues and negotiations within diverse communities, as well as activities that foster social harmony and integration (Lee et al. 2012 a; b; c; Österlund-Pötzsch 2004). However, while multicultural festivals may be forms of a public celebration of differences (Auerbach 1991; McClinchey 2008), they may also be sites of exclusion and divisiveness (Hage 1998; Permezel and Duffy 2007). This will be discussed further in later chapters of this book.

Research on festivals and space

Public space is a highly contested space. The social and spatial relations that occur within this sphere serve to constitute and regulate identity through categories such as race, class, gender, and sexuality. Therefore, although public space may be an arena of social inclusion, it is also a site of social exclusion, and this has significant implications for events such as festivals. Indeed, much of the literature has explored the ways in which festivals are sites of altered social relations that permit challenges to the status quo. Some have proposed that it is through a festival's reversals or inversions of normal, everyday hierarchies that the potential for change may be facilitated (Bakhtin 1984; Turner 1984). An example of this approach is that of Markwell (2002) and Mason and Lo (2009), who examine the potential of the Sydney Gay and Lesbian Mardi Gras to create a space beyond the reach of homophobia (see also Markwell and Waitt 2013, 2009; Johnston 2007). Drawing on the work of Bahktin (1984), scholars have conceptualised the festival (and particularly in the form of a carnival as well as a Mardi Gras celebration) as a paradoxical social process, reinforcing participants' sense of belonging to society. Yet, they also provide a means of reaffirming fragile social bonds and dramatizing and reinforcing collective ideas about society (Frost 2015; Jackson 1988; Jamieson 2004; Quinn 2003, 2005; Shin 2004).

The boundaries between the festival and its geographical and social context have also become increasingly the focus for understanding the influences and effects of a festival. A festival may spill beyond its temporal and spatial boundaries, a process called festivalisation (Cremona 2007; Roche 2011; Yardimci 2007). As Roche (2011) argues, festivalisation processes draw on collective understandings and practices of space, time and agency that are then deployed so as to shape communal notions of identity and belonging. Moreover, these events are interpolated into a community's calendar of "memorable and narratable pasts, with the sociocultural rhythm of life in the present, and with anticipated futures" (Roche 2011: 127–128; see also Duffy et al. 2011). For example, the International Organisation of Book Towns draws on a festival framework to generate sustainable rural development and tourism in small towns and villages that would otherwise suffer economic decline and possible depopulation (Seaton 1996, 1999). The bi-annual festival has successfully incorporated local bibliophile interests into yearly activities of the town or village, as well as helped to establish an international network that attracts considerable tourism interest (www.booktown.net/gi.asp).

The increased mobility of people in the contemporary world has led to greater cultural diversity. Consequently, complex relationships between communal identity and place emerge, as people have various sets of connections to multiple notions of 'place' and 'home'. The number of countries with resident populations that are culturally diverse has led to an awareness of the importance of building well-organised, multicultural societies (Chin 1992; Lee et al. 2012a; Parekh 2006). Festivals can play a significant role in this.

Research on festivals and tourism

Events and festivals are key elements of the tourism product in many destinations (Getz and Page 2016). As Francesco and Oriol (2009) highlight, festivals and cultural events present good tourism products as they tap into the visitor's desire to experience the cultural life in the destination. As a result, festivals and events, in conjunction with tourism, are becoming a realistic policy option for regional development (Moscardo 2007; Robinson et al. 2004). The ability of a festival (and other types of events) to attract visitors to a host region, and to contribute to the economic and social well-being of the region, explains the significance afforded to festivals in many tourism policies and strategies (Mair and Whitford 2013). This contribution is a strong justification for public funding of festivals (Felenstein and Fleischer 2003; O'Hagan 1992). However, festivals do not simply become tourism products as a matter of course, and thus they need to be carefully managed (particularly when organised and staged by volunteers) in order to ensure their effectiveness (Higham and Ritchie 2001; Getz and Frisby 1988). Indeed, Hede and Rentschler (2007) suggest that volunteer managers should be mentored to assist them to achieve the aims of the festival they are managing. Within the body of literature that has built up around festivals and tourism, several key areas – namely, the contribution of festivals to tourism (festival tourism), festivals and destination image; festivals as a tourism development strategy; and the impacts of tourism on festivals – have been the focus of a significant amount of research.

Event tourism as an area of study was established only relatively recently (Getz 2007). It is defined as 'an applied field devoted to understanding and improving tourism through events' (Getz and Page 2016: 3). A full review of current event tourism literature is provided by Getz and Page (2016). According to Getz (2013), there are five core propositions of event tourism: (1) events can attract visitors who may not otherwise visit the area; (2) events can create a positive destination image and branding; (3) events contribute to place marketing by making destinations more attractive; (4) events animate cities, resorts and parks; and (5) event tourism is a catalyst for other forms of development. All of these apply equally to festivals as to any other kind of event. Festival tourism is an important element of event tourism. Festival tourism has been described as essentially instrumentalist, treating festivals as tools in tourism and economic development or as part of the selling of attractions and venues (Getz 2010). However, as Chang (2006) points out, the unique features and cultural dimensions of a particular festival are also important factors in attracting tourists. Picard and Robinson (2006) note that tourists encounter festivals in three main ways: (1) as the key motivator for travel; (2) as part of a package tour; (3) as an incidental component of the destination's cultural attractions. As such, festivals offer unscripted encounters between residents and tourists and are often where the tourist meets 'the other' at the destination (Woosnam et al. 2014). Despite a few examples of research in this area – for example Giovanardi et al. (2014) on using perfomativity to examine host-guest interaction as a way to 'co-perform' place, as Getz and Page (2016) note – host-guest interactions at festivals is a neglected area of research.

Festival tourism is significant to economies tied to certain forms of cultural consumption that construct places, especially cities, as culturally and therefore economically vibrant (Brannas and Nordstrom 2006; Zukin 1995). The role of place branding is very important. Perceptions play a significant role in the tourist's attitude and use of – and, hence, value attributed to – place. Mega events, such as the Venice Biennale or arts festivals associated with the Summer Olympics or Commonwealth Games, help construct and reinforce the reputation of certain places as significant sites within global economic and cultural networks (Franklin 2010; Gold and Gold 2008). In the South African context, Visser (2005) highlights the importance of the links between festivals and urban tourism development. So-called cosmopolitan cities are defined by the cultural and artistic offerings available, including events like White Night (Nuit Blanche). These events also serve to minimise anti-social behaviour such as excessive alcohol consumption (Evans 2012). In other studies, festivals can be important to ongoing art and cultural development (Quinn 2006). Festival cities, such as Edinburgh, have found that the festivals themselves become tourist destinations in their own right (Graham Devlin Associates 2001; Prentice and Anderson 2003; Richards and Palmer 2010). This ties in with Florida's (2002; 2003) work on the rise of the creative classes in cities.

Conclusion

Festivals are an important part of human history, society and community. Celebrating traditions, rituals, important life events and religious occasions, festivals play a vital role in bringing people together. However, in more recent times, festivals have begun to be recognised as a realistic policy option for regional development.

Events and festivals are key elements of the tourism product in many destinations (Getz and Page 2016). Indeed, increasing tourism is one of the key reasons why local governments support and stage festivals. Of course, festivals do not become tourism products simply as a matter of course, and thus they need to be carefully managed in order to ensure their effectiveness (Higham and Ritchie 2001). There are clear benefits to hosting festivals; however, research appears to be lacking in terms of truly comprehending how best to achieve these desired benefits.

References

Ahmed, Z. U. (1992). Islamic pilgrimage (Hajj) to Ka'aba in Makkah (Saudi Arabia): An important international tourism activity. *Journal of Tourism Studies*, 3(1), pp. 35–43.

Allen, K. and Shaw, P. (2000). *Festivals Mean Business: The Shape of Arts Festivals in the UK*. London: British Arts Festivals Association.

Arcodia, C. and Whitford, M. (2006). Festival attendance and the development of social capital. *Journal of Convention and Event Tourism*, 8(2), pp. 1–18.

Auerbach, S. (1991). The brokering of ethnic folklore: Issues of selection and presentation at a multicultural festival. In: Stern, S. and Cicala, J. A. (Eds.) *Creative Ethnicity: Symbols and Strategies of Contemporary Ethnic Life*. Logan: Utah State University Press, pp. 223–238.

Bahktin, M. (1984). *Rabelais and His World*. Bloomington: Indiana University Press.

Boo, S. and Busser, J. A. (2005). Impact analysis of a tourism festival on tourists destination images. *Event Management*, 9(4), pp. 223–237.

Bowdin, G., Allen, J., O'Toole, W., Harris, R. and McDonnell, I. (2011). *Events Management*. Oxford: Butterworth-Heinemann.

Brännäs, K., & Nordström, J. (2006). Tourist accommodation effects of festivals. *Tourism Economics*, 12(2), 291–302.

Brennan-Horley, C., Connell, J. and Gibson, C. (2007). The Parkes Elvis revival festival: Economic development and contested place identities in rural Australia. *Geographical Research*, 45(1), pp. 71–84.

Chang, J. (2006). Segmenting tourists to aboriginal cultural festivals: An example in the Rukai tribal area, Taiwan. *Tourism Management*, 27(6), pp. 1224–1234.

Chhabra, D., Sills, E. and Cubbage, F. W. (2003). The significance of festivals to rural economies: Estimating the economic impacts of Scottish highland games in North Carolina. *Journal of Travel Research*, 41(4), pp. 421–427.

Chin, D. (1992). Multiculturalism and its masks: The art of identity politics. *Performing Arts Journal*, 14(1), pp. 1–15.

Cornish, H. (2015). Not all singing and dancing: Padstow, folk festivals and belonging. *Ethnos: Journal of Anthropology*, 1–17. pp. 631–647.

Costa, X. (2002). Festive identity: Personal and collective identity in the fire carnival of the 'Fallas' (València, Spain). *Social Identities*, 8(2), pp. 321–345.

Cremona, V. (2007). Introduction – the festivalising process. In: (Eds) Hauptfleisch, T., Lev-Aladgem, S., Martin, J. Sauter, W. and Schoenmakers, H. *Festivalising! Theatrical events, politics and culture*. Amsterdam and New York: Rodopi, pp. 5–16.

Crompton, J. L. and McKay, S. L. (1997). Motives of visitors attending festival events. *Annals of Tourism Research*, 24(2), pp. 425–439.

Cudny, W. (2014). Festivals as a subject for geographical research. *Geografisk Tidsskrift-Danish Journal of Geography*, 114(2), pp. 132–142.

Derrett, R. (2003). Making sense of how festivals demonstrate a community's sense of place. *Event Management*, 8(1), pp. 49–58.

Díaz-Barriga, M. (2003). Materialism and sensuality: Visualizing the devil in the festival of our lady of Urkupiña. *Visual Anthropology*, 16(2–3), pp. 245–261.

Dredge, D. and Whitford, M. (2010). Policy for sustainable and responsible festivals and events: Institutionalisation of a new paradigm – A response. *Journal of Policy Research in Tourism, Leisure and Events*, 2(1), pp. 1–13.

Duffy, M. (2003). 'We find ourselves again? Recreating identity through performance in the community music festival. *Australasian Music Research*, 7, pp. 103–112.

Duffy, M. (2005). Performing identity within a multicultural framework. *Social and Cultural Geography*, 6(5), pp. 677–692.

Duffy, M, and Mair, J. (2014). Festivals and sense of community: an Australia case study. In: A Jepson and A Clarke (eds) *Routledge Advances in Events Research Book Series: Exploring Community Festivals and Events*. Oxon and New York: Routledge, pp. 54–65.

Duffy, M. and Waitt, G. (2011). Rural festivals and processes of belonging. In: Gibson, C. and Connell, J. (Eds.) *Festival Places: Revitalising Rural Australia*. Clevedon, UK: Channel View Press, pp. 44–59.

Duffy, M., Waitt, G. R. and Gibson, C. R. (2007). Get into the groove: The role of sound in generating a sense of belonging in street parades. *Altitude: A Journal of Emerging Humanities Work*, 8, pp. 1–32.

Duffy, M., Waitt, G., Gorman-Murray, A. and Gibson, C. (2011). Bodily rhythms: Corporeal capacities to engage with festival spaces. *Emotion, Space and Society*, 4(1), pp. 17–24.

Eade, J. and Sallnow, M. J. (2000). *Contesting the Sacred: The Anthropology of Christian Pilgrimage*. Urbana, Chicago: University of Illinois.

Esu, B. B. (2015). Conceptual Development in Festival Quality Management: Implications for Product Development and Marketing. *International Journal of Academic Research in Business and Social Sciences,* 5(1), pp. 53 - 60.

Evans, G. (2012). Hold back the night: Nuit Blanche and all-night events in capital cities. *Current Issues in Tourism*, 15(1–2), pp. 35–49.

Falassi, A. (1987). *Time Out of Time: Essays on the Festival*. Albuquerque: University of New Mexico Press.

Felsenstein, D., and Fleischer, A. (2003). Local festivals and tourism promotion: the role of public assistance and visitor expenditure. *Journal of Travel Research*, 41(4), pp. 382–392.

Fincher, R. and Iveson, K. (2008). *Planning and Diversity in the City: Redistribution, Recognition and Encounter*. Hampshire, UK: Palgrave Macmillan.

Florida R. (2002). *The Rise of the Creative Class: And How It's Transforming Work, Leisure, Community and Everyday Life*. New York: Basic Books.

Florida, R. (2003), Cities and the creative class. *City and Community*, 2(1), pp. 3–19.

Formica, S. and Uysal, M. (1996). The revitalization of Italy as a tourist destination. *Tourism Management*, 17(5), pp. 323–331.

Fortier, A-M. (1999). Re-membering places and the performance of belonging(s). *Theory, Culture and Society*, 16(2), pp. 41–64.

Francesco, G. R. and Oriol, M. I. (2009). Managing music festivals for tourism purposes in Catalonia (Spain). *Tourism Review*, 64(4), pp. 53–65.

Franklin, A. (2010). *City Life*. London: Sage.

Frey, B. S. (1994). The economics of music festivals. *Journal of Cultural Economics*, 18(1), pp. 29–39.

Frost, N. (2015). Anthropology and festivals: Festival ecologies. *Ethnos: Journal of Anthropology*, 81(4), pp. 569–583.

Getz, D. (2005). *Event Management and Event Tourism* (2nd ed). Putnam Valley, NY: Cognizant Communications.

Getz, D. (2007). *Event Studies: Theory, Research and Policy for Planned Events*. Oxford: Butterworth Heinemann.

Getz, D. (2010). The nature and scope of festival studies. *International Journal of Event Management Research*, 5(1), pp. 1–47.

Getz, D. (2013). *Event Tourism*. Putnam Valley, NY: Cognizant Communications.

Getz, D., Andersson, T. and Carlsen, J. (2010). Festival management studies: Developing a framework and priorities for comparative and cross-cultural research. *International Journal of Event and Festival Management*, 1(1), pp. 29–59.

Getz, D. and Frisby, W. (1988). Evaluating management effectiveness in community-run festivals. *Journal of Travel Research*, 27(1), pp. 22–27.

Getz, D. and Page, S. J. (2016). Progress and prospects for event tourism research. *Tourism Management*, 52, pp. 593–631.

Gibson, C. and Connell, J. (2003). 'Bongo Fury': Tourism, music and cultural economy at Byron Bay, Australia. *Tijdschrift voor economische en sociale geografie*, 94(2), pp. 164–187.

Gibson, C. and Connell, J. (2005). *Music and Tourism: On the Road Again*. Clevedon, Buffalo, Toronto: Channel View Publications.

Giovanardi, M., Lucarelli, A. and Decosta, P. L. E. (2014). Co-performing tourism places: The "Pink Night" festival." *Annals of Tourism Research*, 44, pp. 102–115.

Gold, J. and Gold, M. (2008). *Olympic Cities: City Agendas, Planning, and the World's Games, 1896–2016*. Oxon and NY: Routledge.

Graham Devlin Associates. (2001). *Festivals and the City: The Edinburgh Festivals Strategy*. Edinburgh, Scotland: City of Edinburgh Council.

Hage, G. (1998). *White Nation: Fantasies of White Supremacy in a Multicultural Society*. Annandale, NSW: Pluto Press.

Handelman, D. (1990). *Models and Mirrors: Towards an Anthropology of Public Events*. Cambridge: Cambridge University Press.

Hede, A-M. and Rentschler, R. (2007). Mentoring volunteer festival managers: Evaluation of a pilot scheme in regional Australia. *Managing Leisure*, 12(2–3), pp. 157–170.

Higham, J. E. S. and Ritchie, B. (2001). The evolution of festivals and other events in rural Southern New Zealand. *Event Management*, 7(1), pp. 39–49.

Holloway, I., Brown, L. and Shipway, R. (2010). Meaning not measurement: Using ethnography to bring a deeper understanding to the participant experience of festivals and events. *International Journal of Event and Festival Management*, 1(1), pp. 74–85.

Jackson, P. (1988). Street life: The politics of Carnival. *Environment and Planning D: Society and Space*, 6(2), pp. 213–227.

Jago, L. K. and Shaw, R. N. (1998). Special events: A conceptual and definitional framework. *Festival Management and Event Tourism*, 5(1), pp. 21–32.

Jamieson, K. (2004). Edinburgh the festival gaze and its boundaries. *Space and Culture*, 7(1), pp. 64–75.

Johnston, L. (2007). Mobilizing pride/shame: Lesbians, tourism and parades. *Social and Cultural Geography*, 8(1), pp. 29–45.

Kim, C., Scott, D., Thigpen, J. F. and Kim, S-S. (1998). Economic impact of a birding festival. *Festival Management and Event Tourism*, 5(1–2), pp. 51–58.

Kong, L. and Yeoh, B. S. (1997).The construction of national identity through the production of ritual and spectacle: An analysis of National Day parades in Singapore. *Political Geography*, 16(3), pp. 213–239.

Lavenda, R. H. (1992). Festivals and the creation of public culture: Whose voice(s)? In: Karp, I., Mullen Kreamer, C. and Lavine, S. (Eds.) *Museums and Communities: The Politics of Public Culture*. Washington, DC: Smithsonian Institute Press, pp. 76–104.

Leal, J. (2015). Festivals, group making, remaking and unmaking. *Ethnos: Journal of Anthropology*, 81(4), pp. 584–599.

Lee, I., Arcodia, C. and Lee, T. J. (2012a). Multicultural festivals: A niche tourism product in South Korea. *Tourism Review*, 67(1), pp. 34–41.

Lee, I., Arcodia, C. and Lee, T. J. (2012b). Benefits of visiting a multicultural festival: The case of South Korea. *Tourism Management*, 33(2), pp. 334–340.

Lee, I. S., Arcodia, C. and Lee, T. J. (2012c). Key characteristics of multicultural festivals: A critical review of the literature. *Event Management*, 16(1), pp. 93–101.

Lentz, C. (2001). Local culture in the national arena: The politics of cultural festivals in Ghana. *African Studies Review*, 44(3), pp. 47–72.

Lewis, L. and Dowsey-Magog, P. (1993). The Maleny 'Fire Event': Rehearsals toward neo-liminality'. *The Australian Journal of Anthropology*, 4(3), pp. 198–219.

Mackellar, J. (2013). Participant observation at events: Theory, practice and potential. *International Journal of Event and Festival Management*, 4(1), pp. 56–65.

Mair, J. and Jago, L. (2009). *Business Events and Climate Change: A Scoping Study*. Melbourne: Centre for Tourism and Services Research, Victoria University.

Mair, J. and Laing, J. (2012). The greening of music festivals: Motivations, barriers and outcomes. Applying the Mair and Jago model. *Journal of Sustainable Tourism*, 20(5), pp. 683–700.

Mair, J. and Whitford, M. (2013). An exploration of events research: Event topics, themes and emerging trends. *International Journal of Event and Festival Management*, 4(1), pp. 6–30.

Markwell, K. (2002). Mardi Gras tourism and the construction of Sydney as an international gay and lesbian city. *GLQ: A Journal of Lesbian and Gay Studies*, 8(1), pp. 81–99.

Markwell, K. and Waitt, G. (2009). Festivals, space and sexuality: Gay pride in Australia. *Tourism Geographies*, 11(2), pp. 143–168.

Markwell, K. and Waitt, G. (2013). Events and sexualities. In: R. Finkel, McGillivrary, D. and McPherson, G. (Eds.) *Research Themes for Events*. Wallingford: CABI Publishing.

Mason, G. and Lo, G. (2009). Sexual tourism and the excitement of the strange: Heterosexuality and the Sydney Mardi Gras Parade. *Sexualities*, 12(1), pp. 97–121.

Matheson, C. M. (2005). Festivity and sociability: A study of a celtic music festival. *Tourism Culture and Communication*, 5(3), pp. 149–163.

McClinchey, K. (2015). Something greater than the sum of its parts': Narratives of sense of place at a community multicultural festival. In: Jepson, A. and Clarke, A. (Eds.) *Exploring Community Festivals and Events*. Oxon and New York: Routledge, pp. 137–156.

McClinchey, K. A. (2008). Urban ethnic festivals, neighbourhoods, and the multiple realities of marketing place. *Journal of Travel and Tourism Marketing*, 25(3), pp. 251–264.

Moscardo, G. (2007). Analyzing the role of festivals and events in regional development. *Event Management*, 11(1–2), pp. 23–32.

Nebasifu, A. (2013). Ethnography as consumer-oriented research in event management: A case of Rovaniemi Design Week 2013. *International Journal of Event Management Research*, 8(2), pp. 13–24.

Nicholson, R. and Pearce, D. G. (2000). Who goes to events: A comparative analysis of the profile characteristics of visitors to four South Island events in New Zealand. *Journal of Vacation Marketing*, 6(3), pp. 236–253.

Nolan, M. L. and Nolan, S. (1992). Religious sites as tourism attractions in Europe. *Annals of Tourism Research*, 19(1), pp. 68–78.

O'Hagan, J. (1992). The Wexford Opera festival: A case for public funding? In: Towse, R. and Khakee, A. (Eds.) *Cultural Economics*. Heidelberg, Berlin: Springer, pp. 61–66.

Österlund-Pötzsch, S. (2004). Communicating ethnic heritage: Swedish-speaking Finn descendants in North America. In: Kockel, U. and Craith, M. N. (Eds.) *Communicating Cultures*. Munster: Li, pp. 14–41.

Parekh, B. (2006). *Rethinking Multiculturalism: Cultural Diversity and Political Theory*. New York: Palgrave Macmillan.

Permezel, M. and Duffy, M. (2007). Negotiating cultural difference in local communities: The role of the body, dialogues and performative practices in local communities. *Geographical Research*, 45(4), pp. 358–375.

Peterson, K. I. and Crayton, C. (1995). The effect of an economic impact study on sponsorship development for a festival: A case study. *Festival Management and Event Tourism*, 2(3–4), pp. 185–190.

Picard, D. and Robinson, M. (2006). *Festivals, Tourism and Social Change*. Cleveden, Buffalo, Toronto: Channel View Publications.

Prentice, R. and Andersen, V. (2003). Festival as creative destination. *Annals of Tourism Research*, 30(1), pp. 7–30.

Quinn, B. (2003). Symbols, practices and myth-making: Cultural perspectives on the Wexford Festival Opera. *Tourism Geographies*, 5(3), pp. 329–349.

Quinn, B. (2005). Changing festival places: Insights from Galway. *Social and Cultural Geography*, 6(2), pp. 237–252.

Quinn, B. (2006). Problematising 'Festival Tourism': Arts festivals and sustainable development in Ireland. *Journal of Sustainable Tourism*, 14(3), pp. 288–306.

Richards, G. and Palmer, R. (2010). *Eventful Cities: Cultural Management and Urban Revitalisation*. Oxford: Butterworth-Heinemann.

Robinson, M., Picard, D. and Long, P. (2004). Festival tourism: Producing, translating, and consuming expressions of culture(s). *Event Management*, 8(4), pp. 187–242.

Roche, M. (2011). Festivalisation, cosmopolitanism and European culture: On the sociocultural significance of mage-events. In: Giorgi, L., Sassatelli, M. and Delanty, G. (Eds.) *Festivals and the Cultural Public Sphere*. London, New York: Routledge, pp. 124–141.

Rokam, N. T. (2005). *Emerging Religious Identities of Arunachal Pradesh: A Study of Nyishi Tribe*. New Delhi: Mittal Publications.

Ruback, R. B., Pandey, J. and Kohli, N. (2008). Evaluations of a sacred place: Role and religious belief at the Magh Mela. *Journal of Environmental Psychology*, 28(2), pp. 174–184.

Saayman, M. and Rossouw, R. (2010). The Cape Town international jazz festival: More than just jazz. *Development Southern Africa*, 27(2), pp. 255–272.

Seaton, A. V. (1996). Hay on Wye, the mouse that roared: Book towns and rural tourism. *Tourism Management*, 17(5), pp. 379–382.

Seaton, A. V. (1999). Book towns as tourism developments in peripheral areas. *The International Journal of Tourism Research*, 1(5), pp. 389–399.

Sepp, T. (2014). Pilgrimage and pilgrim hierarchies in vernacular discourse: Comparative notes from the Camino de Santiago and Glastonbury. *Journal of Ethnology and Folkloristics*, 8(1), pp. 23–52.

Shin, H. (2004). Cultural festivals and regional identities in South Korea. *Environment and Planning D: Society and Space*, 22(4), pp. 619–632.

Shukla, S. (1997). Building diaspora and nation: The 1991 'Cultural Festival of India'. *Cultural Studies*, 11(2), 296–315.

Small, K., Edwards, D. and Sheridan, L. (2005). A flexible framework for evaluating the socio-cultural impacts of a (small) festival. *International Journal of Event Management Research*, 1(1), pp. 66–77.

Sofield, T. H. B., Mei, F. and Li, S. (1998). Historical methodology and sustainability: An 800-year-old festival from China. *Journal of Sustainable Tourism*, 6(4), pp. 267–292.

Song, H-J., Lee, C-K., Kim, M., Bendle, L. J. and Shin, C-Y. (2014). Investigating relationships among festival quality, satisfaction, trust, and support: The case of an oriental medicine festival. *Journal of Travel and Tourism Marketing*, 31(2), pp. 211–228.

Tohmo, T. (2005). Economic impacts of cultural events on local economies: An input–output analysis of the Kaustinen folk music festival. *Tourism Economics*, 11(3), pp. 431–451.

Turner, V. (1969). *The Ritual Process: Structure and Anti-Structure*. Chicago: Aldine Press.

Turner, V. (1974). *Dramas, Fields and Metaphors*. Ithaca, NY: Cornell University Press.

Turner, V. (1984). Liminality and performance genres. In: MacAloon, J. (Ed.) *Rite, Drama, Festival, Spectacle: Rehearsals Toward a Theory of Cultural Performance*. Philadelphia: Institute for the Study of Human Issues.

Visser, G. (2005). Let's be festive: Exploratory notes on festival tourism in South Africa. *Urban Forum*, 16(2), pp. 155–175.

Waitt, G. and Duffy, M. (2010). Listening and tourism studies. *Annals of Tourism Research*, 37(2), pp. 457–477.

White, L. (2015). Swiss and Italian identities: Exploring heritage, culture and community in regional Australia. In: Jepson, A. and Clarke, A. (Eds.) *Exploring Community Festivals and Events*. Abingdon, New York: Routledge, pp. 197–211.

Wood, N., Duffy, M. and Smith, S. J. (2007). The art of doing (geographies of) music. *Environment and Planning D: Society and Space*, 25(5), pp. 867–889.

Wood, E. H., Robinson, L. and Thomas, R. (2005). *The Contribution of Community Festivals to Tourism: An Assessment of the Impacts of Rural Events in Wales. Assessing the Impact of Tourist Events*. Juan Les Pins: University Nice, TMP Research Group.

Woosnam, K. M., Aleshinloye, K. D., Van Winkle, C. M. and Qian, W. (2014). Applying and expanding the theoretical framework of emotional solidarity in a festival context. *Event Management*, 18(2), pp. 141–151.

Yardimci, S. (2007). *Festivalising Difference: Privatisation of Culture and Symbolic Exclusion*. Florence: European University Institute.

Yuan, J. and Jang, S. (2008). The effects of quality and satisfaction on awareness and behavioral intentions: Exploring the role of a wine festival. *Journal of Travel Research*, 46(3), pp. 279–288.

Zukin, S. (1995). *The Cultures of Cities*. Oxford: Wiley-Blackwell.

3 Encounter as our underpinning theory

Introduction

Festivals are fundamentally about encounter in its broadest sense; these are events and periods of time in which people meet and interact. Further to this, and as discussed in this book's introduction, festivals are most often held in locations that are potentially open to public access, although it may be that there is some fee for this participation (and so the potential for exclusion, especially if the cost of entry is prohibitive for particular parts of the population). These inclusionary factors are integral to government policies that seek to enhance social connectedness and social cohesion. The role of festivals in public space is important because these are sites for social relations, and it is here that different types and forms of relational networks overlap and meet. However, tensions can arise because of perceived or real fears about crime, violence and terrorism; racial intolerance; uncertainty; and insecurity, such that some groups feel uncomfortable and excluded from public space. As Butler (2015) suggests, such tactics of exclusion may be deliberate. How individuals and groups respond to diversity is itself varied, ranging from celebrating these everyday spaces as a representation of a cosmopolitan sense of shared connectedness, to feeling uncomfortable, excluded or alienated. There are also those who use public space as a means to challenge normative processes of place and community making. Nonetheless, there is a strong argument for the openness of public space, because it is here that we can encounter and engage with the 'vital mix of uses critical to urban life' (Vidler 2001 online), the 'common ground where civility and our collective sense of what may be called "publicness" are developed and expressed' (Francis 1989: 149; see also Iveson 2007).

The constitution of public spaces through encounter

While the notion of encounter has generated fruitful scholarly discussion about urban life, prejudice and differing forms of sociality, Wilson (2016) argues that there has been little critical engagement with how this term is conceptualised, despite its frequent use. 'Encounter' is often embedded within narratives associated with a 'lack of commonality' (Wilson 2016: 2), through use of terms such as 'frontier', 'border', 'boundary', 'margin' and 'borderland' (Leavelle 2004: 915). The encounter is, then, often defined as a politically charged space of highly unequal relations of power (Domosh 2010; Leavelle 2004).

As geographers, architects and planners have long proposed, public space is a site for facilitating social relationships, public discourses and political expression (Hou 2010: 2). Public space, particularly in the Western world, is significant to the social and political life of communities because it is 'predicated on an idealised notion . . . as an open and inclusive stage for social interaction, political action and cultural exchange' (Carmona and Wunderlich 2012: 1). Although there is a narrative of loss and divisiveness occurring within the public sphere – as Brill (1989) points out, this sense of decline of a public life is not new – the activities, engagements and debates that occur in these spaces are part of the ways in which communities represent the public life and social identity of that community. Identity is, as Hetherington argues, 'articulated through the relationship between belonging, recognition or identification and difference' (1998: 15). Moreover, the conceptualisation of public space as an arena for questioning community identity is viewed as inherent to the conceptualisation and everyday workings of democracy (Henaff and Strong 2001). Indeed, Mouffe (1996) suggests that we need to consider a more radical approach to understanding democracy and participation in community and society, one that involves challenging the supposition that group identities are all-inclusive and harmonious. She suggests that notions of 'just' democratic participation and the actual dynamic experiences of that participation could be developed if the notion of 'tension' is incorporated into our thinking. In particular, there will never be a singular version of cultural rights or activity that will achieve just outcomes or social membership. Instead, Mouffe proposes that a productive part of the democratic participatory process is precisely the presence of disagreement and conflict, or what Mouffe calls 'agonism' (Mouffe 1992; 1996). What we need to recognise is that tension and difference are not 'antagonistic'; rather, in conditions that assume the presence of difference and conflict, there is actually room for change, ongoing dialogue and thus the representation and the participation of many voices. Tension can therefore be a tool for exploring how the boundaries and scales of social membership are defined in ways that see certain communities of interest develop and, through this, how notions of social justice are established.

Drawing on the work of Arendt (1958, 2005), Kallio (2016: 2) considers the politics of coexistence as constituted 'through active living in the presence of others.' Arendt's (1958: 199) conceptualisation of the public sphere is that of a 'space of appearance' through which an individual's political subjectivity is constituted, what Kallio (2016: 4) refers to as 'intersubjective socialisation.' In this framework, categories of shared identity (such as gender, race and age) constitute us as social beings who at the same time co-exist with those characteristics that make us individually unique. Socialisation therefore has a fundamentally political nature and arises out of encounters in which 'people take shape and are shaped as political subjects' (Kallio 2016: 1). These are encounters in which the individual displays and reveals his/her self through public acts and words that are witnessed and judged by others also present in that public sphere (Tavani 2013). One's political reality – or *polis* in Arendt's terms – is a relational space that bundles together people, issues, events, ideologies, places and objects, here and there, now, before and in the future. It is a constitutive context for people's view of themselves and (significant) others, influencing their understandings, awareness, and attentiveness and thus shaping them as political subjects. Polis is neither randomly constituted nor does it follow a singular spatial logic, such as territoriality, network, or 'flatness'. Its constituents are brought together by matters that gain importance in polis – issues that politicize and are politicized in a given geosocial realm – making it a dynamic space with a constantly changing shape and composition (Kallio 2016: 5).

In ways that resonate with Mouffe's notion of agonistic social relations, the encounters in the polis are part of an ongoing struggle of 'coexistence and association' through which a community or society is constituted (Kallio 2016: 5). This shaping of a communality is embedded within experiential and contextual relations, a 'phenomenological [. . .] activity related to problems of living together in and through the spaces that this sharing constitutes' (Häkli and Kallio 2014: 188). However, Arendt's focus lies in how we *appear* to others also located within the public sphere, which very specifically operates within the 'realm of acting and speaking' (Arendt 1993: 223). Recent work in the social sciences has sought to critically explore the processes of subjectivity and consider how claims to public space are negotiated between differently *embodied* subjects (Brown 2012). This approach draws attention to a range of modalities that can help us explore and tease apart what is recognised as the much more entangled, embodied and heterogeneous series of relationships fundamental to the constitution of place and subjectivity. Moreover, consideration also needs to be given to understanding how the temporal and spatial contexts we inhabit shape the values and judgements we make. As Valentine and Sadgrove (2012: 2051) explain:

> in the context of new modernity, processes of detraditionalisation, globalisation, and accelerating social and geographical mobility mean that individuals are now exposed to a much wider range of lifestyles, and competing values and attitudes (both positive and negative), and are freer from social constraints to develop more individualised ways of living and to define their own personal values . . . in an increasingly differentiated world it is essential to understand the moral judgements we make about others and the practices to which these judgements give rise in order to manage the antagonisms that are inherent in social relations.

Wilson (2016:1) points out that the phrase "geographies of encounter" has been 'used as a shorthand for a body of work broadly interested in social diversity, urban difference, and prejudice, which has sought to document how people negotiate difference in their everyday lives.' Although this has facilitated scholarly discussion about urban life, prejudice and differing forms of sociality, Wilson (2016) argues that there has been little critical engagement with how the term 'encounter' is conceptualised, despite its frequent use. Much of this work has focused on the urban context, in which urban and social planning seeks to contend with high population density and often markedly high social difference which produces sites of 'throwntogetherness' (Massey 2005: 11). One body of research, drawing on the work of psychologists like Allport (1954), has explored this in terms of the more banal, momentary and insignificant interactions of everyday life, with the premise that 'low-level sociality and banal everyday civilities have enduring effects' (Valentine and Sadgrove 2012: 2050; see also Laurier and Philo 2006). In this framework:

> [t]he freedom to associate and mingle in cafés, parks, streets, shopping malls, and squares is linked to the development of an urban civic culture based on the freedom and pleasure to linger, the serendipity of casual encounter and mixture, the public awareness that these are shared spaces.
>
> (Amin 2002: 967)

Yet as Amin goes on to discuss, this framing of chance encounters in the public sphere is problematic. Visibility and proximity may encourage interaction because of a pragmatic need to accommodate difference, but this does not translate into respect for others (Valentine 2007). Society may encourage certain forms of civil behaviour, but such 'learned grammars of society' (Buonfino and Mulgan 2007: 14) is not the same as respect for difference or for greater openness to diversity (Gawlewicz 2015). Hence simply being co-present in public space fails to lead on to challenging individual and community assumptions about certain individuals and groups and thus enable communities to reconcile ethnic and cultural differences (Amin 2002). Amin (2002) argues that what also needs to be acknowledged are the factors that prevent social cohesion and cultural interchange; racism and prejudice arise out of particular networks of socio-economic and spatial conditions. Conflict arises, he observes, in those spaces where claims to place are 'defended in exclusionary ways' (Amin 2002: 972). In order to enhance social cohesion we need

> initiatives that exploit the potential for overlap and cross-fertilisation within spaces that in reality support multiple publics . . . they are simply mixtures of social groups with varying intensities of local affiliation, varying reasons for local attachment, and varying values and cultural practices.
>
> (Amin 2002: 972)

Such 'sites of encounter' include a range of places with specific social functions, such as the workplace, schools, youth centres, places of worship, sports clubs, and neighbourhoods (Gawlewicz 2015; Hemming 2011; Leitner 2011; Watson 2009). Nevertheless, there is increasing evidence that groups resist mixing with others, preferring instead to self-segregate (Mayblin et al. 2016). This has led to a critical examination as to what types of encounter produce 'meaningful contact' (Mayblin et al. 2016: 962). Amin's (2002: 959) 'micro-publics', where the focus is on purposeful and organised activities regardless of background, offers ways to 'break out of fixed ways of relating' (Mayblin et al. 2016: 67).

The social logic of the encounter

Urban and policy planning are important avenues for improving everyday life and hence issues of social justice such as access and equity. However, urban planners have been criticised for their failure to take into account the diversity of cities and their inhabitants, which has meant that differing perspectives and dissent have been marginalised in the planning process. Yet, difference is not the only factor shaping broader aspects of community identity and belonging. An important critique of the contemporary (Western) world raises questions as to how belonging is also shaped by neoliberal processes that value economic self-sufficiency (Butler 2015). Neoliberal economies have real implications as to who is defined as constituting the community – or, in Butler's (2015: 3) terms, 'the people' – as participation in these economies accord a legitimacy of belonging and the rights attached to that belonging. As Purcell (2002) argues, rather than considering redistribution of goods and services to bring about a more just society, neoliberalist concerns promote competition and greater efficiency as the way to address inequalities. Taking this argument further, Butler (2015: 11) contends that neoliberal economics have restructured public services and institutions to such an extent that 'some populations are considered disposable' and that 'market rationality is deciding whose health and life should be protected and whose health and life should not.'

Many local governments seek to lessen potentially divisive responses to difference and demonstrate a commitment to creating 'a welcoming, inclusive and accessible community' (Cardinia Shire Council 2012: 3) through policy and initiatives that draw on notions of social justice, particularly cultural and associational forms of justice (Cribb and Gewirtz 2003), although access and fair distribution are also important. In these frameworks, social justice underpins policies and programs that encourage participation by all so as to minimise social isolation, increase opportunities for interaction and facilitate greater understanding of difference, as well as the maintenance of minority cultural practices (Lee et al. 2012a). These ideas of social justice are operationalised through strategies of community development, which emphasise the well-being of all residents. Nonetheless, questions as to who has a right to the city continue. Ongoing fears about radicalisation, terrorism, and cultural and class division have led to increased forms of governance and policy that seek to ensure an orderly and safe city, which is often translated into homogeneity, enclosure and surveillance – and which impinges on the civil liberties and rights of particularly the marginalised and vulnerable (Fraser 1995; Mitchell 2003; Sennett 1970; Young 1990).

Fincher and Iveson (2008) propose that a socially just planning process would seek to redress disadvantage, recognise the differing needs of various groups, and facilitate opportunities for increased sociality. In pursuing these goals, they contribute to Lefebvre's concept of the 'right to the city' (originally published in 1967). Lefebvre was critiquing the 'technocratic will to plan cities as if they were machines' (Fincher and Iveson 2008: 8) and hence the ways in which the material forms of the (1960s Parisian) city created marginalisation and segregation. What Lefebvre offers in his right to the city is a rethinking of urban space and how it is constituted. He argues that lived space is not just a passive stage on which social life unfolds but represents an integral element of social life (Lefebvre 1991). Therefore, it is not simply that state decisions around planning create urban space and life, nor is it about the needs and wants of citizens; rather Lefebvre focuses on inhabitants, and this has important implications for social justice. As Purcell (2002: 102) points out:

> [u]nder the right to the city, membership in the community of enfranchised people is not an accident of nationality or ethnicity or birth; rather it is earned by living out the routines of everyday life in the space of the city.

This is a radical reimagining of community and its role in constituting place, one that challenges local government to consider how social life is structured through material and social practices. Whereas earlier social justice reform focused on needs-based approaches, more recent planning practice has turned to a rights-based framework, particularly as a means to enhance notions of urban citizenship and social belonging (Holston 2008; Purcell 2002). This conceptualisation also means that policy will not always readily enact social justice; rather, policy needs to recognise that 'the right to occupy already-produced urban space . . . is also the right to produce urban space so that it meets the needs of inhabitants' (Purcell 2002: 103). In social justice terms, local government policy needs to consider the ways in which factors such as democratic struggles around gender, race, class, sexuality, the environment and other concepts operate at the local scale while keeping in mind the broader regional, national and global contexts and their impacts.

Fincher and Iveson propose that the idea of encounter should be part of planning's normative social logic because urban life 'by definition juxtaposes and mixes people in workplaces, residential areas, public and private spaces of different kinds' (2008: 14) as well as opening up the 'urban inhabitant's own potential for multiplicity' (2008: 145). They argue that it is this social logic that facilitates a 'social differentiation without exclusion' in which 'unscripted encounters' offer opportunities to experience the diversity of communities (2008: 146, 175). Integral to their framework for planning for diversity in the city is the 'unscripted encounter' which facilitates certain opportunities of interaction and engagement. Drawing on the work of Illich (1973), Peattie (1998) and Amin (2002) among others, Fincher and Iveson suggest that public spaces not only are sites of and for developing and consolidating notions of community, but, perhaps more significantly, are sites of conviviality. The term 'conviviality' better captures a wide range of interactions that facilitate temporary identification with others, an 'easy familiarity and conversational warmth' (Fincher 2003: 57) that may go on to produce feelings of belonging and so community – from the casual acknowledgement of others present in public space through to more purposeful activities that may be associated with work, school or community groups (Fincher and Iveson 2008).

Festivals can contribute much to this work of conviviality, and indeed festivals 'have become an established part of the repertoire of contemporary urban planning' (Fincher and Iveson 2008: 176). The effectiveness of festivals lies in the atmosphere created by various scripted and informal activities, as well as the materiality and ambience of the space in which these events are held. The spaces of convivial encounter enable participants to step out of the conventional stances they hold towards one another and enter instead into a shared status of participation. As Fincher and Iveson suggest,

> [t]he notion that festivals offer 'glimpses of the world turned upside down' conveys a hope that through participating in a festive disruption to everyday life, people are not confined to prescribed identities and roles but rather are free to explore potential identities and to share this experience with strangers.
> (2008: 173)

Such contact zones do not minimise difference or agonism; rather, they 'emphasize how subjects are constituted in and by their relations to each other' and to help us consider encounters in terms of 'co-presence, interaction, interlocking understandings and practices' that nonetheless operate 'within radically asymmetrical relations of power' (Pratt 1992: 7, cited in Mayblin et al. 2016). In these exchanges, Peattie (1998) suggests that conviviality is strongly connected to sociability, and this most often occurs in 'third spaces' linked to commerce: the cafes and bars where we eat and drink, supermarkets, post offices, and community or drop-in centres where individuals need to engage in some form of business exchange in order to inhabit that space. This linking of encounter and exchange does open up important questions as to the implicit function of a festival within policy and planning, questions that go beyond the presentation or representation of a community's identity. As will be elaborated in later chapters, there is more to the festival event than simply a possibility for encounter; there is exchange, not necessarily commercial in nature, a process by which those involved acknowledge the encounter.

Conclusion

The notion of encounter is arguably very significant in relation to understanding the relationship between festivals and the various communities that they represent and include. Festivals offer opportunities for unscripted encounters, which allow those present to experience the full diversity of communities. However, it is not enough simply to bring people together; for positive outcomes to ensue, festivals must be planned and managed in ways that allow those attending to share in the atmosphere of the festival, through both formal and informal interactions. Additionally, it is worth remembering that festivals can draw attention to difference and may make some differences more marked. This is not necessarily a negative outcome, as difference can be beneficial and celebrated. However, unless attendees are transformed into active participants, it seems unlikely that the full benefits offered by the festival encounter will be achieved.

References

Allport, G. W. (1954). *The Nature of Prejudice*. Reading, MA: Addison-Wesley.
Amin, A. (2002). Ethnicity and the multicultural city: living with diversity. *Environment and Planning A*, 34, pp. 959–980.

Amin, A. (2008). Collective culture and urban public space. *City*, 12(1), pp. 5–24.

Arendt, H. (1977). *Between Past and Future: Eight Exercises in Political Thought*. New York: Penguin Books.

Arendt, H. (1993). Philosophie und Politik. *Deutsche Zeitschrift für Philosophie*, 41(2), pp. 381–400.

Bell, D. (2007). The hospitable city: Social relations in commercial spaces. *Progress in Human Geography*, 31, pp. 7–22.

Brill, M. (1989). Transformation, nostalgia, and illusion in public life and public place. In: Altman, I. and Zube, E. H. (Eds.) *Public Places and Spaces*. New York: Plenium Press, pp. 7–29.

Brown, K. (2012). Sharing public space across difference: Attunement and the contested burdens of choreographing encounter. *Social and Cultural Geography*, 13(7), pp. 801–820.

Buonfino A. and Mulgan, G. (2007). *Civility Lost and Found*. London: Young Foundation.

Butler, J. (2015). *Notes Towards a Performative Theory of Assembly*. Cambridge, MA: Harvard University Press.

Cardinia Shire Council. (2012). *Cultural Diversity Policy*. Online: www.cardinia.vic.gov.au/downloads/download/59/cultural_diversity_policy_-_cardinia_shire_council

Carmoda, M. and Wunderlich, F. M. (2012). *Capital Spaces: The Multiple Complex Public Spaces of a Global City*. London, New York: Routledge.

Crib, A., Gewirtz, S. (2003). Towards a sociology of just practice: An analysis of plural conceptions of justice. In: Vincent, C. (Ed.) *Social Justice, Education and Identity*. London: RoutledgeFalmer, pp. 15–29.

Domosh M. (2010). The world was never flat: Early global encounters and the messiness of empire. *Progress in Human Geography*, 34(4), pp. 419–435.

Duffy, M. and Waitt, G. (2011). Rural festivals and processes of belonging. In: Gibson, C. and Connell, J. (Eds.) *Festival Places: Revitalising Rural Australia*. Clevedon, UK: Channel View Press, pp. 44–59.

Fincher, R. (2003). Planning for cities of diversity, difference and encounter. *Australian Planner*, 40(1), pp. 55–58.

Fincher, R. and Iveson, K. (2008). *Planning and Diversity in the City: Redistribution, Recognition and Encounter*. Hampshire, UK: Palgrave Macmillan.

Francis, M. (1989). Control as a dimension of public space quality. In: Sorkin, M. (Ed.) *Variations on a Theme Park*. New York: Hill and Wang, pp. 147–172.

Fraser, N. (1995). From redistribution to recognition? Dilemmas of justice in a 'post-socialist' age. *New Left Review*, 212, pp. 68–93.

Gawlewicz, A. (2015). Beyond openness and prejudice: The consequences of migrant encounters with difference. *Environment and Planning A*, 48(2), pp. 256–272.

Häkli, J. and Kallio, K. P. (2014). Subject, action and polis: Theorizing political agency. *Progress in Human Geography*, 38(2), pp. 181–200.

Hemming, P. J. (2011). Meaningful encounters? Religion and social cohesion in the English primary school. *Social and Cultural Geography*, 12, pp. 63–81.

Henaff, M. and Strong, T. B. (Eds.). (2001). *Public Space and Democracy*. Minneapolis: University of Minnesota Press.

Hetherington, K. (1998). *Expressions of Identity: Space, Performance, Politics*. London, Thousand Oaks, California: Sage Publications.

Holston, J. (2008). *Insurgent Citizenship: Disjunctions of Democracy and Modernity in Brazil*. Princeton: Princeton University Press.

Hou, J. (2010). (Not) your everyday public spaces. In: Hou, J. (Ed.) *Insurgent Public Space: Guerrilla Urbanism and the Remaking of Contemporary Cities*. London, New York: Routledge, pp. 1–17.

Illich, I. (1973). *Tools for Conviviality*. New York: Harper and Row.

Iveson, K. (2007). *Publics and the City*. Oxford: Blackwell.

Kallio, K. P. (in press). Shaping subjects in everyday encounters: Intergenerational recognition in intersubjective socialisation. *Environment and Planning D: Society and Space*, doi:10.1177/0263775816654916

Laurier, E. and Philo, C. (2006). Possible geographies: A passing encounter in a café. *Area*, 38, pp. 353–363.

Leavelle, T. N. (2004). Geographies of encounter: Religion and contested spaces in colonial North America. *American Quarterly*, 56, pp. 913–943.

Lee, I., Arcodia, C. and Lee, T. J. (2012a). Benefits of visiting a multicultural festival: The case of South Korea. *Tourism Management*, 33(2), pp. 334–340.

Lefebvre, H. (1991). *The production of space*. Cambridge, MA: Blackwell.

Lefebvre, H. (1996). *Writing on Cities*. Oxford: Blackwell.

Leitner, H. (2011). Spaces of encounters: Immigration, race, class, and the politics of belonging in smalltown America. *Annals of the Association of American Geographers*, 102, pp. 828–846.

Massey, D. (2005). *For Space*. London: Sage.

Mayblin, L., Valentine, G. and Winiarska, A. (2016). Migration and diversity in a postsocialist context: Creating integrative encounters in Poland. *Environment and Planning A*, 48(5), pp. 960–978.

Mitchell, D. (2003). *The Right to the City*. New York, London: Guilford Press.

Mouffe, C. (1996). Democracy, power and the political. In: Benhabib, S., (Ed.) *Democracy and difference*, Princeton, NJ: Princeton University Press, pp. 45–255.

Mouffe, C. (1992) *Dimensions of Radical Democracy: Pluralism, Citizenship, Community*, London: Verso.

Peattie, L. (1998). Convivial cities. In: Douglas, M. and Friedmann, J. (Eds.) *Cities for Citizens*. Chichester: John Wiley and Sons, pp. 247–253.

Pratt, M. L. (1992). *Imperial Eyes: Travel Writing and Transculturation*. London: Routledge.

Purcell, M. (2002). Excavating Lefebvre: The right to the city and its urban politics of the inhabitant. *GeoJournal*, 58, pp. 99–108.

Sennett, R. (1970). *The Uses of Disorder: Personal Identity and City Life*. New York: Knopf.

Tavani, E. (2013). Hannah Arendt: Aesthetics and politics of appearance. *Proceedings of the European Society for Aesthetics*, 5, pp. 466–475.

Valentine, G. (2007). Theorising and researching intersectionality: A challenge for feminist geography. *The Professional Geographer*, 59, pp. 10–21.

Valentine, G. and Sadgrove, J. (2012). Lived difference: A narrative account of spatiotemporal processes of social differentiation. *Environment and Planning A*, 44(9), pp. 2049–2063.

Vidler, A (2001) Aftermath: A city transformed: Designing 'Defensible Space'. *New York Times*, September 23 [online]. Available at: www.nytimes.com/2001/09/23/week inreview/aftermath-a-city-transformed-designing-defensible-space.html?scp=1andsq= september%2023,%202001,%20vidlerandst=cse [Accessed 31 March 2017].

Watson, S. (2009). The magic of the marketplace: Sociality in a neglected public space. *Urban Studies*, 46, pp. 1577–1591.

Wilson, H. (2016). On geography and encounter: Bodies, borders, and difference. *Progress in Human Geography*, doi:10.1177/0309132516645958

Young, I. M. (1990). *Justice and the Politics of Belonging*. Princeton: Princeton University Press.

4 Rituals of community

Encounters of cohesion and subversion

Introduction

We often think about festivals in terms of how they formalize space, time, and behaviour in ways that distinguish these events from everyday events. Although strongly connected to the rhythms of daily life, festivals bring groups and communities together in order to mark out particular religious, socio-political, and historical affiliations. In this way the festival supports notions of boundedness to particular place(s) and people, internal coherence, and the relative unity of the group. These notions of coherence are created through a heightened sense of belonging brought about by rituals and associated symbolic practices. Festivals are an important means of framing and representing the relationship between people and place, communicating relatively coherent ideas about social order, although they possess the possibility of acceptance or challenge to the status quo. Such events are a means to express and celebrate core values of a particular community, with representations of community identity mediated through distinctive cultural artefacts and activities such as music, food, and folk dancing. Hence, contemporary practice and policy draws on discourses that serve to produce an official 'imagined' community (Anderson 1991), which the festival is then planned to address. Celebrating days of national importance, parades for national or sporting heroes, festivals that celebrate the culture and history of particular ethnic groups – all such activities respond to the politics and social dynamics of belonging. The framework of the festival transforms disparate individuals into collective abstractions – community, nation, even race – through engagement of the senses, by inducing action and giving access to knowledge and experience of these public events.

These ideas about the role of festivals have been incorporated into contemporary policy and practice that seeks to enhance social connectedness and community cohesion. Thus the festival event is assumed to function as a community-building activity, be that a community with a long-established connection to a particular place or one that has had a more recent migration and settlement (Auerbach 1991; Lavenda 1992; Purdue et al. 1997). Festivals are viewed as a means to facilitate new forms of belonging and enable active public engagement, as well as foster social harmony and integration (Derrett 2003; Duffy 2003, 2005; Duffy et al.

2007; Gibson and Connell 2005; Keller 2007; Kong and Yeoh 1997; Leal 2015; Lee et al. 2012a; McClinchey 2015; Österlund-Pötzsch 2004; Permezel and Duffy 2007; Quinn 2003; Shukla 1997; White 2015). A focus on enabling active public engagement is understood as especially important for promoting ongoing dialogue and negotiation between members of diverse communities, such as migrant, diasporic and transnational groups (Permezel and Duffy 2007). As Mackley-Crump (2015) suggests, festivals have a powerful and intoxicating effect that is significant to sustaining and transforming social life. Not only, then, do festivals recreate and celebrate a feeling of connection to place and people; they are sites in which notions of community and who belongs can be playfully questioned and at times more rigorously challenged. Hence, festivals and the encounters that take place at these events may also be sites of subversion.

While often used to support such bounded notions of community and place, festivals also can operate as spaces of exclusion, with markers of identity such as race, class, gender and sexuality serving to regulate and reinforce notions of who belongs. So, although festivals may initially seem unproblematic in their celebration of community, these are, in reality, highly contested spaces. Yet, festivals do offer opportunities in which a locale's disparate groups may be brought together in ways that emphasize certain commonalities, albeit often centred on notions of belonging to a (local) place (Auerbach 1991). In this way, festivals have come to be a popular platform for local government and for non-government organizations to create and encourage a sense of social cohesion in our diverse everyday social worlds, often within a discourse of tolerance.

The paradox is that festivals function as both a form of social integration and cohesion as well as sites of dispute and protest – and these conflicting ways of framing the event often occur concurrently (Jackson 1988; refer also to Duffy and Waitt 2011; Kong and Yeoh 1997; Purdue et al. 1997). Yet, as Jackson (1988: 224) notes, this is the source of an event's political significance; the different presentations that circulate within the festival site have political potential because they are 'symbolic expressions of competitive social relations physically inscribed in space.' This chapter explores these differing aspects and roles of festivals. It starts with an overview of the origins of festival culture and practice, with specific reference to anthropological and sociological literature, arguing that the structure and role of festivals in the contemporary world have their origins in religious celebrations and public cultural practices. Indeed, many of these festivals continue and retain links to specific traditions, such as religious pilgrimages, the feast days of saints, and carnival (Ahmed 1992; Diaz-Barriga 2003; Nolan and Nolan 1992; Ruback et al. 2008). This is followed by discussion exploring the two broad ways in which festivals influence and constitute social relations: (1) through activities that reinforce communal bonds and thus minimise potential division within a social group and (2) by allowing – and even at times, enabling – expression of aggression or challenges to authority by providing an emotional outlet. This is not to say that festivals are solely events that reinforce social hegemony, as public displays of conformity may hide transgressive and subversive messages. However, by tracing the ways in which the festival has been conceptualised, we can start to develop a framework that captures such complex meanings. Four key terms are significant to this discussion: *communitas*, 'liminality', 'carnivalesque' and 'festivalisation'. Each of these terms provides a means to uncover the processes of socialisation operating within the festival event as well as how these shape and connect to broader social concerns. In connecting these to the concept of the encounter, we can better understand the simultaneous and often intangible processes of inclusion and exclusion and the emotional and affective drives that are activated.

Rites and rituals

The structure and role of festivals and spectacles in the contemporary world have their origins in religious celebrations and public cultural practices, and many festival events today retain links to specific traditions (Ahmed 1992; Diaz-Barriga 2003; Nolan and Nolan 1992; Ruback et al. 2008). Central to these religious celebrations are rites and rituals, which involve the performance of activities acknowledged to hold certain symbolic value prescribed by religion or the traditions of a group or community that reinforce a particular world view (Addo 2009; Bell 1992). Most scholarly interest has focused on how these activities are embedded within religious behaviour, although some researchers have also considered how much of our everyday social interaction is ritual-like (Hoffman 2012). Our understanding of how a ritual functions is addressed by a number of theoretical perspectives (Kiong and Kong 2000). These include a Freudian psychoanalytic framework that argues rites are symptomatic of unresolved neuroses; that, in line with the work of structuralist Lévi-Strauss (2001), these activities are expressive of symbolic meanings embedded in structures. In work that builds upon that of Robertson Smith and James Frazer, the so-called Cambridge ritualists, the almost counter-intuitive argument is that myth emerges from ritual. However, perhaps the most common approach draws on the work of Durkheim (1915/1976) to argue that participation in rituals – through activities such as singing, chanting, dancing, various practices of abstinence or social isolation, and visiting certain locations at specific times – is a means to create and maintain social structures that reinforce notions of belonging to the community (Durkheim 1915/1995; Frost 2015). Rituals are about binding people together through the festive play and rhythm of special events that encourage enacting a collective consciousness (Eade and Sallnow 2000; Falassi 1987; Handelman 1990; Sepp 2014). Rituals are a means to enact social conflict and tension and move towards a resolution (Turner 1969).

In the framework of ritual, scholars in anthropology and sociology often conceptualise festivals as events set apart from the everyday (Durkheim 1915/1976), what Falassi (1987) refers to as time out of time. Engagement through ritual activities, including religious pilgrimage, the feast days of saints, and carnival, is used to create a spatial and temporal distance from the secular world and enable participants to more fully engage or communicate with a sense of the sacred. Many such religious and festival events continue today, attracting devotees maintaining centuries-old traditions (Maddrell and Scriven 2016) as well as tourists eager to experience some notion of an authentic 'other' that we in the so-called civilised world have apparently lost (Belhassen et al. 2008; MacCannell 1973; Wang 1999). Jepson and Stadler (2017), like Liburd and Derkzen (2009), high-light festivals' links to the generation of positive communal feelings and to quality of life. Recent interest in a better understanding of the emotions aroused while participating in these events has also become important for a tourist market that seeks to participate in a form of modern-day pilgrimage in which experiencing some notion of an authentic 'other' is key (MacCannell 1976). The encounter in ritual practice is, therefore, about transformation, because it facilitates stronger connections to the social group.

Falassi (1987) identifies a number of different ritual acts, or rites, that he considers to form part of a festival. The key rites identified by Falassi (1987) are *the rite of valorisation* (the time or place when the festival begins); *rites of purification* (involving the actual or ceremonial cleansing of a community); *rites of passage* (the transition from one life stage to the next); *rites of reversal* (as explained above); *rites of conspicuous display* (sacred processions, public worship of specific deities, etc.); *rites of conspicuous consumption* (abundance or even excess of food and drink); *ritual dramas* (acting out of stories important to the community); *rites of exchange* (the exchange of information, gifts or mutual visits); *rites of competition* (including athletic or sporting competitions, but also music and dance); and the *rite of devalorization* (to mark the end of the festival time and the return to normal time and space).

Communitas and liminality

Although the habits of ritual engagement may help re-establish social bonds, there needs to be some process whereby an individual comes to feel almost wholly connected with others in the social group. An important part of this process of sociality is the generation of strong, often spontaneous feelings of connectedness, what Durkheim described as the 'collective effervescence of rituals [that] is hard-wired into the human psyche' (Addo 2009: 218). This experience of deep social immersion is what Turner (1969) calls *communitas*.

In simple terms, *communitas* refers to a sense of social interrelatedness, a spontaneous feeling of connectedness and belonging that arises out of involvement in a communal event. In Turner's description, individuals come together to form such a type of alternate community set outside of their usual social structure (Turner 2008/1969). As he writes,

> We are presented, in such rites, with a "moment in and out of time," and in and out of secular social structure, which reveals, however fleetingly, some recognition (in symbol if not always in language) of a generalised social bond that has ceased to be and has simultaneously yet to be fragmented into a multiplicity of structural ties.
>
> (Turner 2008/1969: 96)

Integral to the ways in which *communitas* is activated is another state, one of in-between-ness or ambiguity, defined by anthropologists as a state of liminality.

One form of liminality corresponds to seasonal changes, and associated changes in human activity may be accorded ritual meaning and marked through certain cultural activities (Boland 2013). Yet an individual also progresses through physical changes as s/he matures, and rituals have served to give meaning to these transitions and transformations. As Boland (2013: 228, italics in original) points out,

> Rituals do not just reflect change, they actually enact it. The ritual does not merely ceremonially mark a change which exists neutrally but it defines and gives meaning to the change – it symbolically *performs* the change. Thus, rituals have a distinctive relationship to existing social structures; rituals alter structures, they both put structures temporarily into abeyance and are the source of all social structures.

The period of liminality temporarily suspends conventional social rules (Gluckman 1955; Turner 1957, 1969). For Turner, liminality is a suspension of society's usual structures allowing change to take place; 'there are fewer limits on behaviour, norms are loosely prescribed and scarcely enforced; liminal communitas is beyond the law, at once criminal and untouchable' (Boland 2013: 229). It is this state of liminality that sets the event apart from everyday life and is often the goal of tourists seeking authentic experiences (Edensor and Falconer 2012). The liminal event may offer some contact with the sacred or divine, a threshold moment (Boland 2013), and hence facilitate the attendee's transformation into a full participant of the community or group, exemplified in anthropological literature by ceremonies of initiation (Lewis and Dowsey-Magog 1993). However, what is required is a ritual act that signifies to the group or community that there is this potential and transformation, which may be acknowledged through speech or some culturally symbolic act (Boland 2013). This is followed by some form of celebration and sociability, an important act of closure that signals social structures are renewed and re-established;

> The ritual process renews and reaffirms cultural values which may have been taken for granted, transforming them from mundane aspects of structure into reflexive or even sacred values. Thus, the apparent disorder of ritual creates order.
>
> (Boland 2013: 229; see also Turner 2008/1969)

Research that conceptualises the festival as an event apart from the everyday is a common grounding for many studies on festivals (Turner 1984; Melucci 1989; Bey 1991; Lavenda 1992; Purdue et al. 1997; St John 1997). For example, Graham St John (1997), in his examination of a non-mainstream Australian festival, the ConFest held annually at Tocumwal, uses Turner's idea of liminality as a basis for examining the open-ended and experimental activities of participants at festivals and similar events. Participation, St John argues, can lead to an 'enacting [of] lifestyles (1997: 170)', experiments with identities that, in his study, are created through playing with notions of the authentic and the tribal/primitive other. The (alternative) festival becomes a site for a 'pilgrimage to a location outside the parameters of the everyday where inspired travellers seek affirmation and whole-ness, orchestrat[ing] the (re)production, the becoming, of self, identity, attitude, lifestyle' (St John 1997: 173). Hence the festival event is connected to the rhythms of daily life through a community's calendar of events but also brings groups and communities together in order to mark out particular religious, socio-political, and historical affiliations. A sense of community comes into being within the fes-tival event and then disperses, to be reformed and reactivated at the next festival. In this way the festival supports notions of boundedness to particular place(s) and people, internal coherence, and the relative unity of the group.

Some argue that truly liminal events can occur only within small-scale, inte-grated, or indigenous societies. Indeed, Turner (1982) draws a distinction between liminal events and liminoid events – liminoid events are more ludic in character than liminal events and do not possess the same social obligations as liminal rituals. Further, liminoid events and rituals do not have to take place in specific sites set aside for such purposes, as is the case for liminal events (Hetherington 1996). How-ever, for some scholars *communitas* is generated within contemporary performative events, such as the modern Olympics, as deliberate responses to contemporary feel-ings of alienation and instability (MacAloon 1984). Nonetheless, as some areas of festival research suggest, even while transient, the generation of feelings of attach-ment are important to consolidating feelings of belonging to a specific community. Importantly, these intense feelings of belonging can operate across different social structures, including class, ethnicity and gender, serving to re-affirm the broader group identity and notions of belonging (Costa 2002; Cruikshank 1997; Falassi 1987; Lavenda 1992; Prorok 1998; St John 1997). Yet there needs to be some cau-tion in this approach. Some studies assume a certain stasis with regards to identity creation: that identity or identities are in a sense pre-constructed – in St John's study, these identities are tribal or primitive – and are then brought into the festival space. Yet, as Thrift (2000) has suggested, it is in the event itself that meaning is created. Rather than being something separate from the everyday, a performative event such as the festival is a heightening of everyday behaviour with all its contradictions, in which identity and place are negotiated and (re)constituted in the course of the event. For some scholars, the festival then is not an extra-ordinary event, but better conceptualised as an intensification of the everyday.

Carnivalesque

Scholars drawing on the work of Turner (1982) and Bakhtin (1984) have theo-rised the limited time and space of festivals as sites where uneven social power relationships are temporarily inverted through the space and time of the festival event (Gorman-Murray 2009; Waitt and Gorman-Murray 2008; Markwell 2002).

Festivals are part of the repertoire of constituting a public or community, yet this is a highly contested space. The social and spatial relations that occur within this sphere serve to constitute and regulate identity through categories such as race, class, gender, and sexuality. Therefore, although public space may be an arena of social inclusion, it is also a site of social exclusion, and this has signifi-cant implications for events such as festivals. Indeed, much of the literature has explored the ways in which festivals are sites of altered social relations that permit challenges to the status quo. Some writers have proposed that it is through a festival's reversals or inversions of normal, everyday hierarchies that the potential for change may be facilitated (Bakhtin 1984; Turner 1984). An example of this approach is that of Markwell (2002) and Mason and Lo (2009), who examine the potential of the Sydney Gay and Lesbian Mardi Gras to create a space beyond the reach of homophobia (see also Markwell and Waitt 2013, 2009; Johnston 2007). Drawing on the work of Bahktin (1984), scholars have conceptualised the festival (and particularly in the form of a carnival, as well as a Mardi Gras celebration) as a paradoxical social process, reinforcing participants' sense of belonging to society. Yet, they also provide a means of reaffirming fragile social bonds and of dramatizing and reinforcing collective ideas about society (Frost 2015; Jackson 1988; Jamieson 2004; Quinn 2003, 2005; Shin 2004; Stallybrass and White 1993).

Uncovering what a festival may mean requires exploring the context of the festival. In his analysis of the carnival event held in London's Notting Hill, Jackson (1988) proposes that the symbolic and ritual aspects of carnival are linked and intertwined in its political and economic context. This, he argues, leads to ambiguities in the meaning of these events because, although commonly framed in cultural terms, the interpretation of the materiality and activities of the event remain open. Lavenda (1992) extends this idea, suggesting that once the text and processes of the festival become public property and so public culture, those who have organised the event lose control over what then happens, opening up a 'loophole that lies at the centre of this public culture' (1992: 82). The paradox is that these events function as a form of social integration and cohesion as well as sites of subversion and protest – and these conflicting ways of framing the event often occur concurrently (Jackson 1988; Kong and Yeoh 1997; Purdue et al. 1997). A sociological study of alternative festivals observes that this openness is a characteristic acknowledged and built into this type of festival's structure, and the authors suggest that '[f]estival organisers weave a loose social fabric which the individual may embroider in different ways' (Purdue et al. 1997: 30). Jackson (1988) argues that the inclusion of conflicting elements within the festival structure is the source of a festival's political significance. Others propose that the festival transforms rationalised space into a site in which participants have a certain freedom to experiment with and debate the form and content of performance and hence notions of community identity (Willems-Braun 1994), which in turn may lead to behaviour change (Organ et al. 2015).

Festivalisation

Recent research on festival events, as well as in cultural practice and studies of everyday life, has started to consider how the influences and effects of the festival operate outside the temporal and spatial boundaries of the calendar event (Cremona 2007). Roche (2011) argues that festivalisation processes draw on collective understandings and practices of space, time and agency that are then deployed so as to shape communal notions of identity and belonging. Rather than linked to particular times in the year such as seasonal change, festivals are now regular activities that are not simply about renewing social bonds; rather, they have become a significant component of 'the socio-economic and cultural landscape of the contemporary world' (Bennett et al. 2014: 1).

Festivalisation therefore represents a shift in ideas about community; what we see in this framework is a focus on a public or audience that extends beyond a localised community. Significant to such studies is that the definition of 'culture' has become increasingly fragmented, which in turn has impacted the role of the festival and its audience reach. As Bennett et al. (2014: 1) point out, festivals have 'developed in response to processes of cultural pluralization, mobility and globalization, while also communicating something meaningful about identity, community, locality and belonging.' Festivalisation can also be linked to notions of Florida's (2002) 'creative classes' and the push toward creative cities as a panacea for urban decline. Mega-events, such as the Olympic Games, international sporting events, and expos, are a means to inject finance into a place but also signal that place's position at an international scale. Given the infrastructure, the finance, and the sets of knowledge and skills required, festivalisation is more usually associated with major urban cities, thus consolidating certain networks of (economic, cultural and social) power within a hierarchy of 'global' cities (Sassen 1991). This means that while festivals play a significant role on the places in which they are held, it is mostly in socio-economic terms– and this may be of benefit to only a select few. Some scholars have argued that globalisation and the increased importance of the market and the cultural industry have lessened the Durkheimian notion of festival as an event that binds people together (Giorgi and Sassatelli 2011). Instead, festivals are more likely to be considered as a form of cultural tourism. What we are left with is (a) the branding of a particular location as a desirable destination for investment and expenditure and (b) the festival used as a means to commodify traditions and cultural products in order to construct certain representations that then promote the uniqueness of that place or community (Duffy 2014). Nevertheless, as Roche (2011) argues, the focus and scale inherent in mega-events can locate the processes of festivalisation within discourses of cosmopolitanism, and these work across national borders and boundaries, thus potentially increasing social bonds, notions of connectedness and peaceful coexistence.

Conclusion

The structure and role of festivals and spectacles in the contemporary world have their origins in religious celebrations and public cultural practices, and many festival events today retain links to specific traditions. An important part of this process of sociality is the generation of strong, often spontaneous feelings of connectedness, often referred to as *communitas*. Scholars often report that *communitas*, or a liminal (or liminoid) experience helps to consolidate feelings of belonging to a specific community (geographically based or otherwise). However, it is important to remember that festivals can also be a space for protest or demonstration, leading not to feelings of belonging but to giving vent to feelings of alienation. Whilst festivals are often seen as a way to represent a community, the festival space is highly contested, and so while public space may be an arena of social inclusion, it is also a site of social exclusion. Further, the notion of festivalisation has privileged the various socio-economic benefits to be gained by hosting festivals, and the potential for commodification of heritage and tradition, rather than a focus on the positive social and community outcomes that can be the result of successful festivals.

References

Addo, P-A. (2009). Anthropology, festival, and spectacle. *Reviews in Anthropology*, 38(3), 217–236.

Ahmed, Z. U. (1992). Islamic pilgrimage (Hajj) to Ka'aba in Makkah (Saudi Arabia): an important international tourism activity. *Journal of Tourism Studies*, 3(1), pp 35–43.

Anderson, B. (1991). *Imagined Communities: Reflections on the Origin and Spread of Nationalism*. London, New York: Verso.

Auerbach, S. (1991). The brokering of ethnic folklore: Issues of selection and presentation at a multicultural festival. *Creative ethnicity: Symbols and strategies of contemporary ethnic life*. Logan: Utah State University Press, pp. 223–238.

Bakhtin, M. (1984). *Rabelais and His World*. Bloomington: Indiana University Press.

Belhassen, Y., Caton, K. and Steward, W. P. (2008). The search for authenticity in the pilgrim experience. *Annals of Tourism Research*, 35(3), pp. 668–689.

Bell, C. (1992). *Ritual Theory, Ritual Practice*. Oxford, New York: Oxford University Press.

Bennett, A., Taylor, J., Woodward, I. (2014). Introduction. In: Bennett, A., Taylor, J., Woodward, I. (Eds.) *The Festivalization of Culture*. Surrey, England & Burlington, USA: Ashgate, pp. 1–8.

Bey, H. (1990). *The temporary autonomous zone: ontological anarchy, poetic terrorism*. Autonomedia. Internet 19 May 2000. Available at www.t0.or.at/hakimbey/taz/taz.htm

Boland, T. (2013). Towards an anthropology of critique: The modern experience of liminality and crisis. *Anthropological Theory*, 13(3), pp. 222–239.

Costa, X. (2002). Festive Identity: Personal and Collective Identity in the Fire Carnival of the 'Fallas' (València, Spain). *Social Identities*, 8(2), pp. 321–345.

Cruikshank, J. (1997). Negotiating with Narrative: Establishing Cultural Identity at the Yukon International Storytelling Festival. *American Anthropologist*. 99(1), pp. 56–69.

Derrett, R. (2003). Making sense of how festivals demonstrate a community's sense of place. *Event Management*, 8(1), pp. 49–58.

Díaz-Barriga, M. (2003), Materialism and Sensuality: Visualizing the Devil in the Festival of Our Lady of Urkupiña. *Visual Anthropology*, 16(2–3), pp. 245–261.

Duffy, M. (2005). Performing identity within a multicultural framework. *Social and Cultural Geography*, 6(5), pp. 677–692.

Duffy, M. (2014). The emotional ecologies of festivals. In: A Bennett, I Woodward, J Taylor (eds) *Festivalisation of Culture: Identity, Culture and Politics*. Farnham: Ashgate, pp. 229–250.

Duffy, M., and Waitt, G. (2011). Rural Festivals and Processes of Belonging. In: C Gibson and J Connell (eds). *Festival Places: Revitalising Rural Australia*. Clevedon, UK: Channel View Press, pp. 44–59.

Duffy, M., Waitt, G. R. and Gibson, C. R. (2007). Get into the groove: the role of sound in generating a sense of belonging in street parades. *Altitude: A Journal of Emerging Humanities Work*, 8, pp. 1–32.

Durkheim, E. (1915/1976). *Elementary Forms of Religious Life*. Trans. J.W. Swain. Second edition. London: Allen & Unwin

Edensor, T. and Falconer, E. (2012). Sensuous geographies of tourism. In: Wilson, J. (Ed.) *The Routledge Handbook of Tourism Geographies*. Oxon: Routledge, pp. 74–81.

Falassi, A. (1987). *Time out of Time: Essays on the Festival*. Albuquerque: University of New Mexico Press

Florida, R. L. (2002). *The Rise of the Creative Class: And How It's Transforming Work, Leisure, Community and Everyday Life*. New York: Basic Books.

Frost, N. (2015). Anthropology and Festivals: Festival Ecologies. *Ethnos: Journal of Anthropology*, 81(4), pp. 569–583.

Gibson, C. and Connell, J. (2005). *Music and Tourism: On the Road Again*. Clevedon: Channel View Publications.

Giorgi, L. and Sassatelli, M. (2011). Introduction. In: Delanty, G. (Ed.) *Festivals and the Cultural Public Sphere*, London and New York: Routledge, pp. 1–11.

Gluckman, M. (1955). *Custom and Conflict in Africa*. London: Blackwell.

Gorman-Murray, A. (2009). What's the meaning of Chillout? Rural/urban difference and the cultural significance of Australia's largest rural GLBTQ festival. *Rural Society*, 19(1), pp. 71–86.

Handelman, D. (1990). *Models and Mirrors: Towards an Anthropology of Public Events*, Cambridge: Cambridge University Press.

Hetherington, K. (1996). Identity formation, space and social centrality. *Theory, Culture & Society*, 13(4), pp. 33–52.

Hoffman, J. (Ed.). (2012). *Understanding Religious Ritual Theoretical Approaches and Innovations*. Abingdon, Oxon, New York: Routledge.

Jackson, P. (1988). Street life: the politics of Carnival. *Environment and Planning D: Society and Space*, 6(2), pp. 213–227.

Jamieson, K. (2004). Edinburgh the festival gaze and its boundaries. *Space and Culture*, 7(1), pp. 64–75.

Johnston, L. (2007). Mobilizing pride/shame: lesbians, tourism and parades. *Social and Cultural Geography*, 8(1), pp. 29–45.

Kong, L. and Yeoh, B. S. (1997).The construction of national identity through the production of ritual and spectacle: an analysis of National Day parades in Singapore. *Political Geography*, 16(3), pp. 213–239.

Latour, B. (1999). *Pandora's Hope. Essays on the Reality of Science Studies*. Cambridge, MA: Harvard University Press.

Lau, C., Li, Y. (2015). Producing a sense of meaningful place: evidence from a cultural festival in Hong Kong. *Journal of Tourism and Cultural Change*. 13 (1), pp. 56–77.

Lavenda, R. H. (1992). Festivals and the Creation of Public Culture: whose voice(s)? In: Karp, I., Mullen Kreamer, C. and Lavine, S. (Eds.) *Museums and Communities: The Politics of Public Culture*, Smithsonian Institute Press, Washington, DC, pp. 76–104.

Leal, J. (2015). Festivals, Group Making, Remaking and Unmaking, *Ethnos: Journal of Anthropology*, 81(4), pp. 584–599.

Lévi-Strauss, C. (2001). *Myth and Meaning: Cracking the Code of Culture*. London: Routledge.

Lewis, L., and Dowsey-Magog, P. (1993). The Maleny 'Fire Event': Rehearsals Toward Neo-Liminality'. *The Australian Journal of Anthropology* 4(3), pp. 198 - 219.

Liburd J., Derkzen P. (2009). Emic perspectives on quality of life: the case of the Danish Wadden Sea Festival. *Tourism and Hospitality Research* 9 (2), pp. 132–146

MacAloon, J. Ed. (1984). *Rite, drama, festival, spectacle: rehearsals toward a theory of cultural performance*. Philadelphia: Institute for the Study of Human Issues.

MacCannell, D. (1973). Staged authenticity: Arrangements of social space in tourist settings. *American Sociological Review*, 79, pp. 589–603.

MacCannell, D (1976). *The Tourist: A New Theory of the Leisure Class*. New York: Schocken

Maddrell, A. and Scriven, R. (2016). Celtic pilgrimage, past and present: From historical geography to contemporary embodied practices. *Social and Cultural Geography*, 17(2), pp. 300–321.

Markwell, K. (2002). Mardi Gras tourism and the construction of Sydney as an international gay and lesbian city. *GLQ: A Journal of Lesbian and Gay Studies*, 8(1), pp. 81–99.

Markwell, K. and Waitt, G. (2009). Festivals, space and sexuality: Gay pride in Australia. *Tourism Geographies*, 11(2), pp. 143–168.

Markwell, K. and Waitt, G. (2013). Events and sexualities. In: R. Finkel, McGillivrary, D. and McPherson, G. (Eds.) *Research Themes for Events* CABI Publishing, Wallingford.

Mason, G. and Lo, G. (2009). Sexual tourism and the excitement of the strange: Heterosexuality and the Sydney Mardi Gras Parade. *Sexualities*, 12(1), pp. 97–121.

Melucci, A. (1989). *Nomads of the Present: Social Movements and Individual Needs in Contemporary Society*. London: Hutchinson Radius.

Nolan, M. L. and Nolan, S. (1992). Religious sites as tourism attractions in Europe. *Annals of Tourism Research*, 19(1), pp. 68–78.

Organ, K., Koenig-Lewis, N., Palmer, A., Probert, J. (2015). Festivals as agents for behaviour change: A study of food festival engagement and subsequent food choices. *Tourism Management*. 48, 84–99

Österlund-Pötzsch, S. (2004). Communicating ethnic heritage: Swedish-speaking Finn descendants in North America. In: Kockel, U. and Craith, M. N. (Eds.) *Communicating cultures*. Munster: Li, pp. 14–41.

Permezel, M. and Duffy, M. (2007). Negotiating cultural difference in local communities: the role of the body, dialogues and performative practices in local communities. *Geographical Research* 45(4), pp. 358–375.

Purdue, D., Durrschmidt, J., Jowers, P., O'Doherty, R. (1997). DIY cultural and extended milieux: LETS, veggie boxes and festivals. *Sociological Review*. 45(4), pp. 23–35.

Quinn, B. (2003). Symbols, practices and myth-making: cultural perspectives on the Wexford Festival Opera, *Tourism Geographies*, 5(3), pp. 329–349.

Quinn, B. (2005). Changing festival places: insights from Galway. *Social and Cultural Geography*, 6(2), pp. 237–252.

Roche, M. (2011). Festivalisation, cosmopolitanism and European culture: on the sociocultural significance of mage-events. In: Giorgi, L., Sassatelli, M. and Delanty, G. (Eds.) *Festivals and the Cultural Public Sphere*. London and New York: Routledge, pp. 124–141.

Ruback, R. B., Pandey, J. and Kohli, N. (2008). Evaluations of a sacred place: Role and religious belief at the Magh Mela. *Journal of Environmental Psychology*, 28(2), pp. 174–184.

Sassen, S. (1991). *The Global City: New York, London, Tokyo*. Princeton, NJ: Princeton University Press.

Sepp, T. (2014). Pilgrimage and Pilgrim Hierarchies in Vernacular Discourse: Comparative Notes from the Camino de Santiago and Glastonbury. *Journal of Ethnology and Folkloristics*, 8(1), pp. 23–52.

Shin, H. (2004). Cultural festivals and regional identities in South Korea. *Environment and Planning D: Society and Space*, 22(4), pp. 619–632.

Shukla, S. (1997). Building diaspora and nation: the 1991 'Cultural Festival of India'. *Cultural Studies*, 11(2), 296–315.

St John, G. (1997). Going feral: authentica on the edge of Australian culture. *The Australian Journal of Anthropology* 8(2), pp. 167–189.

Thrift, N. (2000). Afterwords. *Environment and Planning D: Society and Space.* 18 (2), pp. 213–255.

Turner, V. (1957). *Schism and Continuity in an African Society: A Study of Ndembu Village Life.* Manchester: Manchester University Press.

Turner, V. (1969). *The Ritual Process: Structure and Anti-Structure.* Chicago: Aldine Press.

Turner, V. (1982). *From Ritual to Theatre: The Human Seriousness of Play.* New York: Paj Publications.

Turner, V. (1984). Liminality and Performance Genres. In: MacAloon, J. (Ed.). *Rite, Drama, Festival, Spectacle: Rehearsals toward a Theory of Cultural Performance.* Philadelphia: Institute for the Study of Human Issues.

Urry, J. (2008). Moving on the Mobility Turn. In: W Canzler, V Kaufmann, S Kesselring. (eds). *Tracing Mobilities: Towards a Cosmopolitan Perspective.* Aldershot: Ashgate Publishing, pp. 13–23.

Waitt, G., Gorman-Murray, A, (2008). Camp in the country: renegotiating sexuality and gender through a rural lesbian and gay festival. *Journal of Tourism and Cultural Change* 6(3), pp. 185–207.

Wang, N. (1999). Authenticity in tourism experience. *Annals of Tourism Research,* 26(2), 349–370.

White, L. (2015). Swiss and Italian identities: Exploring heritage, culture and community in regional Australia. In: Jepson, A. and Clarke, A. (Eds.). *Exploring Community Festivals and Events.* Abingdon, New York: Routledge, pp. 197–211.

Willems-Braun, B. (1994). Situating cultural politics: fringe festivals and the production of spaces of intersubjectivity. *Environment & Planning D: Society & Space* 12, pp. 75–104.

5   Mobilities and the shaping
of encounter

Introduction

A key characteristic of the contemporary world is that of movement. Globalisation is a particular example of such movement and something that impacts upon
our everyday experiences. We are each able to participate in local and global
networks in a very personal and direct way; for example, we can observe events
as they unfold in almost any part of the world, we can contact and speak directly
to others (whether by phone, text or email or by simply visiting them), and we can
consume or participate in a diverse range of cultures. Such interactions between
different groups of people are not new; communication and economic, cultural
and intellectual transactions have always occurred across state and regional borders. What has changed is the intensity and level of such interaction and engagement. We are more connected than ever before, and this connection seems to mean
that what happens in one place has impacts elsewhere greater than ever before.

Such interactions at local and global scales shape our connections to place and
community in positive and negative ways. Community groups, local stakeholders and governments seek out ways to enhance social connections and community bonds, and the festival has become a particularly popular means to do this
by attempting to anchor diverse groups of people in place and create a sense
of (local) community. This may lead to tension between local and more global
links to place and community. The increasing number of connections we have
are networks beyond our immediate location; a consequence of this is our often
unresolved relationship between bounded notions of identity with a specific location and disruptions to that perceived boundedness brought about by relations to
other locations that nevertheless continue in some form beyond the process of
movement. In considering this, we also need to acknowledge that movements of
people are not necessarily ones that cross national borders; intra-national migration may equally cause tension and disruption; for example, so-called sea- or tree-
change migration of (particularly older, relatively wealthy) residents from major
urban centres to rural locations that offer some sort of Arcadian bliss (Burnley and
Murphy 2004; Duffy and Waitt 2013). These various movements of people can
have significant impacts on the community already resident in that location, from
the level of a national sense of identity (as in the case of Australia's shift from

a pre–World War II 'white Australia' to a post-war multiculturalism) through to ideas about neighbourhood character. Hence, we need to consider what is meant by 'community'.

As discussed earlier in this book, community is most often understood as being those people, usually of a specific locale (be that real or virtual), who share a set of values and social relations characterised by personal connections. Yet many commentators have noted that in Western communities generally there has been a loss of a sense of community. Sennett (2006) has argued that the new global economy has led to increased anxiety and a much more fragmented sense of a shared identity. Furthermore, this new global economy is embedded within processes of globalisation in which the turbulence and uncertainty generated by the rapid circulation of people and ideas, and the sorts of strategies created in response to social change, has led to feelings of social disintegration and disconnection (Sernau 2012). This, in turn, has led to questions over who has the right to belong, a contestation that is played out in the public spaces of cities and towns (Harvey 2003; Lefebvre 1996; Purcell 2002). In a more nuanced reading of public space, Butler (2015) points out that debates about who has freedom of assembly – that is, who can rightly claim to be of 'the people' – is part of a tension inherent to democratic theory.

Public spaces are important sites for social relations, because it is here that different types and forms of relational networks overlap and meet. However, tensions can arise because of perceived or real fears about crime, violence and terrorism; racial intolerance; uncertainty; or insecurity, so that some groups feel uncomfortable and excluded from public space – and, as Butler (2015) suggests, such exclusion is deliberate. Hence, the once common idea that public space is a shared space for social interaction comes under question. As Brown (2012: 801) notes, 'the capacity to share public space has been identified as a crux contemporary issue, especially where claims to space are being made through increasingly diverse subjectivities.' How individuals and groups respond to diversity is itself varied. Some will celebrate the diversity found in everyday spaces as a representation of a cosmopolitan sense of shared connectedness. Others may feel uncomfortable, excluded or alienated, while some will use public space as a means to challenge normative processes of place making. Nonetheless, there is a strong argument for the openness of public space, because it is here that we can encounter and engage with the 'vital mix of uses critical to urban life' (Vidler 2001 online), the 'common ground where civility and our collective sense of what may be called "publicness" are developed and expressed' (Francis 1989: 149; see also Iveson 2007). We therefore need to carefully consider the ways in which power is embedded within public space; that is, how difference is defined within the public sphere and the ways in which otherness and hence 'not belonging' is constructed.

Mobility, diversity and imagined communities

One popular form of creating and/or re-affirming a sense of community has been to generate festival events that foster a sense of shared identity and belonging in ways that can encompass difference (Gibson and Connell 2005; Quinn 2003).

What underpins such festivals is the desire to promote social cohesion through discourses of an official 'imagined' community (Anderson 1983), even as others suggest tension and debate – perhaps better conceptualised as 'agonism' (Mouffe 1992; 1996) – plays an important role in acknowledging the heterogeneity of contemporary life and thus retains the potential to transform democratic politics. Not only do festivals recreate and celebrate a feeling of connection to place and people, they are sites in which notions of community and who belongs can be playfully questioned and at times more rigorously challenged. Therefore, festival events are much more than simply a source of financial gain; the processes of festivals enable notions of place, community, identity and belonging to be to some extent actively negotiated, questioned and experienced. Festivals are significant to a politics of belonging because of the ways in which they are utilised as a common framework for community celebration and for reinvigorating notions of a shared community (Jepson and Clarke 2015). In this framework, these community-oriented events are most often constructed by local government, organisations and audiences as being about local communities situated in a particular place and celebrating a local communal identity (De Bres and Davis 2001; del Barrio et al. 2012; Duffy 2000, 2001; Getz 2007; Jaeger and Mykletun 2013; Lau and Li 2015; van Winkle et al. 2013) or in generating new forms of identification (Auerbach 1991a; Lavenda 1992; Lewis and Dowsey-Magog 1993; Picard 2015; Purdue et al. 1997). This focus on a celebration of community is particularly evident in places of cultural and ethnic diversity, where organisers as well as participants view social cohesion as the goal of the event (Auerbach 1991; Permezel and Duffy 2007). Festivals are viewed as a means to facilitate new forms of belonging and enable dynamic public engagement, as well as foster social harmony and integration (Derrett 2003; Duffy 2003, 2005; Duffy et al. 2007; Gibson and Connell 2005; Keller 2007; Kong and Yeoh 1997; Leal 2015; Lee et al. 2012a; McClinchey 2015; Österlund-Pötzsch 2004; Permezel and Duffy 2007; Quinn 2003; Shukla 1997). A focus on enabling or facilitating public engagement is understood as especially important for promoting ongoing dialogue and negotiation between members of diverse communities, such as migrant, diasporic and transnational groups (Permezel and Duffy 2007). Festivals can facilitate this dialogue because, as Mackley-Crump (2015) suggests, festivals have a powerful and intoxicating effect that is significant to sustaining and transforming social life. A festival can provide a powerful means of garnering these various interactions that serve to create a sense of collective identities, an identity of the place, and a sense of belonging to a place. Thus,

> [a]s arenas for such interaction, it might be hypothesized that festivals can contribute to the development of identities through storytelling, explaining who we are through the concerts and other events, and through the media, which retells those stories to others.
>
> (Jaeger and Mykletun 2013: 215)

Yet the notion of belonging that underpins the festival event is complex and problematic. Defined in terms of a politics of belonging, these feelings of attachment create a sense of connection in particular ways or to particular collective identities, and these attachments and identities are embedded within the narratives that people tell about themselves as a community (Yuval-Davis 2006). We can belong in many different ways and to many different objects, people and places, exacerbated by our global and local mobility. Such senses of belonging and connection range from an abstract feeling about what we think of as 'our' place or community to a much more concrete notion of belonging in which we participate in activities that display our allegiances – such as dance and other cultural performances, the wearing of certain costumes, and the availability of specific foods that are viewed as representative of certain communal identities. These processes and activities, and the feelings they produce, are dynamic things, arising in and out of certain moments of generating community. Festivals have been proliferating in the last two decades in response to a range of social and planning policies that encourage participation by all so as to increase opportunities for interaction, thereby minimising social isolation and facilitating greater understanding of difference. In an increasingly globalised world – where difference, in its broadest sense, is the norm in everyday life – local communities become places through which issues of difference, and the dynamics of coexistence, isolation, inclusion and racism, are played out (and although diversity may be more prevalent in urban areas, it is increasingly found in regional locations; see, for example, de Lima and Wright 2009; Gorman-Murray 2009). Nor is diversity limited to cultural or ethnic identity. Key areas of diversity also include gender, disability, generation, LGBTI, indigenous identity, and religious affiliation. However, there remains a need to critically engage with such ideas and practices, for as Fincher (2003: 55) argues, 'differences between us are continually reproduced by a range of processes and politics, rendering some people mainstream and others marginal.'

Issues around mobility seem especially relevant to culturally diverse communities, where an idea of the 'local,' one who is situated in a place, is unsettled by ethnic and cultural connections to other places. Nonetheless, diversity (and its potential for generating fruitful discussion around agonism) is often muted through official policies of multiculturalism – policies that are about the management of difference – which seek to present a clear and simple relationship between a place and community and its representation in such things as a community festival. That is, a community is defined as ethnically and culturally diverse, so performing within that festival marks the individual as 'other' to that of the dominant community. What is striking about this is the emphasis on identity as more often than not expressed as a display of cultures. In this context, some scholars point out that it is state and local government policies on multiculturalism that give meaning and cohesion to this type of festival model (Smith and Brett 1998). This does not mean the potential for difference in rethinking social relations is lost. As Jacobs (1998) argues, the presentation or staging of ethnic and racial diversity within postmodern capitalism is a site of the political, disruptive potential of difference. Difference is understood as a key element in 'the aestheticization of city life' that 'only ever marks the familiar, albeit now more instrumentally semiotic, appropriative force of postmodern capitalism' (Jacobs 1998: 253). Ethnic and cultural diversity is about access to forms of (social) capital, because these sources of difference are a means to competitively mark out the distinctiveness of a place.

However, as Jacobs (1998) cautions, this diversity is often just a play of difference rather than a politics of difference, a set of surface markers that remain subordinate to the workings of consumption.

While acknowledging Hage's (1998) critique that a multicultural festival is a mode for regulating minority groups, there needs to be some consideration as to how such festival events are performed, experienced and interpreted. Such a festival simultaneously emphasises the connections of the various communities that constitute a culturally diverse 'local' to the world of the outside. Establishing and maintaining these connections may correspond to a desire on the part of communities to create a different sense of belonging – because, for example, migrant communities are faced with a sense of belonging neither 'here' nor 'there' but in both imagined and remembered homelands simultaneously that then shapes a potential new 'home' space.

Mobility and immobility

Policies that utilise the festival event for community connectedness and social cohesion are most often structured around an underlying assumption that strongly links the festival to a bounded sense of place and community. Although participants, including audience members, may be from elsewhere – and attracting people from elsewhere is part of the logic for the festival in economic development strategies – the focus of the event is on a resident community. The creation of place identities is tied to policies and practices of economic or community development and the benefits derived for resident communities and businesses (Derrett 2003; van Winkle et al. 2013; Jaeger and Mykletun 2013; Quinn 2005). Nonetheless, what is missing from this focus of community-in-place is the importance of movement and mobility – of people, ideas, practices into *and* out of the festival and its location – and how these shape the meanings and experience attributed to the festival event.

A location and a community are not interchangeable; rather, the festival constitutes a place and community for that time. This means that when we consider the processes and practices of the festival we need to be mindful that such an event is not simply about face-to-face interactions. As Massey (1994: 120) explains, the concept of place arises out of particular moments of intersecting social relations, 'nets of which have over time been constructed, laid down, interacted with one another, decayed and renewed.' The identity of a place is, therefore, the product of such interactions, linked to individual and collective memories and constituted within the heterogeneous relations of the social world. However, as Massey reminds us, the construction of a place's identity is a dynamic process, created out of numerous social relations that connect that place to a much larger social fabric.

This conceptualisation of place (and community) also means that social interaction is more than that of an immediate presence, or even a more or less direct co-presence; rather, there 'are multiple forms of "imagined presence" occurring through objects, people, information and images travelling, carrying connections across, and into, multiple other social spaces' (Urry 2008: 13–14). Competing narratives, ideologies and ideas inform who (and what) constitutes a place and community. Moreover, such a reconfiguration of mobility raises issues of *immobility*. In their studies of sexual and gender minorities, Gorman-Murray and Nash (2014: 623) suggest that the research 'has tended to focus on either "place making" and "territories" *or* "movement" and "mobility" ' (Gorman-Murray and Nash 2014: 623; italics in original) and thus has overlooked 'the potentially networked, intertwined and mutually constitutive relationships among and between' different groups and communities. A focus on the ways in which movement and fixity interact conceptualises a space and community/communities in terms of transformation, which in their study of Sydney's LGBTQ neighbourhoods arises out of 'flows of people, knowledge, and capital [that] have intersected with particular formations of sexual and gender politics to in turn coalesce into territories based on recognizable sexuality and gender difference' (Gorman-Murray and Nash 2014: 624). This notion of a 'mooring' (Gorman-Murray and Nash 2014: 624) of identity is a means to integrate mobilities and relational spaces; [. . .] it is the 'incessant movement of mobile things – bodies, materials, ideas – that interconnect to create the spaces of everyday life' (Gorman-Murray and Nash 2014: 625).

The 'new mobilities paradigm' provides a framework for addressing the complex sets of mobility/immobility, relations and networks that constitute contemporary social relations in terms of what it means to be mobile and how this impacts upon society (Sheller and Urry 2006; see also Adey et al. 2013). As Urry (2008: 13) explains,

> Social relations are never only fixed or located in place but are to very varying degrees constituted through various entities or what Latour terms "circulating entities" (1999). There are many such circulating entities that bring about relationality within and between societies at multiple and varied distances.

A fuller discussion of new mobilities can be found elsewhere; however, in exploring the intersection of festivals and the concept of encounter, a number of aspects within this field of study offer potentially fertile ways to rethink social relations in terms of circulating and dynamic forces and affects.

The new mobilities literature has its origins in the work undertaken by researchers in transport geography and its underlying infrastructure, as well as migration and population studies. Yet, since the late 1990s – and so interacting with and arising out of interest in globalisation – theorists from a range of disciplines have argued that we need to recognise mobility as the central fact of modern (or postmodern) life. This is significant to understanding contemporary social relations and how community is realised, because of the scale and temporality of social relations. As Cresswell (2011: 551) notes, scholars have argued that we need to 'question the perceived prioritization of more rooted and bounded notions of place as the locus of identity.' The new mobilities paradigm brings to our attention the ways we have tended to ignore or trivialise the importance of mobility in its impact and takes seriously the impact of movement at all scales on contemporary life (Sheller and Urry 2006). Bringing together frameworks from the sciences, social sciences and humanities enables thinking through contemporary life in terms of 'complex assemblages between these different mobilities that may make and maintain social connections across varied and multiple distances' (Urry 2008: 13). Conceptualising the festival as networked within an assemblage that comprises mobility *and* various forms of stasis can better capture the fluidity of community formation and processes of identity and identification. Belonging emerges through numerous activities, processes, networks and social relations, as well as such things as the aesthetics through which identity is created and performed, all of which impacts upon the individual and his or her embeddedness in the social. As Cresswell notes, '[m]obility here is as much about meaning as it is about mappable and calculable movement. It is an ethical and political issue as much as a utilitarian and practical one' (2011: 552). Thus, the new mobilities framework is

> part of a broader theoretical project aimed at going beyond the imagery of 'terrains' as spatially fixed geographical containers for social processes, and calling into question scalar logics such as local/global as descriptors of regional extent.
>
> (Sheller and Urry 2006: 209)

All places are tied through networks of connections, and the significance of this is that what we have is more than a *geographic* mobility and its associations with migration at differing scales. Mobility is thus reconceptualised in terms of making and maintaining social connections across varied and multiple distances (Urry 2008; see also Sheller and Urry 2006: 209; Kaufman and Montulet 2008). As Cresswell and Merriman (2011: 5) point out, 'mobile, embodied practices are central to how we experience the world, from practices of writing and sensing, to walking and driving. Our mobilities create spaces and stories – spatial stories.' This reframing of mobility helps uncover a more nuanced understanding as to how individuals and communities experience social and material transformations; there are narratives about identity, belonging, exclusion and so on that are activated within the event of a community festival time and space.

Events, mobilities, encounters

Scholars working in tourism and events have productively drawn on the new mobilities paradigm to critically examine events as part of relations and networks that consist of people, places, and politics 'at the myriad conjunctures in which they collide' (Hannam et al. 2016: 2). This can open up our understanding of the festival event as an encounter: it is not simply about how people, ideas, things and so on are connected but also about how this varied movement impacts on the bodies, actions, and even feelings of individuals, which then shapes our social world. In this way, the new mobilities intersects with the concerns of performativity and non-representational theory.

Performativity calls into question assumptions about a stable and coherent identity. As Butler's (1990) examination of gendered identity points out, identity is not based on a set of essentialised or pre-given characteristics. The body is a 'variable boundary, a surface whose permeability is politically regulated' (Butler 1990: 139).

Although Butler's focus is on gender, her conceptualisation of identity as a performative practice suggests that we articulate a particular identity through

> a stylized repetition of acts . . . which are internally discontinuous [so that] the appearance of substance is precisely that, a constructed identity, a performative accomplishment which the mundane social audience, including the actors themselves, come to believe and to perform in the mode of belief.
>
> (Butler 1990: 215)

Thus, it is not that the physical body confers identity onto the subject; rather, identity is attributed to the subject through signifying practices that construct an identity. These signifying practices are embedded within discourse about appropriate forms of behaviour associated with specific constructions of identity. In a similar way, Fortier's (1999) 'terrains of belonging' is a means to capture how 'practices of group identity are about manufacturing cultural and historical belongings which mark out terrains of commonality that delineate the politics and social dynamics of "fitting in"' (1999: 42). However, Butler demonstrates how it is not linguistic structure alone that creates a subject position; equally important is bodily and non-verbal discourse. As Nash (2000: 655) explains, our identity as a particular '[g]ender does not exist outside its "doing" but its performance is also a reiteration of previous "doings" that become naturalized as gender norms' (Nash 2000: 655).

The significance of the body is also a concern within non-representational approaches (or even more-than-representational, as suggested by Lorimer 2005) and is discussed in more detail in the following chapter. Non-representational theory (NRT) considers the body's movements as integral to knowing, engaging with and communicating through the everyday world, yet, unlike performativity, NRT is 'resolutely . . . pre-individual. It trades in modes of perception which are not subject-based' (Thrift 2008: 7). Consciousness is simply one aspect of perceiving the world, and we need to acknowledge the significance of the pre-cognitive aspects of embodied life (Simpson 2010).

What the new mobilities offers the study of festivals is a means to critically unpack 'the embodied nature and experience of different modes of travel, seeing these modes in part as forms of material and sociable dwelling-in-motion, places of and for various activities' (Hannam et al. 2016: 4). The intersection of various social relations constitutes a place and community (Massey 1994; see also Bissell 2013) and is an ongoing process that can facilitate new forms of social and cultural life, through which 'hosts, guests, buildings, objects and machines' are brought together to produce certain performances about place (Hannam et al. 2016: 13). This understanding of mobility also acknowledges Latour's (1993) conceptualisation of the social realm as heterogeneous; human, non-human and the materiality of everyday life are integral to the constitution of place and thus community. As with Gorman-Murray and Nash's (2014) notion of moorings, thinking of the festival event in terms of mobilities emphasises the importance of various forms of movement not as an 'undifferentiated flow' but 'instead as a series of identifiable activities' (Hannam et al. 2016: 2) that connect individuals and groups into a location or community. The new mobilities paradigm therefore brings to the study of festivals an attention to bodily movement within a broader mobility framework. Yet, as Hannam et al. (2016) also point out, the 'mooring' of new distinct social lives arises out of the *event* of the festival, which interjects into the already-present networks that constitute place.

Conclusion

What does this mean in the context of the festival? In ways that resonate with the notion of carnival, as well as Turner's (1984) work on *communitas* and liminality, the festival can be conceptualised as a time and space of change that has the potential for danger, excess, even violence. Drawing on the work of Žižek (2014), Hannam et al. (2016) suggest that the event is an 'intrusion of something new which remains unacceptable for the predominant view' (Žižek 2014: 77). Thus, the event offers 'a change of the very frame through which we perceive the world and engage in it' (Žižek 2014: 10). Yet a differing view is that offered by Edensor (2007: 199), who suggests that rather than transcending the 'stresses and strains' of mundane, everyday life, tourism events are themselves 'fashioned by culturally coded escape *attempts*' (199: 200; italics added). The 'ubiquity of tourist practice' (Edensor 2007: 200; see also Urry 2002) and its common deployment in development strategies, particularly in the regeneration of urban economies, has produced a feeling of malaise. Edensor argues that the

> penetration of the exotic into everyday lives and banal urban spaces, and the dense intertextual and interspatial resonances which resound between similarly themed and designed spaces, have the effect of rendering the exotic mundane, diluting its power to confound normativity . . . tourism has consequently lost much of its power as a practice through which the everyday might be transcended via a confrontation with otherness.
>
> (2007: 201)

Yet, as Edensor goes on to argue, the routines, performances and habits of the everyday serve an important social function in that 'habits organise the social life of individuals' (2007: 211). Everyday life is more than unthinking habit and 'rigid praxis' (Edensor 2007: 211); rather, the everyday is 'open-ended, fluid and generative, concerns becoming rather than being, is a sensual experiencing and understanding' (Edensor 2007: 212; see also Harrison 2000). Bringing these two differing approaches of Žižek and Edensor to the meaning of 'event', then, helps us conceptualise the festival as an encounter in terms of an intensification of performative, habitual, mundane, deliberate, extra-ordinary and ongoing processes and practices that never fully settle.

This chapter has examined mobilities as a lens through which to examine festivals and their impacts on communities. In particular, the new mobilities paradigm offers a useful perspective for research in this area. Hannam et al. (2016) offer a valuable set of conceptual dimensions through which to critically engage with festivals in terms of mobilities – interruptions, transitions, framings and materialities – in order to capture this complexity. Such an approach also facilitates thinking of the body as 'an affective vehicle through which we sense place and movement, and construct emotional geographies' (Sheller and Urry 2006: 216) that give rise to feelings of connectedness (or alienation). Hence, when considering mobilities we need to consider how movement impacts on bodies, not only as to how movement constitutes our everyday lives but also as to how our bodily presence can shape the experiences, and therefore meaning attributed to festival events. These dimensions are taken up in the case studies presented in the latter part of this book.

References

Adey, P., Bissell, D., Hannam, K., Merriman, P., Sheller, M. (2014). *The Routledge Handbook of Mobilities*. Abingdon and New York: Routledge.

Anderson, B. (1983). *Imagined Communities: Reflections on the Origin and Spread of Nationalism*. London: Verso.

Bissell, D. (2013). Pointless mobilities: Rethinking proximity through the loops of neighbourhood. *Mobilities*, 8(3), pp. 1–19.

Brennan, T. (2004). *The Transmission of Affect*. Ithaca: Cornell University Press

Brown, K. (2012). Sharing public space across difference: Attunement and the contested burdens of choreographing encounter. *Social and Cultural Geography*, 13(7), pp. 801–820.

Burnley, I. and Murphy, P. (2004). *Sea Change: Movement From Metropolitan to Arcadian Australia*. Sydney: UNSW Press.

Butler, J. (1990). *Gender Trouble: Feminism and the Subversion of Identity*. New York, Routledge.

Butler, J. (2015). *Notes Towards a Performative Theory of Assembly*. Cambridge, MA: Harvard University Press.

Cresswell, T. (2011). Mobilities I: Catching up. *Progress in Human Geography*. 35(4), pp. 550–558.

Cresswell, T., Merriman, P. (2011). Introduction: Geographies of mobilities – Practices, spaces, subjects. In: Cresswell, T., Merriman, P. (Eds.) *Geographies of Mobilities: Practices, Spaces, Subjects*. Surrey, England; Burlington, USA: Ashgate, pp. 1–18.

De Bres, K., and Davis, J. (2001). Celebrating group and place identity: A case study of a new regional festival. *Tourism Geographies*, 3(3), pp. 326–337.

del Barrio, M., Devesa, M., Herrero, L. (2012) Evaluating intangible cultural heritage: The case of cultural festivals. *City, Culture and Society*. 3, pp. 235–244

De Lima, P. and Wright, S. (2009). Welcoming migrants? Migrant labour in rural Scotland. *Social Policy and Society*, 8(3), pp. 391–404.

Derrett, R. (2003). Making sense of how festivals demonstrate a community's sense of place. *Event Management*, 8(1), pp. 49–58.

Duffy, M. (2005). Performing identity within a multicultural framework. *Social and Cultural Geography*, 6(5), pp. 677–692.

Duffy, M. and Waitt, G. (2013). Home sounds: Experiential practices and performativities of hearing and listening. *Social and Cultural Geography*, 14(4), pp. 466–481.

Duffy, M., Waitt, G. R. and Gibson, C. R. (2007). Get into the groove: the role of sound in generating a sense of belonging in street parades. *Altitude: A Journal of Emerging Humanities Work*, 8, pp. 1–32.

Fincher, R. (2003). Planning for cities of diversity, difference and encounter. *Australian Planner* 40(1), pp. 55–58.

Edensor, T. (2007). Mundane mobilities, performances and spaces of tourism. *Social and Cultural Geography*, 8(2), pp. 199–215.

Francis, M. (1989). Control as a dimension of public space quality. In: Sorkin, M. (Ed.) *Variations on a Theme Park*. New York: Hill and Wang, pp. 147–172.

Fortier, M. (1999). Re-membering places and the performance of belonging(s). *Theory, Culture and Society: Performativity and Belonging*. 16 (2), pp. 41–64.

Getz, D. (2007). *Event Studies: Theory, Research and Policy for Planned Events*, Oxford: Butterworth-Heinemann.

Gibson, C. and Connell, J. (2005). *Music and Tourism: On the Road Again*. Clevedon: Channel View Publications.

Gorman-Murray, A. (2009). What's the meaning of chillout? Rural/urban difference and the cultural significance of Australia's largest rural GLBTQ festival. *Rural Society*, 19(1), pp. 71–86.

Gorman-Murray, A. and Nash, C. (2014). Mobile places, relational spaces: Conceptualizing change in Sydney's LGBTQ neighborhoods. *Environment and Planning D: Society and Space*, 32(4), pp. 622–641.

Hage, G. (1998). *White Nation: Fantasies of White Supremacy in a Multicultural Society*. Annandale, NSW: Pluto Press.

Hannam, K., Mostafanezhad, M. and Rickly, J. (2016). *Event Mobilities: Politics, Place and Performance*. London, New York: Routledge.

Harrison, P. (2000). Making sense: Embodiment and the sensibilities of the everyday. *Environment and Planning D: Society and Space*, 18, pp. 497–517.

Harvey, D. (2003). The right to the city. *International Journal of Urban and Regional Research*, 27(4), pp. 939–941.

Iveson, K. (2007). *Publics and the City*. Oxford: Blackwell.

Jacobs, J.M. (1998). Staging difference: aestheticization and the politics of difference in contemporary cities. In: Fincher, R., Jacobs, J. (Eds.) *Cities of Difference*. New York: The Guildford Press. pp. 252–278.

Jaeger, K., Mykletun, R. J. (2013). Festivals, identities, and belonging. *Event Management*, 17(3), pp. 213–226.

Jepson, A., Clarke, A (Eds.) (2015). *Routledge Advances in Events Research Book Series: Exploring Community Festivals and Events* Oxon & New York: Routledge

Kaufmann, V. and Montulet, B. (2008). Between social and spatial mobilities: The issue of social fluidity. In: Canzler, W., Kaufmann, V. and Kesselring, S. (Eds.) *Tracing Mobilities: Towards a Cosmopolitan Perspective*. Aldershot: Ashgate, pp. 37–56.

Kong, L. and Yeoh, B. S. (1997). The construction of national identity through the production of ritual and spectacle: an analysis of National Day parades in Singapore. *Political Geography*, 16(3), pp. 213–239.

Latour, B. (1993). Ethnography of a "High-tech"Case: About Aramis. In: In P. Lemonnier (Ed.) *Technological Choices: Transformations in Material Culture since the Neolithic*, Oxon & New York: Routledge and Kegan Paul, pp. 372–398

Latour, B. (1999). *Pandora's Hope. Essays on the Reality of Science Studies*. Cambridge, MA: Harvard University Press.

Lau, C., Li, Y. (2015) Producing a sense of meaningful place: evidence from a cultural festival in Hong Kong. *Journal of Tourism and Cultural Change*. 13(1), pp. 56–77.

Leal, J. (2015). Festivals, Group Making, Remaking and Unmaking, *Ethnos: Journal of Anthropology*, 81)4), pp. 584–599.

Lefebvre, H. (1996). *Writing on Cities*. Oxford: Blackwell.

Lewis, L., and Dowsey-Magog, P. (1993). The Maleny 'Fire Event': Rehearsals Toward Neo-Liminality'. *The Australian Journal of Anthropology* 4(3), pp. 198–219.

Lorimer, H. (2005). Cultural geography: The busyness of being "more-than-representational." *Progress in Human Geography*, 29, pp. 83–94.

Mackley-Crump, J. (2015) *The Pacific Festivals of Aotearora New Zealand: Negotiating Place and Identity in a New Homeland*. Honolulu: University of Hawai'i Press.

Massey, D. (1994). *Space, Place and Gender*. Cambridge: Polity Press.

Mouffe, C. (1992) *Dimensions of Radical Democracy: Pluralism, Citizenship, Community*, London: Verso.

Mouffe, C. (1996). On the itineraries of democracy: an interview with Chantal Mouffe. *Studies in Political Economy*, 49, pp. 131–148.

Nash, C. (2000). Performativity in practice: some recent work in cultural geography. *Progress in Human Geography* 24(4), pp 653–664.

Österlund-Pötzsch, S. (2004). Communicating ethnic heritage: Swedish-speaking Finn descendants in North America. In: Kockel, U. and Craith, M. N. (Eds.) *Communicating Cultures*. Munster: Li, pp. 14–41.

Permezel, M. and Duffy, M. (2007). Negotiating cultural difference in local communities: the role of the body, dialogues and performative practices in local communities. *Geographical Research* 45(4), pp. 358–375.

Picard, D. (2015). The festive frame: festivals as mediators for social change. *Ethnos: Journal of Anthropology*, 81(4), pp. 600–616.

Purcell, M. (2002). Excavating Lefebvre: The right to the city and its urban politics of the inhabitant. *GeoJournal*, 58, pp. 99–108.

Quinn, B. (2003). Symbols, practices and myth-making: cultural perspectives on the Wexford Festival Opera, *Tourism Geographies*, 5(3), pp. 329–349.

Quinn, B. (2005). Changing festival places: insights from Galway. *Social and Cultural Geography*, 6(2), pp. 237–252

Shukla, S. (1997). Building diaspora and nation: the 1991 'Cultural Festival of India'. *Cultural Studies*, 11(2), 296–315.

Sernau, S. (2012). *Global Problems: The Search for Equity, Peace, and Sustainability*. Boston: Pearson.

Sheller, M., Urry, J. (2006). The new mobilities paradigm. *Environment and Planning A*, 38, pp. 207–226.

Simpson, P. (2010) Ecologies of Street Performance: Bodies, Affects, Politics.[online] Unpublished PhD Thesis, University of Bristol. Available at: https://psimpsongeography. wordpress.com/2011/06/07/what-is-non-representational-theory/ [Accessed 31 March 2017].

Simpson, P. (2016). Sonic affects and the production of space: 'Music by handle' and the politics of street music in Victorian London. *Cultural Geographies*, 24(1), pp. 89–109.

Smith, G., Brett, J. (1998). Nation, authenticity and social difference in Australian popular music: folk, country, multicultural. *Journal of Australian Studies* 58, pp. 3–17.

Thrift, N. (1996). *Spatial Formations*. London: Sage.

Thrift, N. (2008). *Non-Representational Theory: Space/ Politics/ Affect*. London, New York: Routledge.

Turner, V. (1984). Liminality and Performance Genres. In: MacAloon, J. (Ed.). *Rite, Drama, Festival, Spectacle: Rehearsals toward a Theory of Cultural Performance*. Philadelphia: Institute for the Study of Human Issues.

Urry, J. (2002) Mobility and proximity. *Sociology*. 36(2), pp. 255–274

Urry, J. (2008). Moving on the Mobility Turn. In: W Canzler, V Kaufmann, S Kesselring. (eds). *Tracing Mobilities: Towards a Cosmopolitan Perspective*. Aldershot: Ashgate Publishing, pp. 13–23.

Van Winkle, C., Woosnam, K. and Mohammed, A. (2013). Sense of community and festival attendance. *Event Management*, 17(2), pp. 155–163.

Vidler, A. (2001). Aftermath: A city transformed: Designing 'Defensible Space'. *New York Times*, September 23 [online]. Available at: www.nytimes.com/2001/09/23/week inreview/aftermath-a-city-transformed-designing-defensible-space.html?scp=1andsq= september%2023,%202001,%20vidlerandst=cse [Accessed 31 March 2017].

White, L. (2015). Swiss and Italian identities: Exploring heritage, culture and community in regional Australia. In: Jepson, A. and Clarke, A. (Eds.). *Exploring Community Festivals and Events*. Abingdon, New York: Routledge, pp. 197–211.

Yuval-Davis, Nira. 2006. Belonging and the politics of belonging. *Patterns of Prejudice* 40: 197–214.

Žižek, S. (2014). *Event: Philosophy in Transit*. Harmondsworth: Penguin.

6 Festivals, non-representation theory and encounter

Introduction

Non-representational theory (NRT) has become an important focus of debate in human geography specifically, but its overarching approach to exploring the everyday has been readily taken up in a range of disciplinary areas. NRT's conceptualisation of the body, affect and the unfolding of an event resonate with the ideas of *communitas*, liminality, carnivalesque and festivalisation discussed in Chapter 4, as well as the ideas of mobility presented in Chapter 5. Yet, what is particular to NRT is that it draws our attention to the ways in which the totality of human and non-human worlds are emergent and that these worlds are 'relationally constituted' (Anderson and Harrison 2010: 15). One exciting possibility for festival studies is NRT's conceptualisation of what Anderson and Harrison (2010: 11) refer to as 'life and the social,' which they argue is the 'starting point for all non-representational theories.' Taking this position as a reference point for what unfolds in a festival may enable significant insights into the festival event as a space of encounter, because this framework opens up ideas of how we might consider the complex processes inherent in social cohesion and exclusion. Nevertheless, providing a clear summary of NRT's diverse set of ideas and focus is difficult (Cresswell 2012). Rather than a single theoretical perspective, NRT's focus is on emergent, more often than not mundane, phenomena of our everyday lives and

> how life takes shape and gains expression in shared experiences, everyday routines, fleeting encounters, embodied movements, precognitive triggers, practical skills, affective intensities, enduring urges, unexceptional interactions and sensuous dispositions.
>
> (Lorimer 2005: 84)

Yet, as some critics of NRT have noted, these concerns are already present in the work of scholars in feminism, cultural Marxism and poststructuralism who also question the taken-for-grantedness assumed within representation practices (Cresswell 2012) and who seek to 'think through locally formative interventions in the world' (Lorimer 2005: 84). Nonetheless, the lively debate provoked by NRT serves to critically engage with unfolding of social life in all of its messiness.

NRT is associated with Nigel Thrift's work that began in the 1990s, a response to and development out of the 1980s 'cultural turn' in specifically British but also Australian and North American human geography. The 'new cultural geography' challenged the universal notions of culture and normative values and beliefs that were argued to underpin the work of social scientists associated with Carl Sauer and the Berkeley school (Valentine 2001). In the new cultural geography, culture is understood as a signifying process, so drawing on poststructuralist and post-colonial theories, and thus is concerned with cultural politics (Valentine 2001; see also Jackson 1989; Crang 1998; Anderson and Harrison 2010). Thrift, in turn, questioned the apparent dominant mode of representational thinking in human geography, arguing that this framework failed to capture what happens outside of discourse (Cadman 2009). Instead, Thrift argues for a 'geography of what happens' (Thrift 2008: 2). This is because

> [t]he contours and content of what happens constantly change: for example, there is no stable 'human' experience because the human sensorium is constantly being re-invented as the body continually adds parts to itself; therefore how and what is experienced as experience is itself variable.
>
> (Thrift 2008: 2)

Thrift's questioning as to how knowledge is created in embodied, performative, and non-discursive ways that constitute the 'elusory nature of the everyday world' (Cadman 2009: 456) occurred during a period of geography's burgeoning interest in ideas in and aligned with continental philosophy, including the work of Spinoza, Benjamin, Whitehead, Merleau-Ponty, de Certeau, Deleuze and Guattari, Latour, Massumi, and Serres. For Thrift, NRT is about 'the construction of new counterpublics through assembling of more performative political ecologies' (2008: 22) and to do this we need to critically explore 'bare life [. . .] that small space of time between action and cognition' (2008: 24). Yet, as Thrift himself cautions, NRT is not a theory as such, nor does it set out one unique methodological framework or a means of communicating research (Vannini 2015). Rather, it is 'a mosaic of theoretical ideas . . . a synthesizing effort to amalgamate diverse but interrelated theoretical perspectives' (Vannini 2015: 3) and more 'a style of thinking which values practice' (Simpson 2010). Nonetheless, NRT is interested in emergent practices, 'an attention to events and the new potentialities for being, doing and thinking that events may bring forth' (Anderson and Harrison 2010: 19). In this sense, NRT is open-ended and focused on what is in process or unfolding (Cadman 2009), and so also aligned to the ideas originating in the mobilities literature (Lorimer 2007), especially with reference to performance, dance and affect. NRT's emphasis on practice can be difficult to grasp in the act of doing research, because it has an emphasis that 'cannot adequately be spoken of, that words cannot capture, that texts cannot convey'; instead, the focus is 'on forms of experience and movement that are not only or never cognitive' (Nash 2000: 655).

There have been important critiques of NRT, particularly from feminist scholars, who are concerned with the apparent withdrawal from the politics of the body and (renewed) focus on 'individualistic and universalizing sovereign subject'

(Nash 2000: 662; see also Cresswell 2012) – acknowledging difference and diversity is central to feminist approaches as well as post-colonial critiques. Lively discussion on emotion and affect between NRT proponents and feminist scholars has also raised issues of underlying assumptions about how gender operates in the networks and relations of feelings. As Thien (2005: 452) argues, the use of the terms 'affect' and 'emotion' in NRT literature seems to re-inscribe 'masculinist reason [that is, affect] and feminized emotion' as well as 'the false distinction between "personal" and "political"' which feminist scholars have extensively critiqued. Instead, affective geographies should draw our attention precisely because they dissolve such public/private boundaries (see also Tolia-Kelly 2006). Lorimer's (2005, 2007, 2008) set of progress reports on NRT also points to potential frustrations for those new to NRT, not least its 'seemingly unforgiving language' (2007: 97). As a number of scholars have stated, there is a need to ensure NRT is grounded or connected to existing issues and concerns (Lorimer 2007), otherwise such research will not address injustice and inequalities (Smith 2005).

What might NRT tell us about the festival experience? A "successful" festival in terms of social connectedness brings about a feeling of togetherness, a collective joy that transforms individuals into a community (Ehrenreich 2007). Waitt and Duffy (2010) depict the impact of this affective ambience in their examination of a classical music festival held in a small Australian coastal town. While acknowledging the specific capacities for participation and social relations inherent in music, they refer to one attendee at this festival who described this affective force: 'People come together as a whole instrument – made up of the many human beings and form a new living being – it is just transitory – and then it is gone' (Waitt and Duffy 2010: 458). This short quote aptly captures the emergence of everyday life; how we can be swept up into a place, a scene, or community perhaps without being aware as to why. Or, as Lorimer (2008: 552) writes, '[o]ur sensual worlds catalyse complexly and dissipate unexpectedly. Social fabrics and practices are not locked in to rational or predictable logics, and often are visceral and instinctive.' But how to make sense of such fleeting moments that nonetheless can have significant impact on the constitution of a community? Although this chapter does not set out to provide a definitive overview of its theoretical perspectives, a summary of some of NRT's key tenets will help us think through how this approach offers a means to explore the importance of bodies, emotions, affect and intensities in constituting the festival event as an encounter, as well as what these may mean for communities and social connectedness.

Senses and festival bodies

We are well aware as to how we can be affected by a range of cognitive and bodily sensations – and this happens not simply through discourse alone – that interpolate us into our everyday worlds (Boyd and Duffy 2012; Duffy et al. 2011). As discussed in Chapter 4, the generation of strong, often spontaneous feelings of connectedness arise out of the participants' responses to the sensual; that is, the visual, oral, olfactory and haptic elements of an event. These responses are a significant part of the process of sociality, producing *communitas* (Turner 1982).

Importantly, these intense feelings of belonging can operate across different social structures including class, ethnicity and gender, serving to re-affirm group identity and belonging (Costa 2002; Falassi 1987; Lavenda 1992; St John 1997). Nevertheless, feelings of exclusion, disgust and even alienation can also be aroused. Integral to the generation of each of these feelings is the participant's body and the ways in which the activities of the festival event engage and impact upon our various senses. Although Durkheim and Turner describe joyous and exultant feelings as integral to a deep social immersion, there is less consideration as to how the individual comes to be enmeshed within the social such that a heightened sense of belonging arises. Indeed, some scholars have noted a curious absence of bodies in studies of the everyday as well as events. NRT can contribute to this research through its broader questioning of the significance of the body in the social.

A focus on the ways in which bodily experiences constitute bonds of social connectedness is a fundamental part of the emotional, affective and sensual dimensions of festivals. Indeed, for some scholars, it is necessary to foreground the body in its seeking to explore experience (Hayes-Conroy and Hayes-Conroy 2010; Hockey and Allen-Collinson 2009). Bodies and the spaces they inhabit are inseparable (Merleau-Ponty 1962; Lefebvre 2004; Edensor 2010; Duffy et al. 2011), and this theoretical stance has its origins in the works of Heidegger and Merleau-Ponty. However, this phenomenological focus is of a *conscious* experience of events; that is, the ways in which we knowingly live through experience and communicate this from a first-person point of view, identifying phenomena as we perceive them in any given situation (Cohen 1979). This approach is deliberately subjective, for, as Merleau-Ponty (2002: 275) argued,

> [M]y body is not only an object among all objects . . . but an object which is sensitive to all the rest, which reverberates to all sounds, vibrates to all colours, and provides words with their primordial significance through the way in which it receives them.

In this framework, our senses mediate 'the relationship between mind and body, idea and object, self and environment (both physical and social)' (Howes 2006: 122). Work in the social sciences in the last few decades has emphasised the significance of the senses in instituting forms of sociality, because of the ways in which sensory experience contributes to concepts of the self and culture (Low 2012). As Ingold (2011: 315) argues, 'the senses are not keyboards or filters that mediate the traffic between mind and world. They are rather – as Gibson (1966) always insisted – aspects of the functioning of the living being and its environment'. Yet an important part of the critique of this 'empire of signs' (Howes 2005: 1) has been our inclination to ignore the sensations of the body and instead position ourselves in the modern framework of the subject/object distinction (Brennan 2004). This has important implications when considering cross-cultural events, such as in comparative anthropology, for, as Low (2012: 272) points out,

> the hierarchy of the sensorium is a product of cultural construction, of the "phylogenetic development of the human species" [Jütte 2005: 61], and of

the advancements in technology that run parallel to processes of civilization. Where vision took the lead in the order of things, other senses such as smell or touch occupied positions of "animality" given the associations with lust, gluttony, and savagery.

From a phenomenological perspective, it is through our physical body's perceptions that we respond to, make sense of and find ways to talk about the world. Yet, earlier studies in anthropology and sociology erroneously established Eurocentric and gendered hierarchies of being which were then 'affirmed' by the role of the senses in constituting social life (Grasseni 2007; Low 2005; Stoller 1997). A hierarchy of the senses serves to reinforce cultural assumptions about the non-White world that 'privilege[s] vision and consider[s] touch and taste as bestial and base' (Paterson 2009: 767). Critics of these phenomenological frameworks point out that in this approach there is an assumption of stability of the body in terms of such things as gender and race, yet we now recognise this notion of stability as incorrect.

Rather than a framework that assumes a stable and bounded body, NRT seeks to address the porosity of bodies and what this means for the everyday. For some scholars working in this field, this means drawing on Deleuze's reconceptualisation of the body as an assemblage rather than 'as raw material, prosocial or *fixed* containers for biology' (Waitt and Duffy 2010: 461; italics in original). The question posed is not 'what is the body?' rather it shifts towards the Spinozan 'what can a body do?' (in both its human and inhuman forms). Within such a question there is an acknowledgement of the ways in which bodies are intimately connected to the world – or, as Thrift points out, 'the human body is what it is because of its unparalleled ability to co-evolve with things . . . the human body is a tool-being' (2008: 10). However, Thrift cautions us not to consider all such embodied interaction as possessing a 'kind of continuous intentionality' because

[t]he experience of embodiment is not like that at all; not everything is focused intensity. Embodiment includes tripping, falling over, and a whole host of other such mistakes. It includes vulnerability, passivity, suffering, even simple hunger. It includes episodes of insomnia, weariness and exhaustion, a sense of insignificance and even sheer indifference to the world. In other words, bodies can and do become overwhelmed. The unchosen and unforeseen exceed the ability of the body to contain or absorb. And this is not an abnormal condition: it is a part of being as flesh.

(2008: 5)

Hence, NRT brings to our attention the ordinary encounters in ordinary places and the vibrancy of life to be found there (Boyd and Duffy 2012). The implication for empirical work is an imperative to expose the affective content of 'tacit' knowledges – ways and forms of knowing that are 'active, practical and sensory' (Wood and Smith 2004: 535). As Vannini (2015: 5) notes, bodies are therefore especially significant because of their affective capacities; that is, bodies are integral to the series of relations and networks through which affect operates and generates connectivity (or conversely, exclusion).

Affect and emotion

Since the late 1990s, there has been a renewed interest in emotion and affect in the humanities and social sciences. What is meant by these two terms remains contentious, reflecting differing disciplinary epistemologies, yet in the social sciences (e.g. geography), the emotional and affect literatures are not entirely discrete. Indeed, some argue that separating affect and emotion is counterproductive (Kenway and Youdell 2011), instead arguing they have a shared ontology in that both are considered mobile, moving between people and things, which in turn 'privileges proximity and intimacy' (Pile 2010: 10; see also Bondi 2005). However, those working within the NRT framework tend to make 'an analytic distinction between the corporeality inherent in a notion of affect and the more mindful conception of emotion' (Watkins 2011: 137). Therefore, *emotion* is restricted to psychological states such as anger, disappointment, resentment, and so on, whereas *affect* is conceptualized as non- or precognitive and transpersonal (Thrift 2008), although this division is complicated by associations both concepts have with such things as emotion, feeling, sensation, mood, passion and intensity (Anderson 2006). Some scholars point out, for example, that emotions are embedded within cultural knowledge and discursively produced and socially formed (Clarke et al. 2006) and, therefore, understood as not simply something felt within an individualised body but produced within networks of relations, both human and nonhuman (Bondi et al. 2005). This conceptualisation of emotion means that within such relational contexts, individuals will witness and, to some extent, be able to interpret and give meaning to bodily expressions of emotion.

Influenced by the work of Massumi (2002) and Deleuze, affect is most commonly used by NRT scholars in the Spinozan sense as a bodily capacity to act and be acted upon. Yet, 'in this ostensibly simple definition there is significant complexity, for it refers to a range of processes from the affected states of bodies, to the relaying of movement by individual bodies and the connection between bodies' (Duffy and Atkinson 2014: 107). As with emotion, the meaning of affect is further complicated by its association with terms such as 'emotion', 'feeling' and 'sensation'. However, scholars working within NRT perceive a distinct conceptual break with the geographies of emotion. Affect is defined as 'beyond' cognition and is relational, moving between, 'as a vehicle connecting individuals to one another and the environment . . . connecting the mind or cognition to bodily processes' (Brennan 2004: 19). In this way, affect can be distributed across a complex range of networks (biological, neurological, social, and psychological). Hence, work within this framework seeks to explore the importance of the affective relations in between the human and non-human elements of a space, as well as the in-betweenness of the body itself – the ways in which the body's chemical and neural processes influence our experiences of daily life, for example (McCormack 2006). Yet, this raises a methodological difficulty, as this conceptualisation of affect means that, unlike emotions, affects cannot be made known or represented (Pile 2010). Research continues to explore what sort of empirical approach addresses the concerns of NRT (Vannini 2015), yet what is clear is that this is the 'geography of what happens' (Thrift 2008). NRT highlights the failures of representational thinking to understand 'the palpable relevance of "thought-in-action" as the foreground (rather than the background) of our lives' (Boyd and Duffy 2012 online).

Returning to the example of the music festival's affective force on participants presented earlier in this chapter, individuals come to feel connected through a shared sense of consciousness, built around a form of cooperation that accommodates difference through a range of affective resources (social, cultural, economic, material and political). Numerous studies have sought to understand such responses through a focus on representation, with a focus on the role of musical genres as 'texts' that serve to shape and represent identities that participants then identify with (Gibson and Connell 2005; Quinn 2003). Yet, while an examination of musical genres and texts is useful in the tourism industry's framing of festival events and thus garnering audience interest, what is also significant are the affective, emotional and bodily responses that draw festival attendees into the thrill of an event in ways that bring individuals 'into the groove together' (Keil and Feld 1994: 167). In a study on a rural classical music festival, Waitt and Duffy (2010) suggest that understanding how a sense of connectivity arises requires reconsidering the body as embedded within networks with other (human and non-human) bodies constituted through neurological, psychological and culturally situated processes. The robustness of these affective relations increases the vitality of communities and is fundamental to the forming of social life and connectedness.

NRT and the encounter: Affective political terrains

Anderson and Harrison (2010: 19) argue that "the event" is a central concern within NRT scholarship because 'it opens up the question of how to think about change.' In ways that resonate with the new mobilities paradigm and its notion of event as simultaneously transformative and mundane, NRT conceptualises the event in terms of an emergent potential, a 'transforming moment that releases from the grip of the present and opens up the future in a way that makes possible a new birth, a new beginning, a new invention of ourselves, even as it awakens dangerous memories' (Caputo 2007: 19). Thus, the event is not benign or neutral; rather, it is better conceptualised within NRT thought as a provocation that can enable creative and inventive responses (Anderson and Harrison 2010). Whether this be the 'always just happened or . . . about to happen' (Anderson and Harrison 2010: 20) as described by Whitehead (1920), or Derrida's suggestion that the event is a 'rare surprise that breaks with how . . . a specific social-material configuration is assembled' (Anderson and Harrison 2010: 21), the event requires a different way of thinking and acting. How might this framing of the event, and its associations with affect, contribute to scholarship on festivals?

One way to respond to this question is to draw on the contributions of affect to forms of sociality that arise out of the transmission of forces across and between bodies. Those fleeting moments of connectedness – or the sense of 'being in the groove together', as described by Keil and Feld (1994) – often occur without human cognition or individual consciousness. And yet these can form powerful bonds between individuals, as well as between individuals and non-human elements. The notion of 'affective political terrain' presented here arises out of work conducted by Duffy, Slater and Waitt and out of attempts to understand how the transmission of affect can operate beyond linguistic or discursive construction. The ontological ground of the 'affective political terrain' is formed first by drawing on Gatens (1996) in her use of Spinoza's understanding of affect as a matter of sad and joyful passions and second through Fortier's (1999) concept of 'terrains of belonging'. Although neither Gatens nor Fortier would profess to be an NRT scholar, here we bring their ideas into a NRT framework in the spirit of NRT's inclusivity and eclectic nature (Vannini 2015) and because of their interest in how identities, place and notions of belonging are relationally constituted, a focus that is fundamental to NRT scholarship. Fortier's work on culturally diverse communities offers a productive means to understand the festival encounter. Her use of the word 'terrain' refers to the politics and practices that delineate social boundaries of who 'fits in' (Fortier 1999: 41–42). She uses this concept specifically to understand the ways in which migrant groups activate notions of belonging through shared histories and experiences that then serve to attach these (re)imagined communities to particular places. By introducing the term 'affective terrains', we wish to draw attention to the potential of the powerful emotive and affective politics embedded in the festival encounter and how these can be harnessed to understand our present and live with and in multiple sets of community belonging. This does not mean we avoid or ignore uncomfortable moments that can arise through difference. As with Mouffe's notion of agonism, the affective, bodily and ephemeral moments of encounter make present the vulnerable and uncertain complex terrain of sociability.

Conclusion

Increasingly, researchers are exploring the ways in which the emotions, feelings and sensations triggered at festivals either inspire or deter different expressions of individual and collective belonging. One important avenue for understanding how connectedness or alienation occurs is through a focus on the relations of affect and how these operate in and through particular (social, cultural economic, material) networks. Thus, in addition to research that emphasises how festivals are key sites through which communities are imagined and performed, it is equally important to think through the embodied affects of emotion in and through festival spaces.

NRT offers an important framework for exploring the festival encounter as part of a dynamic and embodied set of responses. By focusing on the ways in which the body is embedded within a series of emotional, material, social, economic and other contexts, we can come to different understandings as to how people develop social networks and connections through bodily, sensual and affective relations and how these, in turn, can shape notions of connectedness and belonging. These ideas will be discussed further in relation to specific festivals in later chapters of this book.

References

Anderson, B. (2006). Becoming and being hopeful: towards a theory of affect. *Environment and Planning D: Society & Space* 24, pp. 733–752.

Anderson, B. and Harrison, P. (2010). *Taking-Place: Non-Representational Theories and Geography*. Farnham, UK, Burlington, CA: Ashgate.

Bondi, L. (2005). 'Making Connections and Thinking Through Emotions: Between Geography and Psychotherapy. *Transactions: Institute of British Geographers* 30(4), pp. 433–448.

Bondi, L., Smith, M. and Davidson, J. (eds). (2005). *Emotional Geographies*, London: Ashgate

Boyd, C. and M. Duffy (2012). Sonic Geographies of Shifting Bodies. *Interference: A Journal of Audio Culture*. [online]. Available at: www.interferencejournal.com/articles/a-sonic-geography/sonic-geographies-of-shifting-bodies [Accessed 31 March 2017].

Brennan, T. (2004). *The Transmission of Affect*. Ithaca: Cornell University Press

Cadman, L. (2009). Non-representational theory/non-representational geographies. In: Kitchin, R. and Thrift, N. (Eds.) *International Encyclopaedia of Human Geography*, Volume 10, Oxford: Elsevier, pp. 456–463.

Caputo, J. (2007). *The Weakness of God*. Bloomington & London: Indiana University Press.

Cohen, E. (1979). A Phenomenology of Tourist Experiences. *Sociology* 13(2), pp. 179–20.

Costa, X. (2002). Festive Identity: Personal and Collective Identity in the Fire Carnival of the 'Fallas' (València, Spain). *Social Identities,* 8(2), pp. 321–345.

Crang, M. (1998). *Cultural Geography*. London: Routledge.

Cresswell, T. (2012). Review essay: Nonrepresentational theory and me: Notes of an interested sceptic. *Environment and Planning D: Society and Space*, 30(1), pp. 96–105.

Duffy, M., Atkinson, P. (2014). Unnatural Movements: Modernism's shaping of intimate relations in Stravinsky's *Le sacre du printemps*. *Affirmations: of the Modern* 1(2), pp. 95–119.

Duffy, M., Waitt, G., Gorman-Murray, A. and Gibson, C. (2011), Bodily rhythms: Corporeal capacities to engage with festival spaces. *Emotion, Space and Society,* 4(1), pp. 17–24.

Edensor, T. (2010). Walking in rhythms: place, regulation, style and the flow of experience. *Visual Studies.* 25(1), pp. 69–79.

Ehrenreich, B. (2007). *Dancing in the Streets: A History of Collective Joy*. London: Granta Books.

Falassi, A. (1987). *Time out of Time: Essays on the Festival*. Albuquerque:University of New Mexico Press.

Fortier, A.-M. (1999). Re-membering places and the performance of belonging(s). *Theory, Culture and Society,* 16(2), pp. 41–64.

Gatens, M. (1996). *Imaginary Bodies: Ethics, Power and Corporeality*. London: Routledge.

Gibson, J. (1966). *The Senses Considered as Perceptual Systems*. Oxford, England: Houghton Mifflin.

Grasseni, C. (2007). Communities of practice and forms of life: towards rehabilitation of vision. In: M. Harris (ed) *Ways of Knowing: New Approaches in the Anthropology of Evidence and Learning*. Oxford: Berghahn.

Hayes-Conroy, J., and Hayes-Conroy, A. (2010). Visceral Geographies: Mattering, Relating, and Defying. *Geography Compass*, 4(9), pp. 1273–1283.

Hockey, J, and Allen-Collinson, J. (2009). The sensorium at work: the sensory phenomenology of the working body. *The Sociological Review,* 57(2), pp. 217–239.

Howes, D. (2005). Introduction: Empire of the senses. In: D. Howes (Ed.), *Empire of the senses: The sensual cultural reader.* Oxford, New York: Berg (1–17)

Howes, D. (2006). Charting the sensorial revolution, *Senses and Society,* 1(1), pp. 113–128.

Ingold, T. (2011). Debare Section: Worlds of sense and sensing the world: a response to Sarah Pink and David Howes. *Social Anthropology/ Anthropologie Sociale,* 19(3), pp. 313–317.

Jackson, P. (1989). *Maps of Meaning: An Introduction to Cultural Geography.* London: Routledge.

Jütte, R. (2005). *A History of the Senses: From Antiquity to Cyberspace.* Cambridge: Polity Press.

Keil, C., Feld, S. (1994). *Music Grooves.* Chicago & London: University of Chicago Press.

Kenway, J., and Youdell, D. (2011). The emotional geographies of education: Beginning a conversation. *Emotion, Space and Society* 4(3), pp. 131–136.

Lefebvre, H. (2004). *Rhythmanalysis: Space, Time and Everyday Life.* London: Continuum.

Lorimer, H. (2005). Cultural geography: The busyness of being "More-Than-Representational." *Progress in Human Geography,* 29, pp. 83–94.

Lorimer, H. (2007). Cultural geography: Worldly shapes, differently arranged. *Progress in Human Geography,* 31(1), pp. 89–100.

Lorimer, H. (2008). Cultural geography: Non-representational conditions and concerns. *Progress in Human Geography,* 32, pp. 551–559.

Low, K. (2012). The social life of the senses: charting directions. *Sociology Compass* 6(3), pp. 271–282

Massumi, B. (2002). *Parables for the virtual: movement, affect, sensation.* Durham, N.C.: Duke University Press

McCormack, D. (2006). For the love of pipes and cables: A response to Deborah Thien. *Area,* 38, pp. 330–332.

Merleau-Ponty, M. (1962). *Phenomenology of perception,* In: Smith, C. (Ed.) London: Routledge and Kegan Paul.

Merleau-Ponty, M. (2002). *The Phenomenology of Perception,* trans. C. Smith, London: Routledge.

Nash, C. (2000). Performativity in practice: Some recent work in cultural geography. *Progress in Human Geography,* 24(4), pp. 653–664.

Paterson, M. (2009). Haptic Geographies: ethnography, haptic knowledges and sensuous dispositions. *Progress in Human Geography* 33, pp. 766–788

Pile, S. (2010). Emotions and affect in recent human geography. *Transactions of the Institute of British Geographers,* 35(1), pp. 5–20.

Quinn, B. (2003). Symbols, practices and myth-making: cultural perspectives on the Wexford Festival Opera, *Tourism Geographies,* 5(3), pp. 329–349.

Simpson, P. (2010) *Ecologies of Street Performance: Bodies, Affects, Politics.* Unpublished PhD Thesis, University of Bristol [online]. Available at: https://psimpsongeography.wordpress.com/2011/06/07/what-is-non-representational-theory/ [Accessed 31 March 2017].

Smith, N. (2005). Neo-critical geography, or, the flat pluralist world of business class. *Antipode,* 37(5), pp. 887–899.

St John, G. (1997). Going feral: authentica on the edge of Australian culture. *The Australian Journal of Anthropology* 8(2), pp. 167–189.

Stoller, P. (1997). *Sensuous Scholarship* Philadelphia, PA: University of Pennsylvania Press.

Thien, D. (2005). After or beyond feeling? A consideration of affect and emotion in geography. *Area*, 3(4), pp. 450–456.

Thrift, N. (2008). *Non-Representational Theory: Space/ Politics/ Affect*. London, New York: Routledge.

Tolia-Kelly, D. (2006). Affect – An ethnocentric encounter? Exploring the 'Universalist' imperative of emotional/ affectual geographies. *Area*, 38(2), pp. 213–217.

Turner, V. (1982). *From Ritual to Theatre: The Human Seriousness of Play*. New York: Paj Publications.

Valentine, G. (2001). Whatever happened to the social? Reflections on the 'cultural turn' in British human geography. *Norsk Geografisk Tidsskrift – Norwegian Journal of Geography*, 55(3), pp. 166–172.

Vannini, P. (2015). *Non-Representational Methodologies: Re-Envisioning Research*. New York, London: Routledge.

Waitt, G. and Duffy, M. (2010). Listening and tourism studies. *Annals of Tourism Research*, 37(2), pp. 457–477.

Watkins, M. (2011). Teachers' tears and the affective geography of the classroom. *Emotion, Space and Society,* 4(3), pp. 137–143.

Whitehead, A. (1920). *The Concept of Nature*, Cambridge: Cambridge University Press.

Wood, N., Smith, S. J. (2004). Instrumental routes to emotional geographies. *Social and Cultural Geography* 5, pp. 533–548.

7 Festivals and social justice

Introduction

Social justice is a complex construct. Social justice is defined by the Oxford English Dictionary as 'justice in terms of the distribution of wealth, opportunities and privileges within a society'; however, within that relatively straightforward definition lies a web of conflicting ideologies. Ideas of social justice become important when we consider how particular decisions and actions affect people – that is, how the distribution of certain benefits and burdens affects different individuals and groups (Rawls 1973; see also Butler 2015). Festivals and events have been argued to contribute to social justice objectives, particularly those of local authorities, but the main challenge for understanding, identifying and measuring the impacts of events on the local community is the intangibility of social justice and associated components of civic pride, community cohesion, community identity or sense of belonging. Further complexity arises as a result of the frequent use of festivals to showcase local government responses to culturally diverse communities, which may lead to individuals and groups feeling excluded from such expressions of community belonging, thus calling into question the value of festivals as a tool to promote multiculturalism (See Chapter 11 for more on multiculturalism and events). This chapter will introduce the concept of social justice and discuss how it is perceived and conceptualised at various levels (globally, nationally and locally) and will consider how festivals may, or may not, be operating in a socially just way or contributing to the broader government policies on social justice.

Social justice – Background to the concept

Inequity is a pervasive issue around the world. Inequality in the distribution of income at global, national, regional and even local levels is commonplace, and unequal distribution of opportunities affects a disproportionate number of people at the lower end of the socio-economic scale (UN 2006). Additionally, there is an uneven geography as to how social justice and vulnerability play out. Social justice at the global level may be broadly understood as the fair and compassionate distribution of the fruits of economic growth (UN 2006). However, it is not appropriate to frame social justice solely in economic terms. Indeed, the UN Sustainable Development Goals (SDGs), otherwise known as the Global Goals, address social justice in a different way. These goals are a call to end poverty, protect the planet and ensure that all people enjoy peace and prosperity (UNDP 2017). The goals cover areas such as climate change, economic inequality, innovation, sustainable consumption, peace and justice, and the interconnected nature of these goals is acknowledged (UNDP 2017).

The United Nations is committed to justice for all people: 'faith in fundamental human rights, in the dignity and worth of the human person, [and] in the equal rights of men and women.' This requires the promotion of 'social progress and better standards of life in larger freedom' and of 'the economic and social advancement of all peoples.' Social justice underlies the third stated purpose of the United Nations (after maintaining peace and friendly relations among nations), which is 'to achieve international cooperation in solving international problems of an economic, social, cultural or humanitarian character, and in promoting and encouraging respect for human rights and for fundamental freedoms for all without distinction as to race, sex, language, or religion' (Article 1; UN 2006: 14).

The application of social justice requires a geographical, sociological, political and cultural framework within which relations between individuals and groups can be understood, assessed, and characterized as just or unjust (UN 2006: 12). Individuals, institutions, Governments and international organizations make judgements about what is just and what is unjust based on a range of moral and political values and frameworks, and such frameworks vary considerably across cultures and over time. However, three key dimensions appear to be common to most conceptualisations of social justice: equality of rights; equality of opportunities; and equity in living conditions. The United Nations has also identified six key areas of inequality which contribute to a lack of social justice for those affected: inequalities in the distribution of income; inequalities in the distribution of assets; inequalities in the distribution of opportunities for work and remunerated employment; inequalities in the distribution of access to knowledge; inequalities in the distribution of health services, social security and the provision of a safe environment; and inequalities in the distribution of opportunities for civic and political participation (UN 2006).

On a national level, many Western democracies have incorporated social justice principles and ideals into their government policies and structures. However, the nature of social justice and the ways in which is it conceptualised appear to differ. In Australia, the Commonwealth Government states that its social justice strategy seeks to redress inequalities that continue to exist in Australian society. The current Government defines a socially just Australia as one in which there is a fair distribution of economic resources; equal access to essential services such as housing, health care and education; equal rights in civil, legal and industrial affairs; and equal opportunity for participation by all in personal development, community life and decision-making (Australian Government Department of Social Services). Australia thus has a strong focus on accessibility and inclusivity in community life as a pillar of social justice. In the United Kingdom, the Centre for Social Justice was created in 2004 as an independent think tank for generating policy recommendations to tackle the root causes of poverty, which was seen as being caused by social breakdown. Social justice in the UK therefore appears to focus more on economic justice as a way to bring about social justice; on lifting people out of poverty by trying to address five fundamental issues – family breakdown; educational failure; worklessness; addiction; and serious personal debt (Centre for Social Justice 2017). Interestingly, the standing of social justice issues in the United States appears uncertain since the inauguration of President Donald Trump; however, a search for 'social justice' on the White House website displayed no results, suggesting perhaps that social justice and equality are not current priorities of the presidential administration (whitehouse.gov 2017).

In a different cultural context, Chinese scholars have begun to examine social justice 'with Chinese characteristics' (Wei 2013). However, caution has been advised in applying the Western understanding of social justice to collectivist cultures (Wei 2013). Although an in-depth discussion of cultural differences is beyond the scope of this book, broadly speaking, collectivism refers to a preference for a tightly knit social framework in which individuals can expect their relatives, clan, or other in-group to look after them in exchange for unquestioning loyalty. Individualism, on the other hand, refers to a preference for a loosely knit social framework wherein individuals expect to take care of themselves and their immediate families only (Hofstede 1984). Wei (2013) advocates reimagining social justice in Chinese collectivist culture in an open way, to allow for different understandings of social justice and to bridge the gaps between differences and integration, divergence and common understanding, and diversity and unity, and Liang (2014) highlights issues of powerlessness and feelings of constraint in light of the current social and political reality in China.

In addition to considering social justice in the framework of different nations, it is important to include notions of social justice within countries in relation to indigenous communities. In some ways, there may be similarities between social justice as it is understood in collectivist cultures and as it is perceived in indigenous cultures. However, the impact of colonisation and boundaries/borders set up by colonising powers increases the complexity of social justice, because such artificially imposed boundaries fail to take into account different understandings and workings of what is just.

Social justice in the local context

Despite the multifaceted nature of the concept, the way it has been interpreted and the priorities attached to it by different governments and countries, social justice is an important component of national government policy in many countries. However, it is interesting to look at how this national conceptualisation translates into local action.

A content analysis using Leximancer of a range of social justice policies and charters from the East Coast of Australia highlighted the key themes that were apparent in these documents. The overall themes included community, social, services, people, support, needs, access and culture. Of particular interest are groups of words such as "life" and "rights"; "opportunities"; "information" and "education"; "development" and "future"; and "health"; "support"; "needs" and "services", as these point to specific areas that are considered important in these documents.

Taking one particular case as an example, in 2011, the City of Port Phillip, in Victoria, Australia, launched its first Social Justice Charter, based on six principles (City of Port Phillip 2017):

- Participation in decision-making and Council processes
- Partnership with our Indigenous community
- Access: equality of access to information, facilities and services
- Respect: valuing diversity
- Addressing the rising cost of living: reducing disadvantage
- Enjoying the City: being connected

A key part of this Social Justice Charter is a requirement for all City of Port Phillip Council policy to reflect its goals and aspirations, highlighting the relationship between social justice aims and local government policy. This Charter appears, at least, to be in line with the proposition of Fincher and Iveson (2008) that a socially just planning process should seek to redress disadvantage, recognise the differing needs of various groups and facilitate opportunities for increased sociality.

However, policy and planning is not always met with universal support; indeed, there have been strident criticisms of the failure of policymakers to take into account the diversity of cities and their inhabitants, which has meant that differing perspectives and dissent have been marginalised in the planning process (Fincher and Iveson 2008). Additionally, rather than considering redistribution of goods and services to bring about a more just society (Purcell 2002), neoliberalist concerns promote competition and greater efficiency as the most appropriate way to address inequalities. In the process, the restructuring of governance has meant significant shifts in how policy discourse is framed and used to address social justice, as well as the lessening role of the state in such matters.

At the local level, urban and regional planning are important avenues for improving everyday life and, hence, issues of social justice such as access and equity. The concept of the 'right to the city', developed by Henri Lefebvre and originally published in 1967, provides a useful framework to consider how urban planning and social justice may complement each other. His work rethinks how urban space is constituted, and he argues that lived space is not just a passive stage on which social life unfolds; rather, it represents an integral element of social life (Lefebvre 1991). This approach requires local government to reconsider how social life is structured through material and social practices and is a radical reimagining of community and its role in constituting place (Mair and Duffy 2015). Building on this notion, Purcell (2002: 102) argues that under the right to the city, membership in the community of enfranchised people is not an accident of nationality or ethnicity or birth; rather, it is earned by living out the routines of everyday life in the space of the city. In social justice terms, local government policy needs to consider the ways in which factors such as democratic struggles around gender, race, class, sexuality, and the environment operate at the local scale while keeping in mind the broader regional, national and global contexts and their impacts. Such an approach highlights the importance of local government decisions around planning and how they create urban space and life, but also fails to recognise that 'the right to occupy already-produced urban space . . . is also the right to produce urban space so that it meets the needs of inhabitants' (Purcell 2002: 103). This is not simple, but it is important in facilitating social encounters between more established and emerging communities.

Festivals and social justice

Festivals 'have become an established part of the repertoire of contemporary urban planning' (Fincher and Iveson 2008: 176), particularly through re-imagining who has a right to the city. As has been highlighted throughout this book, festivals offer a space for encounter. Citizenship, community and culture are important parts of event policy debates and discussions, but the degree to which they influence decision-making varies widely (Foley et al. 2011). However, there is increasing recognition that the economic impacts and benefits of festivals and events are not the only, or indeed necessarily the most important, way to evaluate them (Wood 2008). The social dimensions of festivals (along with their environmental impacts) has been the subject of significantly more research in the past decade than previously (Mair and Whitford 2013). Researchers have examined social impacts of festivals (e.g. Delamere 2001; Delamere et al. 2001; Rollins and Delamere 2007; Woosnam et al. 2013), festivals and social inclusion (Laing and Mair 2015), and celebrating a local communal identity (e.g. De Bres and Davis 2001; Duffy 2000, Jaeger and Mykletun 2013). Derrett's (2003) research suggests that festivals and events contribute to community well-being through the creation and enhancement of sense of place, which contributes to social identity. Community involvement in, and support for, events and festivals has also been recognised as significant to their success (Moscardo 2007). According to Moscardo (2007), various facets of festivals contribute to community well-being, such as the opportunities for residents and participants to socialise and have fun, the celebration of achievement and the relevance of the event to the local community. However, and perhaps more relevant to a discussion of social justice, at least in relation to improving access to paid employment and income opportunities, Moscardo (2007) also argued that participation in the planning and in the running of the event increased community capacity, by giving local people opportunities to extend their administration, organisational and leadership skills. Of course, as always, it is vital to remember that communities are not homogenous entities; therefore, in order to contribute to social justice aims and policies, events and festivals must have elements that appeal to a range of community sub-groups (Pugh and Wood 2004).

It does not appear to be in doubt that festivals have the potential to make significant contributions towards community building and other social cohesion processes. However, there has been very little research on how festivals respond to specific social justice issues as they are articulated in local government policy (Pugh and Wood 2004). The emphasis has been on how the social benefits for the economy generated through festivals and tourism can contribute towards social justice policy aims (Whitford 2009), and this is naturally an important component of the roles and responsibilities of local authorities. There has been a growing recognition that festivals, other events and tourism can all be used as ways to promote economic growth and regeneration, particularly in rural and regional areas with limited alternative livelihood options (Stokes 2006). Brennan-Horley et al. (2007) draw on the example of the Parkes Elvis Festival and explore the way in which a remote place with few economic prospects created a tourism product, and subsequently captured national attention, through a festival based around commemoration of the birthday of Elvis Presley. The findings of this study demonstrate how small places, even in remote areas, can develop economic activities through festivals.

Florida's (2002, 2003) creative industries framework is an important framework for conceptualising the role of festivals in local economic development (Cudny 2014). Festivals are understood as part of a range of cultural activities that attract the so-called creative classes into economically depressed urban areas that then help initiate urban regeneration through a cultural economy (Scott 2000). As a result, festivals and tourism can bring not only improved economic prospects but also increased vibrancy and liveability for communities (Mair and Duffy 2015).

However, simply creating a policy does not automatically bring the desired results, as policies rely on the political environment, values and ideologies, power distribution, institutional frameworks and decision-making processes (Hall and Jenkins 1995). Additionally, while many local authorities have developed or are developing local tourism policies, the same cannot be said for event policies. Whitford (2009: 677) even stated that 'many local governments have not attempted the development of event policy'. However, the development of cohesive and specific event policies would arguably facilitate regional development on many levels, with the important caveat that the needs and wishes of local people should be balanced with the development of projects that will offer sustainable benefits to visitors and locals alike (Pugh and Wood 2004).

Our previous work on the subject of festivals and social justice highlighted differences between the approaches taken by two different local authorities in relation to using events to meet social justice policy objectives (Mair and Duffy 2015). One council introduced a multicultural event (Experience! The Casey Multicultural Festival) with the specific aim of addressing particular priorities, whereas the other council relied on an existing festival (Yakkerboo) to meet its social justice policy (both of these festivals will be discussed in greater depth in Chapters 10 and 11). The festival designed to meet social justice aims was, not surprisingly, more successful in addressing these issues than the festival that had no such design, although such intangibles are difficult to measure. However, in different ways, both festivals arguably made positive contributions to some of the key domains of social justice, particularly in terms of improving equity of access. Examples include the fact that both festivals were free of charge, and both were held in locations easily accessed by public transport. However, other aspects of social justice did not appear to be so well addressed. For example, even where the community is recognised as culturally plural, one of these festivals appears to reiterate an ideal notion of community, rather than reflect how the community is actually constituted. Even when a festival is expressly designed to celebrate cultural diversity, the ideals of social cohesion and community identity are given meaning through local government policies, and through this official discourse, an 'imagined' community is produced (Smith and Brett 1998). Such outcomes are arguably unlikely to increase mutual respect or encourage increased civic and political participation.

Conclusion

Social justice is a complex concept and can be viewed in many ways. Common to most conceptualisations of social justice are notions of ensuring equality of rights; providing equality of opportunities; and enabling equity in living conditions. Taking a more grassroots perspective, social justice in the local context is often seen as relating to improving opportunities for participation in community life for all; developing partnerships across all levels of society (including with indigenous community members) to improve decision-making; improving equality of access to information, facilities and services; reducing economic disadvantage; and promoting respect and tolerance of diversity in all its various forms.

Festivals and events offer the opportunity to contribute to social justice aims, particularly those of local authorities tasked with improving the economic and social conditions of rural and regional communities. As discussed, this can include improving access to paid employment and income opportunities; extending community capacity by giving local people opportunities to participate in the planning and in the running of the event; contributing to community well-being; and providing opportunities for residents and participants to socialise and have fun.

However, an important caveat, as noted here and in other parts of this book, is that communities are not homogenous, and, while festivals may bring benefits to some parts of the community, others may not get equal access to these benefits. Festivals can act as spaces of exclusion, or as places where particular beliefs, ideologies or agendas are forefronted. Therefore, any automatic assumption that festivals will always contribute to broad social justice goals is unwarranted. Researchers and policymakers must be aware of the multifaceted nature of the communities they are investigating or supporting, and, while using festivals instrumentally to achieve certain goals, local authorities must bear in mind the potential for festivals to actively work against some of these goals.

References

Australian Government Department of Social Services. (2017). *Social Justice*. [online]. Available at: www.dss.gov.au/our-responsibilities/settlement-and-multicultural-affairs/programs-policy/a-multicultural-australia/national-agenda-for-a-multicultural-australia/participation/social-justice [Accessed 31 March 2017].

Brennan-Horley, C., Connell, J. and Gibson, C. (2007). The Parkes Elvis revival festival: Economic development and contested place identities in rural Australia. *Geographical Research*, 45(1), pp. 71–84.

Butler, J. (2015). *Notes Towards a Performative Theory of Assembly*. Cambridge, Mass.: Harvard University Press.

Centre for Social Justice. (2017). *The CSJ Story*. [online]. Available at: www.dss.gov.au/our-responsibilities/settlement-and-multicultural-affairs/programs-policy/a-multicultural-australia/national-agenda-for-a-multicultural-australia/participation/ social-justice [Accessed 31 March 2017].

City of Port Phillip. (2017). *Social Justice Charter*. [online]. Available at: www.portphillip. vic.gov.au/social-justice.htm [Accessed 31 March 2017].

Cudny, W. (2014). Festivals as a subject for geographical research. *Geografisk Tidsskrift- Danish Journal of Geography*, 114(2), pp. 132–142.

De Bres, K. and Davis, J. (2001). Celebrating group and place identity: A case study of a new regional festival. *Tourism Geographies*, 3(3), pp. 326–337.

Delamere, T. A. (2001). Development of a scale to measure resident attitudes toward the social impacts of community festivals, Part II: Verification of the scale. *Event Management*, 7(1), pp. 25–38.

Delamere, T. A., Wankel, L. M. and Hinch, T. D. (2001). Development of a scale to measure resident attitudes toward the social impacts of community festivals, Part I: Item generation and purification of the measure. *Event Management*, 7(1), pp. 11–24.

Derrett, R. (2003). Making sense of how festivals demonstrate a community's sense of place. *Event Management*, 8(1), pp. 49–58.

Duffy, M. (2000). Lines of drift: Festival participation and performing a sense of place. *Popular Music*, 19(1), pp. 51–64.

Fincher, R. and Iveson, K. (2008). *Planning and Diversity in the City: Redistribution, Recognition and Encounter*. Hampshire, UK: Palgrave Macmillan.

Florida, R. L. (2002). *The Rise of the Creative Class: And How It's Transforming Work, Leisure, Community and Everyday Life*. New York: Basic Books.

Florida, R. L. (2003). Cities and the creative class. *City and Community*, 2(1), pp. 3–19.

Foley, M., McGillivray, D. and McPherson, G. (2011). Events policy: The limits of democracy. *Journal of Policy Research in Tourism, Leisure and Events*, 3(3), pp. 321–324.

Hall, C. M. and Jenkins, J. (1995). *Tourism and Public Policy*. London: Routledge.

Hofstede, G. (1984). Cultural dimensions in management and planning. *Asia Pacific Journal of Management*, 1(2), pp. 81–99.

Jaeger, K. and Mykletun, R. J. (2009). The festivalscape of finnmark. *Scandinavian Journal of Hospitality and Tourism*, 9(2–3), pp. 327–348.

Jaeger, K., and Mykletun, R. J. (2013). Festivals, identities, and belonging. *Event Management*, 17(3), pp. 213–226.

Laing, J. and Mair, J. (2015). Music festivals and social inclusion – The festival organizers' perspective. *Leisure Sciences*, 37(3), pp. 252–268.

Lefebvre, H. (1991). *The Production of Space*. Cambridge, MA: Blackwell.

Liang, Y. (2014). *Exploring the Meaning of Social Justice in Chinese Context*. Yokohama, Japan: XVIII ISA World Congress of Sociology, 13–18 July 2014.

Mair, J. and Duffy, M. (2015). Community events and social justice in urban growth areas. *Journal of Policy Research in Tourism, Leisure and Events*, 7(3), pp. 282–298.

Mair, J. and Whitford, M. (2013). An exploration of events research: Event topics, themes and emerging trends. *International Journal of Event and Festival Management*, 4(1), pp. 6–30.

Moscardo, G. (2007). Analyzing the role of festivals and events in regional development. *Event Management*, 11(1–2), pp. 23–32.

Pugh, C. and Wood, E. H. (2004). The strategic use of events within local government: A study of London Borough Councils. *Event Management*, 9(1–2), pp. 1–12.

Purcell, M. (2002). Excavating Lefebvre: The right to the city and its urban politics of the inhabitant. *GeoJournal*, 58, pp. 99–108.

Rawls, J. (1973). *A Theory of Justice*. London: Oxford University Press.

Rollins, R. and Delamere, T. (2007). Measuring the social impact of festivals. *Annals of Tourism Research*, 34(3), pp. 805–808.

Scott, A. J. (2000). *The Cultural Economy of Cities: Essays on the Geography of Image-Producing Industries*. London: Sage.

Smith, G. and Brett, J. (1998). Nation, authenticity and social difference in Australian popular music: Folk, country, multicultural. *Journal of Australian Studies*, 22, pp. 3–17.

Stokes, R. (2006). Network-based strategy making for events tourism. *European Journal of Marketing*, 40(5/6), pp. 682–695.

United Nations (2006). *Social Justice in an Open world. The Role of the United Nations. International Forum for Social Development*. New York: United Nations. [online]. Available at: www.un.org/esa/socdev/documents/ifsd/SocialJustice.pdf [Accessed 31 March 2017].

United Nations Development Program (2017). *Sustainable Development Goals*. New York: United Nations [online]. Available at: www.undp.org/content/undp/en/home/sustainable-development-goals.html [Accessed 31 March 2017].

Wei, Z. (2013). *The Chinese Dream and China's Social Justice Theory*. [online]. Available at: www.china.org.cn/china/Chinese_dream_dialogue/2013-12/06/content_30819892.htm [Accessed 31 March 2017].

Whitehouse.gov (2017). *The White House Website*. [online]. Available at: www.whitehouse.gov/ [Accessed 31 March 2017].

Whitford, M. (2009). A framework for the development of event public policy: Facilitating regional development. *Tourism Management*, 30(5), pp. 674–682.

Wood, E. H. (2008). An impact evaluation framework: Local government community festivals. *Event Management*, 12(3–4), pp. 171–185.

Woosnam, K., Van Winkle, C. and An, S. (2013). Confirming the festival social impact attitude scale in the context of a rural Texas cultural festival. *Event Management*, 17(3), pp. 257–270.

8 Social inclusion, social exclusion and encounter

Introduction

As Fincher and Iveson (2008) note, festivals are considered to be places where people can experience and explore multiple identities; yet, as such, festivals need careful management if they are to facilitate this aim. The activities, engagements and debates that occur in public spaces are part of the ways in which communities represent the public life and social identity of that community. Further, events that take place in these public spaces provide an important opportunity for fostering interactions between individuals who may not otherwise meet. Both of these are key dimensions of developing inclusive festivals that represent the wider community, both the geographically local community and other communities of interest. Limited research has examined encounter in the tourism context, which questions how geographical knowledge is produced through engagements with places and people that are in some way considered "other" (Crouch and Desforges 2003). This suggests that encounters between tourists and both place and other people help to develop the visitor's knowledge (Crouch and Desforges 2003). However, there is more to the festival event than simply a possibility for a brief, or chance, encounter. Festivals allow for exchange of knowledge, networks, trades, goods and services. Therefore, encounter plays out particularly in relation to notions of inclusion and exclusion.

Social policy debates about inclusion v exclusion

Social inclusion and exclusion have been important components of European social policy debates for more than thirty years. Social exclusion can be conceptualised as encompassing five dimensions: exclusion from material resources, exclusion from social relations, exclusion from civic activities, exclusion from basic services, and neighbourhood exclusion (Scharf et al. 2002). Initially, the notion underpinning social exclusion was that those who were excluded from society had in some senses brought this upon themselves, perhaps through a lack of individual responsibility or through failing to adjust to the accepted norms of a capitalist Western democracy (Sandell 1998). Naturally, social exclusion may also apply in other contexts, but the initial literature focused on this Western perspective. Wilson (2006) viewed the issue of social exclusion through the common exclusionist discourses, highlighting three discourses – a redistributive, egalitarian discourse; a moralistic discourse; and a mutual obligations discourse. The first of these presumes that it is the role of the state to intervene financially and redistribute wealth to prevent the social exclusion of individuals. The second discourse brings a moral argument to bear, suggesting that the individual is at fault and that his or her exclusion is the result of laziness or shirking responsibilities; thus, the state shouldn't intervene. Finally, there were those who believed that in the capitalist system, there were mutual obligations – individuals should be able to receive assistance from the state where necessary but, at the same time, should be obliged to contribute back to the state.

However, over time, the debates moved away from a focus on blame and responsibility and instead moved towards the issue of how to facilitate and encourage fuller participation in society by all individuals. Social exclusion can be explained thus: 'An individual is socially excluded if (a) he or she is geographically resident in a society but (b) for reasons beyond his or her control, he or she cannot participate in the normal activities of citizens in that society, and (c) he or she would like to so participate' (Burchardt et al. 2002: 32). In the United Kingdom in particular, and in Europe more broadly, policy on social inclusion featured education, social policy, cultural diversity and poverty alleviation (Bates and Davis 2004). In Asia, however, perhaps as a result of differing social norms and social structures, social exclusion appeared to remain more closely related to issues of race and inward migration, particularly of low-skilled workers (Ngan and Chan 2013). However, there are signs that the neoliberalist discourse in the West generally is moving towards exclusion based on "not us". Butler (2015: 25) talks about this in terms of 'each of us [being] responsible for ourselves, not others, and that responsibility is first and foremost a responsibility to become economically self-sufficient under conditions where self-sufficiency is structurally undermined.'

Rather than seek reasons for why some groups are disadvantaged and excluded, governments began seeking ways to remove barriers to participation by disadvantaged social groups (O'Sullivan 2012). Johnson et al. (2011) proposed a list of the positive outcomes sought from increasing social inclusion, namely, (1) greater confidence and the development of social support networks, (2) increased self-determination and control for communities, (3) improved mental health and happiness, (4) learning new skills and improved access to education, and (5) improved opportunities for employment. Participation in mainstream social, cultural, economic, and political activities is at the core of most definitions of inclusion (Burchardt et al. 2002). Criticisms remain as to the efficacy of government efforts in this regard (Allison and Hibbler 2004); however, the removal of barriers to participation at least offers a practical solution to some of the social exclusion issues faced by Western democracies.

Leisure and the arts have a long association with social inclusion (Laing and Mair 2015). For example, according to Sandell (1998), although museums may appear to be spaces of exclusion (for financial, cultural and class reasons), they may take active steps to increase their relevance to a wider audience, perhaps by including artefacts and exhibits representing the history and culture of minority groups. This type of inclusivity may lead to an improvement in accessibility to the museum services by the wider community (Sandell 1998). Sharp et al. (2005) investigated how urban regeneration and public art are linked, and they concluded that public art can play an important role in promoting inclusion. Inclusive access to libraries, art and cultural institutions contributes to community and social inclusion, particularly in rural areas (McHenry 2009). There is also increasing recognition that festivals, particularly community festivals, may encourage social inclusion, although there is little research that documents this or clarifies the mechanisms through which festivals facilitate social inclusion. This will be discussed further later in this chapter.

Inclusion and exclusion at festivals

Whilst there is ample research on social inclusion and exclusion more generally, there is far less on inclusion and exclusion at festivals and events. Finkel (2010) suggests that social inclusion is one of the key reasons given by community events organisers for staging events and festivals. Mair and Duffy (2015) give an example of how a local authority sees the rationale for staging festivals: to demonstrate a commitment to creating 'a welcoming, inclusive and accessible community' (Mair and Duffy 2015: 3). Socialization or social interaction is one of the main ways that festival organisers see themselves contributing to social inclusion (Laing and Mair 2015). This is usually achieved by providing an atmosphere of tolerance and inclusivity, in which all are welcomed. Jepson and Clarke (2015) even state that the primary role of a community festival is to enhance engagement and inclusivity. However, it is also important that the planning process for community festivals be inclusive (Jepson and Clarke 2015). One final point worth noting is that there are significant difficulties associated with the measurement of social inclusion. In other words, even if a festival aims to create social inclusion, it is near impossible to judge whether it has achieved this aim (Foley and McPherson 2007). There is evidence to suggest that festivals do offer opportunities to encourage and facilitate inclusion and interaction across social strata, ethnic background, and gender divides, but, at the same time, there are occasions when festivals can clearly be seen as involving exclusionary practices. Festivals are complex processes and may involve division, and, as Clarke and Jepson (2011) note, may intentionally or otherwise operate as spaces of exclusion.

Social inclusion and festivals

In terms of inclusion, there appear to be several dimensions which affect how inclusive a festival can be considered to be. These can be tangible factors such as whether the festival is financially accessible (or indeed physically accessible) or contributes to filling knowledge and skills gaps; or they can be more intangible, such as issues of belonging and identity and diversity issues. Laing and Mair (2015), writing from the festival organiser perspective, posit that festival organisers may contribute to social inclusion across four areas of society – consumption, production, political engagement, and social interaction or *communitas*.

Consumption of a festival relies heavily on the ability of people to access the festival. Festivals and events can be expensive, and this cost can be a barrier to entry for a range of different groups. A number of initiatives were documented in the Laing and Mair (2015) study relating to how organisers can make it easier for residents and visitors to access a festival. Festivals can strive for greater inclusivity by removing structural barriers such as costs by staging festivals that are free of charge, providing free or discounted tickets for local residents or those from disadvantaged communities, or offering entry for locals at nominal charge. This allows lower socio-economic groups to access the event and take part in cultural activities that may otherwise be unattainable for them (Arcodia and Whitford 2006; Waitt and Duffy 2010). It may also allow local residents into spaces not normally accessible to them, such as city halls, or landmarks, if they are being used as festival venues. However, inclusivity is not only about cost but also about location. Certain venues will reinforce feelings of exclusion for those who wouldn't normally go, for example, to a classical festival/concert. Finally, opening festivals to local schools and community groups at low prices can assist with inclusion aims. However, at the same time, Mair and Laing (2012) noted that not all organisers publicised the availability of free tickets to local residents, suggesting that budgetary pressures may overcome the desire of festival organisers to make their festivals more inclusive. Other ways in which festivals can operate inclusively include the provision of disabled access above and beyond meeting the minimum legal requirements. Even something as simple as choosing an informal outdoor venue for a festival also helps to broaden access to many activities, particularly arts and culture (Carlsen et al. 2007).

Social inclusion has a strong connection with levels of education and participation in wider society, and participating ('consuming') activities such as festivals offers people the opportunity to develop positive relationships and learn new skills that may lead to positive outcomes in the 'hard' indicators of inclusion such as employment (Johnson et al. 2011). Laing and Mair (2015) also conceptualise *consumption* as being greater than simply accessing a festival, but rather including what an attendee might learn as a result of working at, volunteering for, or attending a festival. Festivals offer the opportunity for local people to become involved in the organisation and perhaps pick up some work experience or qualifications, such as Responsible Service of Alcohol certificates, or food handling and hygiene certification (Johnson et al. 2011). This contributes to local capacity building and upskilling, also identified as being connected to social inclusion (Johnson et al. 2011).

The second component of social inclusion identified by Laing and Mair (2015) is *production*. This relates to how a festival is produced and how this can be considered an inclusive process. Examples include using local suppliers, developing public-private partnerships with community-based organizations, encouraging local community members to be involved in festivals through volunteering, and using festivals as tools to contribute towards the regeneration of deprived areas (Laing and Mair 2015). Finally, festivals can present a significant opportunity for local talent, for example by commissioning local artists or by discovering and presenting new local musicians. In relation to this, Rogers and Anastasidou

(2011) point to the way that festivals can be more inclusive of local residents and businesses, by using local artists/performers; involving local businesses as suppliers and as sponsors; involving the local community in festival decision-making; and by facilitating close liaison between festival organisers and local residents. The notion of 'local' is, of course, variable – what is perceived to be 'local' in a large city (for example, products grown or produced within 100 kilometres of the city) may be perceived differently in a small rural village, where 'local' may imply products grown or produced in the immediate neighbourhood. Thus festival organisers need to work with business, residents and artist/performers to develop a collaborative approach to identifying and defining what is meant by "local".

Volunteering at festivals may also result in positive inclusion outcomes, as people mix with other community members across a broad range of backgrounds, abilities and interests (Finkel 2010; Lockstone-Binney et al. 2010). Rogers and Anastasidou (2011) proposed that festivals can encourage inclusion by attracting local residents to attend festivals as volunteers, thus mixing people from different walks of life. Additionally, research is demonstrating that those who volunteer at festivals and other events are more likely to consider volunteering in other areas, such as for charities, and for health-related causes (Gallarza et al. 2013). Therefore, volunteering at festivals can arguably benefit not only the festivals and the volunteers themselves, but also other charities and causes in the community into the future. In this way, volunteering not only contributes to the creation of social inclusion, but also is an outcome of social inclusion.

Many communities struggle to deal with diversity, and festivals can offer a way to allow the broader community to access and understand different cultures, sexualities and ethnicities (among others). Festivals often include a range in programming, which can highlight diversity and present it in a positive way, thus encouraging tolerance and contributing to a more inclusive community (Carlsen et al. 2007; Finkel 2006). Research has shown that festival organisers can act as champions for ethnic diversity and multiculturalism, either by including local and indigenous artists in their programming to better reflect the cultural mix of the wider society or by expressly and overtly including migrant and refugee communities in their festival (Laing and Mair 2015; Permezel and Duffy 2007). Mair and Duffy (2015) note the example of the Experience! multicultural festival in Australia, a festival expressly designed by a local authority to fulfil a particular policy objective – celebrating diversity. (See also Chapter 11 on encounter with the other).

Political engagement can be considered an important component of social inclusion. It may refer to willingness to be engaged with particular political causes, or it may refer to active civic participation – voting, standing for election or being a committee member in a community group, for example. Being involved in a festival organising committee (even as a volunteer) can give participants a greater sense of awareness of the broader local or regional political landscape and can provide an entry point into other community roles. Going further, festivals can be spaces where political causes are publicised – often local or national pressure groups or campaigns will have a presence at a festival – thus, attendees are made aware of issues that they may not yet have known about. Such issues can range from very small-scale local protests and grievances like the proposed loss of a children's community playground all the way up to issues of national and international importance like terrorism, anti-war protests and environmental activism. Additionally, festivals can be places for contesting societal norms – outdoor festivals have traditionally provided a counterculture space for anti-authoritarianism, experimentation with sexual relationships and drug consumption with minimum interference from society in general (Anderton 2011). This has been referred to as the countercultural carnivalesque, which incorporates, amongst other things, a critique of the materialism and consumerism of mainstream capitalist society and which nurtures a strong interest in environmental, social and broadly alternative or New Age beliefs among attendees (Anderton 2008).

Finally, Laing and Mair (2015) propose that *social interaction* is crucial to generating social inclusion. Festivals have the potential to act as spaces of integration and encounter and thus have an important role to play in helping people to build and sustain a stronger sense of belonging and identity. Festivals are also strongly connected with a sense of local or community identity (Morgan 2008). Derrett (2003) suggests that festivals can help to break down barriers within a community and thus lead to stronger communities. For O'Sullivan (2012), festivals can provide opportunities for social advantage, identity, and improved self-esteem, whilst Gorman-Murray (2009) proposes that festivals might encourage tolerance of diversity and encourage acceptance of difference in the wider community. As Picard (2015) notes, festivals can offer opportunities for participants to generate a sense of community among themselves. He refers to participants talking to each other about the event, sharing anecdotes, and creating a narrative that becomes 'a common reference of belonging' (p. 9). He also suggests that festival attendance facilitates the dissolving of normally accepted boundaries, such as between genders or between ethnic groups. Festivals offer 'a licence to mix with each other' (p. 9) when such groups would not normally mix. This suggests that in relaxing social norms, rules and prohibitions, festivals are creating an inclusive atmosphere.

According to Jaeger and Mykletun (2013), festivals are part of a larger notion of how place is socially constructed through human interaction. Storytelling and tales about a place can be used to create boundaries and to delineate who belongs in a space and who does not. Festivals can either contribute to inclusiveness by strengthening feelings of belonging or create divisiveness and exclusion by strenuously demarcating belonging. In their study on the Kangaroo Island Art Feast, George et al. (2015) document how festival organisers use communication to emphasise the focus of the event on the local and to identify festival attendees as locals (whether they are residents or not). This is done by the use of informal email contact, and use of first names for festival organisers and supporters, thus implying that attendees are familiar with these community members and thus are themselves considered members of the local community.

Social exclusion and festivals

Although most festivals would argue that they strive to stage inclusive and accessible events, it is accepted that on occasion, festivals operate to exclude sections of the community (Laing and Mair 2015). Historic and cultural factors may be the source of division – for example, where women are traditionally excluded from cultural or religious celebrations, or where festivals have contested meanings. Alternatively, financial considerations may intervene to prevent some community members from attending festivals. As Lockstone-Binney et al. (2010) suggest, there is also widespread under-representation of socially disadvantaged groups among festival volunteers, which is likely to lead to positive inclusion outcomes for those already included in society, rather than those on the margins.

Sometimes, festivals that are designed to be inclusive fail in this endeavour. One potential reason for this is a failure to consult with local community residents, businesses and groups. George et al. (2015) note that in the case of the Kangaroo Island Surf Festival, which closed after only one year, a lack of engagement with local knowledge led to the festival's demise.

Literature suggests that on occasions, festivals are intentionally designed as contested spaces, allowing a socially sanctioned forum for unleashing societal tensions (Quinn 2006). This by nature suggests that some parties may be excluded intentionally – according to Quinn (2006), for example by marching on particular routes, wearing particular clothing, playing particular music and displaying particular flags and banners that have religious or political significance and are designed expressly to consolidate or demonstrate resistance against in-group solidarity.

However, in most instances, exclusionary practices at festivals can be considered unintentional or the result of a lack of engagement with all sections of the community. There are two key issues in relation to organising festivals that may result in exclusion – these are the presence of multiple stakeholders, and the way that festivals manage issues of diversity.

Given the diversity of stakeholders involved in a community festival, it is arguably very difficult to please everyone. Organisers, community groups, local residents (both those who attend and support the event and those who do not), visitors, local businesses, local authorities and local media all have a stake in an event, and it is difficult to imagine one event being able to satisfy the needs and wants of so many diverse groups. Tensions are bound to arise, and where there is disagreement or dissent between the wishes of one or more stakeholders, there is a risk that those not fully satisfied by the way an event is organised or run will feel excluded.

In Cornwall, UK, each year, the Obby Oss Festival takes place in Padstow. With roots going back at least 200 years, the festival celebrates May Day and may even have pagan roots (Cornish 2015). The festival is associated with a deep connection with place: '[t]he Oss Societies are made up of old Padstow families' and 'residents echo the clothing of the two Oss Societies to mark their town membership, wearing white clothes and a headscarf or neckerchief (red or blue depending on the Oss), their black hats adorned with flowers' (Cornish 2015: 4). Street parades are normally opportunities for people to celebrate a collective identity in a civic space (Duffy et al. 2007), and anthropological literature demonstrates that these events are important to strengthening the social fabric (see for example Lewis and Dowsey-Magog 1993). Yet practices such as those at the

Obby Oss Festival may be seen as exclusive, given that non-residents among the festival attendees are not allowed to participate in the parade. Similarly, work by Finkel (2010: 277) highlights the importance to local residents of the Up Helly Aa Festival in Shetland as 'a celebration and reaffirmation of community identity [. . .] which interprets and reinterprets what it means to be a Shetlander'. Although visitors may spectate (and each year around 5,000 do, according to Finkel [2010]), they may not take part in the parade. Even attending parties after the parade is mostly limited to local residents. Finkel (2010) refers to this as protecting the 'sacred space' of the festival from outsiders. Tourists were marginalized or excluded from involvement and treated as "outsiders," and there was community resistance to widespread publicity for this festival.

The choice of genre for a festival may be problematic in terms of inclusion. Festivals have been described as elitist, and it has been suggested that focusing on "high culture" excludes large segments of the local population (Waterman 1998). Some scholars have even suggested that, far from contributing to community development, festivals simply reflect the desire of a small elite group to pursue its interests (Ritchie 1984). Further, in her work on an opera festival, Quinn (2003) showed that local residents felt a sense of dissatisfaction and exclusion in relation to the way that the festival privileged visiting audiences and tourists over the wishes and needs of local residents.

In relation to addressing diversity concerns, Clarke and Jepson (2011) highlight issues around power differentials in the community events space, noting that although festivals can provide a platform for marginalised or minority groups, festivals can also be seen as a demonstration of power if the existing majority can use a festival as a way to exercise hegemony over less powerful groups. Mair and Duffy (2015) demonstrate how a traditional festival that fails to adapt to the changing nature of place can risk excluding (albeit unintentionally) new sections of the community, yet Mair and Duffy also highlight how a top-down approach to providing a multicultural festival may lack buy-in from marginalised communities, thus isolating or further excluding these community groups. Clarke and Jepson (2011, p. 14) also highlight a lack of ownership of community festivals by the communities they are intended to serve – as they point out: 'a community festival was being constructed without the local communities whose lack of inclusion and voice laid the foundations for hegemony and a minority to exercise and retain power within the festival planning process.' This lack of inclusion (although not overtly intended to exclude) contributed to apathy among large sections of the local community, who were not empowered to make any changes to the festival.

Foley and McPherson (2007) argue that stating that a festival is intended to serve the needs of all citizens and races is not enough to ensure the inclusion of diverse religious and ethnic groups and thus secure the engagement of these communities. They further point to the difficulties in measuring whether a festival has indeed met such goals, casting doubt on the usefulness of such festival objectives.

Another issue highlighted by Finkel (2010) in her work on Up Helly Aa is the exclusion of women for traditional and historical reasons. Only men can take part in the procession, while women can be involved in other ways, usually by cooking, cleaning and engaging in other traditionally female occupations. However, most of the women in Finkel's study did not seem to want to change this accepted tradition (Finkel 2010). In this case, it is difficult to argue whether this is an exclusionary practice or not.

Conclusion

Festivals are closely connected with social inclusion, and they have tremendous potential to be inclusive activities. The most important ways that festivals encourage and promote social inclusion are through facilitating access for all (residents and visitors alike); using local resources, suppliers and producers; incorporating local artists and performers, using local volunteers, encouraging civic participation and providing a space where people can get together to celebrate identity, community and belonging. However, in many instances, and often unintentionally, festivals appear to act as spaces of exclusion, where visitors are privileged over locals, where minority groups are further marginalised, where diversity is not celebrated and where divisions are entrenched.

References

Allison, M. T. and Hibbler, D. K. (2004). Organizational barriers to inclusion: Perspectives from the recreation professional. *Leisure Sciences*, 26, pp. 261–280.

Anderton, C. (2008). Commercializing the carnivalesque: The V festival and image/risk management. *Event Management*, 12(1), pp. 39–51.

Anderton, C. (2011). Music festival sponsorship: Between commerce and carnival. *Arts Marketing: An International Journal*, 1(2), pp. 145–158.

Arcodia, C. and Whitford, M. (2006). Festival attendance and the development of social capital. *Journal of Convention and Event Tourism*, 8(2), pp. 1–18.

Bates, P. and Davis, F. A. (2004). Social capital, social inclusion and services for people with learning disabilities. *Disability and Society*, 19(3), pp. 195–207.

Burchardt, T., Grande, J. L. and Pichaud, D. (2002). Degrees of exclusion: Developing a dynamic, multidimensional measure. In: Hills, J., Grande, J. L. and Pichaud, D. (Eds.) *Understanding Social Exclusion*. Oxford, England: Oxford University Press, pp. 30–43.

Butler, J. (2015). *Notes Towards a Performative Theory of Assembly*. Cambridge, Mass.: Harvard University Press.

Carlsen, J., Ali-Knight, J. and Robertson, M. (2007). Access – A research agenda for Edinburgh festivals. *Event Management*, 11(1–2), pp. 3–11.

Clarke, A. and Jepson, A. (2011). Power and hegemony within a community festival. *International Journal of Event and Festival Management*, 2(1), pp. 7–19.

Cornish, H. (2015). Not all singing and dancing: Padstow, folk festivals and belonging. *Ethnos: Journal of Anthropology*, 1–17. pp. 631–647.

Crouch, D. and Desforges, L. (2003). The sensuous in the tourist encounter. Introduction: The power of the body in tourist studies. *Tourist Studies*, 3(1), pp. 5–22.

Derrett, R. (2003). Making sense of how festivals demonstrate a community's sense of place. *Event Management*, 8(1), pp. 49–58.

Duffy, M., Waitt, G. R. and Gibson, C. R. (2007), Get into the groove: The role of sound in generating a sense of belonging in street parades. *Altitude: A Journal of Emerging Humanities Work*, 8, pp. 1–32.

Fincher, R. and Iveson, K. (2008). *Planning and Diversity in the City: Redistribution, Recognition and Encounter*. Hampshire, UK: Palgrave Macmillan.

Finkel, R. (2006). Tensions between ambition and reality in UK combined arts festival programming: Case study of the Lichfield Festival. *International Journal of Event Management Research*, 2(1), pp. 25–36.

Finkel, R. (2010). Dancing around the ring of fire: Social capital, tourism resistance, and gender dichotomies at up Helly Aa in Lerwick, Shetland. *Event Management*, 14(4), pp. 275–285.

Foley, M. and McPherson, G. (2007). Glasgow's winter festival: Can cultural leadership serve the common good? *Managing Leisure*, 12(2/3), pp. 143–156.

Gallarza, M. G., Arteaga, F. and Gil-Saura, I. (2013). The value of volunteering in special events: A longitudinal study. *Annals of Tourism Research*, 40, pp. 105–131.

George, J., Roberts, R. and Pacella, J. (2015). Whose festival? Examining questions of participation, access and ownership in rural festivals. In: Jepson, A. and Clarke, A. (Eds.) *Routledge Advances in Events Research Book Series: Exploring Community Festivals and Events*. Oxon, New York: Routledge, pp. 79–92.

Gorman-Murray, A. (2009). What's the meaning of Chillout? Rural/urban difference and the cultural significance of Australia's largest rural GLBTQ festival. *Rural Society*, 19(1), pp. 71–86.

Jaeger, K. and Mykletun, R. J. (2013). Festivals, identities, and belonging. *Event Management*, 17(3), pp. 213–226.

Jepson, A., & Clarke, A. (2015). Defining and exploring community festivals and events. In: Jepson, A. and Clarke, A. (Eds.) *Routledge Advances in Events Research Book Series: Exploring Community Festivals and Events*. Oxon, New York: Routledge, pp 1–14.

Johnson, V., Currie, G. and Stanley, J. (2011). Exploring transport to arts and cultural activities as a facilitator of social inclusion. *Transport Policy*, 18, pp. 68–75.

Laing, J. and Mair, J. (2015). Music festivals and social inclusion – The festival organizers' Perspective, *Leisure Sciences*, 37(3), pp. 252–268.

Lewis, L. and Dowsey-Magog, P. (1993). The Maleny 'Fire Event': Rehearsals toward neo-liminality'. *The Australian Journal of Anthropology*, 4(3), pp. 198–219.

Lockstone-Binney, L., Holmes, K., Smith, K. and Baum, T. (2010). Volunteers and volunteering in leisure: Social science perspectives. *Leisure Studies*, 29(4), pp. 435–455.

Mair, J. and Duffy, M. (2015). Community events and social justice in urban growth areas. *Journal of Policy Research in Tourism, Leisure and Events*, 7(3), pp. 282–298.

Mair, J. and Laing, J. (2012). The greening of music festivals: Motivations, barriers and outcomes. Applying the Mair and Jago model. *Journal of Sustainable Tourism*, 20(5), pp. 683–700.

McHenry, J. A. (2009). A place for the arts in rural revitalisation and the social wellbeing of Australian rural communities. *Rural Society*, 19(1), pp. 60–70.

Morgan, M. (2008). What makes a good festival? Understanding the event experience. *Event Management*, 12(2), pp. 81–93.

Ngan, L. L. S. and Chan, K. W. (2013). An outsider is always an outsider: Migration, social policy and social exclusion in East Asia. *Journal of Comparative Asian Development*, 12(2), pp. 316–350.

O'Sullivan, D. (2012). Public events, personal leisure. In: Connell, J. and Page, S. (Eds.). *The Routledge Handbook of Events*. Abingdon: Routledge, pp. 87–103.

Permezel, M. and Duffy, M. (2007). Negotiating cultural difference in local communities: The role of the body, dialogues and performative practices in local communities. *Geographical Research*, 45(4), pp. 358–375.

Picard, D. (2015). The festive frame: Festivals as mediators for social change. *Ethnos: Journal of Anthropology*, 81(4), pp. 600–616.

Quinn, B. (2003). Symbols, practices and myth-making: cultural perspectives on the Wexford Festival Opera, *Tourism Geographies*, 5(3), pp. 329–349.

Quinn, B. (2006). Problematising 'Festival Tourism': Arts festivals and sustainable development in Ireland. *Journal of Sustainable Tourism*, 14(3), pp. 288–306.

Ritchie, J. B. (1984). Assessing the impact of hallmark events: Conceptual and research issues. *Journal of Travel Research*, 23(1), pp. 2–11.

Rogers, P. and Anastasidou, C. (2011). Community involvement in festivals: Exploring ways of increasing local participation. *Event Management*, 15(4), pp. 387–399.

Sandell, R. (1998). Museums as agents of social inclusion. *Museum Management and Curatorship*, 17(4), pp. 401–418.

Scharf, T., Phillipson, C., Smith, A. E. and Kingston, P. (2002). *Growing Older in Socially Deprived Areas: Social Exclusion in Later Life*. London, England: Help the Aged.

Sharp, J., Pollock, V. and Paddison, R. (2005). Just art for a just city: Public art and social inclusion in urban regeneration. *Urban Studies*, 2(5/6), pp. 1000–1023.

Waitt, G. and Duffy, M. (2010). Listening and tourism studies. *Annals of Tourism Research*, 37(2), pp. 457–477.

Waterman, S. (1998). Carnivals for elites? The cultural politics of arts festivals. *Progress in Human Geography*, 22(1), pp. 54–74.

Wilson, L. (2006). Developing a model for the measurement of social inclusion and social capital in regional Australia. *Social Indicators Research*, 75(3), pp. 335–360.

9 Festivals and social capital

Introduction

Social capital is the product of social interactions, and if generated and shared successfully, it can contribute to the social, civic, or economic well-being of individuals and communities (Halpern 2005; Putnam 1995). As Falk and Kilpatrick (2000) note, social capital is produced and used in everyday interactions. Fincher and Iveson (2008) propose that festivals are significant in urban and social planning because they provide an important opportunity for fostering encounters and interactions between individuals who may not otherwise meet. Such encounters may be valuable in terms of building social capital. Sharpley and Stone (2012: 356) suggest that 'social capital provides a framework for developing a deeper understanding of the socio-cultural impacts of events on communities'. Festivals and events, it has even been suggested, provide one of the more pleasurable ways a community facing a common crisis or shared danger (such as floods or bush fires) can come together and build or strengthen social capital (Jamieson 2014). Although this is an area of limited research, there have been suggestions that social capital can be built through major and mega sport events (Chalip 2006; Misener and Mason 2006; Schulenkorf 2009, 2010), as well as through arts and leisure activities (Dowling 2008; Blackshaw and Long 2005). However, the extent to which festivals can encourage or build social capital remains somewhat unknown.

Social capital

Social capital, although a somewhat contested term, has increasingly been recognised as an important component of society. Although the concept arose in the sociology field, Portes (2000) argues that social capital has become one of the most popular terms from sociology to make it into everyday language. Social capital has been described as 'the glue that holds society together' (Serageldin 1996: 196). The positive outcomes from high levels of social capital within a community can be summarised as the creation of a civil society; a strong sense of community; community cooperation and community empowerment (Ooi 2014). Although there is a plethora of research on social capital in various contexts, the ideas of three key theorists – Bourdieu, Putnam and Coleman – have come to dominate the discussion and use of social capital. For Bourdieu (1986: 248), social capital is defined as 'the aggregate of the actual or potential resources which are linked to possession of a durable network of more or less institutionalised relationships of mutual acquaintance'. Bourdieu's view of social capital arose from his work on social struggles of power and politics. For Bourdieu, social capital is one of three capitals – economic, cultural and social. In his framing, social capital is something that is used by individuals, and primarily by elites, who use their membership of various networks and associations to benefit their social position. In this sense, his view differs from both Putnam and Coleman, both of whom view social capital as something that can be accessible to all members of a community or society. Coleman (1988) emphasises the fact that social capital does not exist by itself; rather, social capital is made up of a variety of different entities with two features in common – social capital pertains to social structures and to the actions and interactions within these social structures. Social capital, therefore, inheres in the structure of relationships between actors and among actors (Coleman 1988). For Coleman (1988), social capital consists of the obligations, expectations and trustworthiness of social structures, the information channels available within these structures and the norms and effective sanctions that encourage individuals to forego self-interest and act in the interests of the collective. Putnam (1995: 67) considers social capital to be 'those features of social organisation such as networks, norms and social trust that facilitate coordination and cooperation for mutual benefit'. Networks are those social structures, both formal and informal, that allow members to communicate and access information. Norms refer to shared values that exist within a community, with key norms identified by Putnam (2000) being trust and reciprocity. Trust is a generalised notion – individuals choose to or are persuaded to do something for others or for the general good, because they trust that their own actions will be rewarded, either directly or more generally in the form of positive development of communal relations (Siisiainen 2003). This leads to reciprocity, which resolves the problems associated with collective actions and which binds communities together. Generalised reciprocity is argued to transform individuals from self-seeking agents to members of a community with shared interests, a common identity and a commitment to the common good (Putnam 2000). Within social capital, there is also the notion of resources – those goods which are valued in society and embedded within an individual's network or associations (Lin 1999).

It is important to note that social capital is not a given; rather, it must be constructed through investment strategies oriented to the institutionalisation of group relationships, which are then usable as a source of other benefits (Bourdieu 1986). Also, as Adler and Kwon (2002) note, social capital needs maintenance – if they are not periodically renewed and reaffirmed, social bonds lose efficacy. Social capital is argued to be a vital ingredient in economic development – grassroots associations and networks can be as essential to community growth as physical investment and appropriate technology (Putnam 1993).

However, there are also important criticisms of social capital. A particular concern regarding the conceptualisation of social capital at the level of the community and beyond includes the common assumption that the benefits accrued belong to the collective as a whole (Portes 2000). This overlooks the fact that communities, states, and nations are not homogenous in nature, with social capital unevenly distributed within and across societies (Fukuyama 1995). In particular, much of the literature has tended to focus on the positive outcomes of social capital, failing to acknowledge some of the more negative outcomes. Some of these outcomes have been identified as social exclusion (see Chapter 6 for a full discussion on social inclusion and exclusion), and social isolation, where people find themselves without social support or connectedness to others (Hawthorne 2006). Additionally, the tightly knit connections that social capital can foster and strengthen can also result in a sense of "us" and "them," which views those on the outside as threatening (Fukuyama 1995). This can reinforce inequality and lead to a situation in which people of various groups have unequal opportunities to participate in community life (Ooi 2014). At worst, this type of segregation can manifest itself in the form of powerlessness and feelings of mistrust (Mirowsky and Ross 1983). Finally, outright discrimination and adversity to mainstream society can result in the creation of downward levelling norms. These norms seek to discourage individual efforts to fit into mainstream society, with individual success stories seen as undermining group cohesion (Portes 2000). Therefore, the categorisation of social capital as something that is inherently good is overly simplistic.

There are other criticisms of social capital too, in part due to its seemingly elastic nature (De Filippis 2001). The lack of a universally accepted definition of social capital opens the concept up to accusations of vagueness and expediency. In addition, the work of Putnam (2000) has been criticised for 'logical circularity' – in which the components that determine the existence of social capital are also used to measure its outcomes (Portes 1998). Finally, as Creed (2006) points out, we can, and should, expect the meanings of community to vary according to social, cultural, geographic and historical circumstances, as well as according to the identity, common interests or shared beliefs (or lack thereof) of any community being examined (Creed 2006). As a result, the definition of community will affect levels of social capital in any given location.

Bridging, bonding and linking social capital

Social capital has been categorised in a variety of ways. For example, Nahapiet and Ghosal (1998) characterised social capital as being structural (relating to networks), relational (norms and trust) and cognitive (resources and goals). In addition to this, differing types of social capital have been identified. The concepts of bridging, bonding and linking social capital may also be relevant to the event context (Wilks 2011). Bonding social capital refers to the trust and reciprocity that exists within tightly knit networks, which reinforces exclusive identities and homogeneity (Adler and Kwon 2002). Putnam (2000) explains that bonding social capital is inward looking, creating strong in-group loyalty, but also encouraging exclusionary practices. Bonding social capital refers to increased solidarity with people who are already similar, which leads to a focus on a narrow conceptualisation of the self and creates strong in-group loyalty (Putnam 2000). Bridging social capital was proposed by Putnam in 2000 as referring to open and inclusive networks, which encourage membership and underpin generalised trust and reciprocity. Bridging social capital is outward looking, promoting connections between diverse individuals and connecting people to others who move in different circles. Finally, linking social capital refers to the creation of opportunities for vertical linkages – alliances or associations formed between individuals and groups at different levels of society – which are useful for community building and social engagement (Halpern 2005). There are clear connections with power and how it is shared in a community – such vertical bonds allow less affluent individuals to build connections with those in more powerful positions (usually in formal institutions). Linking social capital can be central to a process of breaking down power relations and allowing for positive community development (Misener 2013).

It is acknowledged that bridging, bonding and linking social capital are fluid concepts, and breaking social capital down into these relatively arbitrary distinctions is, perhaps justifiably, an oversimplification (Blackshaw and Long 2005). Additionally, these concepts do not adequately incorporate the role of emotions and affect – or the fact that festivals and events can generate certain atmospheres or ambiences that may encourage, or discourage, the formation of social relations. However, these concepts can be a framework to help us understand how social capital can contribute to community cohesion by spanning the boundaries between groups of people (Wilks 2011).

Social capital and events

Nationally and internationally, event research has been increasing over the past decade, with a particular focus on event tourism and maximising economic impacts (Getz 2013). Negative social impacts of events are also well understood; however, the positive impacts of events on the communities which host them have been the subject of significantly fewer studies (Mair and Whitford 2013). Foley et al. (2011: 93) argue that 'there is a cogent argument to be made for events and festivals working as the social glue of communities by aiding capacity building and reinforcing a sense of place identity'. This notion of social glue resonates with a similar description of the concept of social capital as 'the glue that holds society together' (Serageldin 1996: 196). As Misener (2013) notes, there has been substantial research on the physical, human and financial capital of planning and managing events; however, Foley et al. (2011) suggest that the potential contribution of events and festivals to social capital should not be underestimated.

Social capital has been proposed as a potential theoretical framework for exploring how events may contribute to community resilience (Foley et al. 2011; Misener and Mason 2006), but this proposition remains untested. Social capital is essential to both economic development and to strong communities (Putnam 2000). It has been demonstrated that leisure activities create informal social networks, which are part of social capital, and can help participants acquire skills – such as planning, organising and administration – that are conducive to formal participation in the workplace, thus further strengthening social capital (Van Ingen and Van Eijck 2009). However, few empirical studies have examined social capital and events of any kind, particularly festivals (Misener 2013). Given that arts, music and community festivals are a chance for a group celebration of shared values, it seems likely that they would provide the possibility of the development of social capital (Wilks 2011).

In a study focused on sporting events, Misener (2013) identifies four essential elements of events which may promote the development of social capital. According to Misener (2013), sporting events can (1) encourage behaviours such as joining, participating actively in, and leading new/renewed civic institutions; (2) help people, particularly disengaged citizens or those with less status in the community, acquire new civic skills, allowing for a greater equity in community life; (3) build more extensive, boundary-spanning and resource-rich networks and (4) build supportive new norms that value and enable collectivities.

Further, Misener (2013) proposes four broad strategies to assist in developing social capital through sport and sporting events: (1) enhancing the abilities of individuals (education, leadership development); (2) making community organisations stronger (capacity development); (3) building links among individuals (community organizing); and (4) building links among organisations (through collaborations, partnerships). Misener's argument is that this will allow for the broadening and solidifying of community participation and active citizen engagement. However, although Misener (2013) attempted to demonstrate how these elements and strategies may be used in the planning and management of large-scale sporting events, she acknowledges that considerable further empirical research is needed to test these propositions.

Schulenkorf et al. (2011) also examined sporting events, but rather than focus on large-scale events, they chose to examine an inter-community sporting event in Sri Lanka, an ethnically divided country. Schulenkorf et al. (2011) posit hypothetically that events might contribute to social capital by offering opportunities for socialising; offering a neutral space for diverse groups to come together; supporting reciprocity through active engagement; strengthening networks already existing between groups and individuals and establishing new networks between groups; and facilitating cooperation between event organisers and communities, providing locals with learning and skills development opportunities. However, this study also found evidence of negative attitudes among community members towards one another, as well as significant tensions associated with managing the event. Perhaps greater consideration of the role of emotions and affect on the building of social relations would be useful in this case.

As noted, most of the research into the links between events and social capital has focused on large-scale sport and music events. There is very little research examining how community festivals may contribute to social capital. Several features of social capital are assumed to be connected with community events. Arcodia and Whitford (2006) proposed that events help to develop community resources by providing opportunities for new networks between previously unrelated groups and organisations or opportunities for revitalising existing networks and also by encouraging effective use of community resources. Events also promote social norms by offering members of a community the opportunity to unite and share a world view, as well as developing a common social purpose. Finally, events provide an opportunity for public celebration by encouraging participation, strengthening community ties and facilitating community well-being. Generally, events are proposed to contribute to social capital by strengthening and maintaining networks, norms and resources, as well as by supporting economic development through tourism revenues as shown in Figure 9.1. However, events may also contribute to some of the negative outcomes of social capital – for example, where they exclude some members of the community (because of high ticket prices or other exclusionary practices) (Mair and Duffy 2015), and this element should not be ignored.

In terms of networks, community festivals and other events are proposed to contribute to the development of social capital in three main ways – building new networks for individuals and organisations (bridging); strengthening existing networks for individuals and organisations (bonding); and strengthening relationships between individuals, organisations and the public sector (linking) – with the result being improved structures for formal and informal community consultation.

Community festivals can also make good use of local resources, another contribution towards developing social capital. It is proposed that this is done by providing learning and skills development for individuals; encouraging effective use of local community resources, providing opportunities for volunteering; and encouraging membership of community organisations.

Finally, it can be suggested that community festivals can contribute to social capital in relation to norms, in terms of providing opportunities for socialising and coming together in celebration; supporting cooperation and reciprocity and trust; facilitating a public expression of shared values, giving a voice and a neutral space to sub-groups or minorities and being part of the shared life of a community, including its rituals and traditions.

However, although there are many reasons to consider that festivals and events may contribute to the development of social capital, research suggests that this contribution is not clear-cut. For example, Wilks (2011) examined the case of attendees at music festivals and found three key discourses among her study participants – the 'persistent connection' discourse; the 'temporary connection' discourse and the 'detachment' discourse. *Persistent connection* refers to those attending the festival

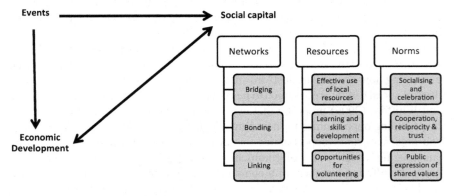

Figure 9.1 Social Capital and Events Conceptual Framework.

with an existing group of close friends or those meeting up with old friends or previous contacts at the festival, and it clearly has connections with bonding social capital (among known social groups). It also included reinforcing existing relationships with friends who didn't attend the festival, by telling them about the experience after the event. This was the most common type of social capital reported by Wilks's participants. *Temporary connection* refers to casual conversations with strangers – encounters – which have the potential to help with the development of bridging social capital (forming new social relationships). However, no participants in this particular study reported that these conversations resulted in any lasting connections, thus showing that bridging social capital did not appear to have been created. Finally, there were even some participants in this study who reported a *detachment* discourse – people avoided contact with other festival attendees and in some cases even felt apart from the festival community. This suggests that although festivals may offer the opportunity to build social capital, in practice, only bonding social capital was evident (Wilks 2011). Similar findings come from a study by Quinn and Wilks (2013), which demonstrated that bonding social capital was prevalent among family and friendship groups, yet bridging social capital was not identified within the sets of social actors in this study. Yet again, another study by Jamieson (2014) found that the event under investigation contributed to the building of bonding social capital in the communities investigated but had a negligible effect on bridging social capital. Additionally, Jamieson (2014) also found virtually no linking social capital in the same study, a finding which he put down to the government's reluctance to be involved in the rural event component and a lack of skills in community development. Finally, a study by Gibson et al. (2014) on the FIFA Soccer World Cup in South Africa showed that perceptions of social capital were only moderately high at all stages in the study. It may be the case that while the celebratory nature of these events appeared to encourage *communitas* (Turner 1974), and perhaps link to the generation of emotion and affect, in reality this is only a temporary notion, concealing divisions rather than healing them; papering over the cracks rather than addressing inequalities and divisions within a community. Further research in this area is badly needed.

Although it is likely that there are many reasons why festivals and events fail to maximise the opportunities to create social capital of different types, we can learn from these and identify ways to help festival organisers and planners to improve in future. For Quinn and Wilks (2013), the geographical place of the festival was identified as a key feature in anchoring the inter-connections and providing a sense of community, thus forming the foundation for social capital. Jamieson (2014) advocates better planning and more concerted efforts at collaboration, engagement and consultation to build a feeling of community among those involved. It has also been argued that the limited time frame of festivals hinders the development of social capital; however, this ignores the fact that a core group of festival staff (either paid staff or volunteers) work throughout the year to plan and stage a festival, and social capital can be – and, indeed, often is – nurtured and developed in all aspects of festival planning and management. It also overlooks the importance of social capital in the community hosting the event, rather than just among attendees or those directly involved in the festival.

Conclusion

The relationship between social capital and community events remains uncertain. However, it seems highly likely that festivals offer significant opportunities to strengthen social capital within a community, and, therefore, this is an area worth investigating further. The fact that festivals bring so many people together, not just during the event itself but throughout the year as part of the planning process, suggests that festivals may provide excellent opportunities to promote and develop bridging, bonding and linking social capital. However, the research to date appears to suggest that only bonding social capital has been evidenced. Given that festival organisers work with so many varied stakeholders (including local authorities, community organisations, local businesses, local residents, artists and performers), there is certainly potential to develop both bridging and linking social capital. However, it is apparent that this potential remains as yet untapped. Future research should focus on ascertaining how to maximise the benefits that may be yielded from the use of festivals as tools to improve both bridging and linking social capital.

It is also worth highlighting once again that social capital, although generally viewed as a good thing, can also have negative consequences, and these apply particularly to bonding social capital. Bonding within a group can lead to strengthened relationships and ties; however, such bonds can also be exclusive, leading to the potential exclusion of segments of a community. It is notable that the research to date shows that bonding social capital is the most prevalent form of social capital associated with festivals. This is similar to the contention by Mayblin et al. (2016) that there is increasing evidence that groups resist mixing with others, preferring instead to self-segregate. Given these findings, it may be the case that festivals are acting as spaces of both inclusion (for certain groups) and exclusion (for other groups). This may result in higher levels of social capital for the first group (the included) but reduced levels of social capital for the second group (the excluded).

Finally, it should be noted that much of the research that has examined how festivals may contribute to community social capital has not differentiated well between different sections of the communities under study. Much of the work that has examined social capital and festivals has heavily focused on the attendees, rather than on the community that hosts the festival. Indeed, few of the existing studies in this area have acknowledged that community is a multifaceted and contested term. Research is badly needed to help us understand these dynamics and to ensure that festivals can work for the benefit of all community members.

References

Adler, P. S. and Kwon, S. W. (2002). Social capital: Prospects for a new concept. *Academy of Management Review*, 27(1), pp. 17–40.

Arcodia, C. and Whitford, M. (2006). Festival attendance and the development of social capital. *Journal of Convention and Event Tourism*, 8(2), pp. 1–18.

Blackshaw, T. and Long, J. (2005). What's the big idea? A critical exploration of the concept of social capital and its incorporation into leisure policy discourse. *Leisure Studies*, 24(3), pp. 239–258.

Bourdieu, P. (1986). The forms of capital. In: Richardson, J. G. (Ed.). *Handbook of Theory and Research for the Sociology of Education.* Westport, CT: Greenwood Press, pp. 241–253.

Chalip, L. (2006). Towards social leverage of sport events. *Journal of Sport and Tourism,* 11(2), pp. 109–127.

Coleman, J. S. (1988). Social capital in the creation of human capital. *American Journal of Sociology,* 94, pp. 95–120.

Creed, G. W. (Ed.). (2006). *The Seductions of Community: Emancipations, Oppressions, Quandaries.* Santa Fe, NM: SARP.

De Filippis, J. (2001). The myth of social capital in community development. *Housing Policy Debate,* 12(4), pp. 781–806.

Dowling, M. (2008). Fiddling for outcomes: Traditional music, social capital, and arts policy in Northern Ireland. *International Journal of Cultural Policy,* 14(2), pp. 179–194.

Falk, I. and Kilpatrick, S. (2000). What is social capital? A study of interaction in a rural community. *Sociologia Ruralis,* 40, pp. 87–110.

Fincher, R. and Iveson, K. (2008). *Planning and Diversity in the City: Redistribution, Recognition and Encounter.* Hampshire, UK: Palgrave Macmillan.

Foley, M., McGillivray, D. and McPherson, G. (2011). Events policy: The limits of democracy. *Journal of Policy Research in Tourism, Leisure and Events,* 3(3), pp. 321–324.

Fukuyama, F. (1995). *Trust.* New York: Free Press Paperbacks.

Getz, D. (2013). *Event Tourism.* Putnam Valley, NY: Cognizant Communications.

Gibson, H. J., Walker, M., Thapa, B., Kaplanidou, K., Geldenhuys, S. and Coetzee, W. (2014). Psychic income and social capital among host nation residents: A pre – post analysis of the 2010 FIFA World Cup in South Africa. *Tourism Management,* 44, pp. 113–122.

Halpern, D. (2005). *Social Capital.* Cambridge: Polity Press.

Hawthorne, G. (2006). Measuring social isolation in older adults: Development and initial validation of the friendship scale. *Social Indicators Research,* 77(3), pp. 521–548.

Jamieson, N. (2014). Sport tourism events as community builders – How social capital helps the "Locals" cope. *Journal of Convention and Event Tourism,* 15(1), pp. 57–68.

Lin, N. (1999). Building a network theory of social capital. *Connections,* 22(1), pp. 28–51.

Mair, J. and Duffy, M. (2015). Community events and social justice in urban growth areas. *Journal of Policy Research in Tourism, Leisure and Events,* 7(3), pp. 282–298.

Mair, J. and Whitford, M. (2013). An exploration of events research: Event topics, themes and emerging trends. *International Journal of Event and Festival Management,* 4(1), pp. 6–30.

Mayblin, L., Valentine, G. and Winiarska, A. (2016). Migration and diversity in a post-socialist context: Creating integrative encounters in Poland. *Environment and Planning A,* 48(5), pp. 960–978.

Mirowsky, J. and Ross, C. E. (1983). Paranoia and the structure of powerlessness. *American Sociological Review,* 48(2), pp. 228–239.

Misener, L. (2013). Events and social capital. In: Finkel, R et al. (Eds.). *Research Themes for Events.* Ashgate: CABI, pp. 18–30.

Misener, L. and Mason, D. (2006). Creating community networks: Can sporting events offer meaningful sources of social capital? *Managing Leisure,* 11(1), pp. 39–56.

Nahapiet, J. and Ghoshal, S. (1998). Social capital, intellectual capital, and the organizational advantage. *Academy of Management Review,* 23(2), pp. 242–266.

Ooi, N. (2014). *Socio-Cultural Sustainability of Mountain Resort Tourism: A Case Study of Steamboat Springs.* Unpublished PhD Thesis, The University of Queensland.

Portes, A. (2000). Social capital: Its origins and applications in modern sociology. In: Lesser, E. L. (Ed.) *Knowledge and Social Capital.* Boston: Butterworth-Heinemann, pp. 43–67.

Putnam, R. D. (1993). The prosperous community: Social capital and public life. *American Prospect*, 13, pp. 35–42.

Putnam, R. D. (1995). Bowling alone: America's declining social capital. *Journal of Democracy*, 6(1), pp. 65–78.

Putnam, R. D. (2000). *Bowling Alone: The Collapse and Revival of American Community.* New York: Simon and Schuster.

Quinn, B. and Wilks, L. (2013). Festival connections: People, place and social capital. In: Richards, G., de Brito, M. P. and Wilks, L. (Eds.). *Exploring the Social Impacts of Events.* Abingdon: Routledge, pp. 15–30.

Schulenkorf, N. (2009). An ex ante framework for the strategic study of social utility of sport events. *Tourism and Hospitality Research*, 9(2), pp. 120–131.

Schulenkorf, N. (2010). The roles and responsibilities of a change agent in sport event development projects. *Sport Management Review*, 13(2), pp. 118–128.

Schulenkorf, N., Thomson, A. and Schlenker, K. (2011). Intercommunity sport events: Vehicles and catalysts for social capital in divided societies. *Event Management*, 15(2), pp. 105–119.

Serageldin, I. (1996). Sustainability as opportunity and the problem of social capital. *The Brown Journal of World Affairs*, 3(2), pp. 187–203.

Sharpley, R. and Stone, P. (2012). Socio-cultural impacts of events: Meanings, authorized transgression and social capital. In: Page, S. and Connell, J. (Eds.) *The Routledge Handbook of Events.* London: Routledge, pp. 347–360.

Siisiainen, M. (2003). Two concepts of social capital: Bourdieu vs. Putnam. *International Journal of Contemporary Sociology*, 40(2), pp. 183–204.

Turner, V. (1974). *Dramas, Fields and Metaphors.* Ithaca, NY: Cornell University Press.

Van Ingen, E. and Van Eijck, K. (2009). Leisure and social capital: An analysis of types of company and activities. *Leisure Sciences*, 31(2), pp. 192–206.

Wilks, L. (2011). Bridging and bonding: Social capital at music festivals. *Journal of Policy Research in Tourism, Leisure and Events*, 3(3), pp. 281–297.

10 Encounter with past, present and future

Yakkerboo and the rural-urban fringe

Introduction

In many countries around the world, increasing urbanisation is becoming commonplace and somewhat problematic. Particularly in developing countries, the flood of people leaving the land for jobs and better prospects in rapidly multiplying mega-cities is leading to slum conditions, poverty and even a sense of hopelessness. In other, predominantly Western developed countries, the boom in city populations, and the concomitant urban sprawl, is associated less with a rush away from the countryside and more with the dream of home ownership and a life in the suburbs. Inward migration too is pushing up demand for homes in many cities, leading to the development of peri-urban, or "ruration", suburbs at the rural-urban interface.

Yet the recent push behind the development of peri-urban regions raises a number of important challenges because of the strategic, spatial, economic and environmental significance of these sites (Buxton and Tieman 2005). High housing prices, rising costs of petrol, economic restructuring and changing employment opportunities, as well as growing anxieties about environmental sustainability in the face of climate change, have combined in different ways to challenge the taken-for-granted processes of urban and suburban growth. Moreover, many rural communities that experience the advancing urban frontier have expressed frustration over their loss of a sense of place, as farming land and pastures are transformed and subdivided into "amenity" or "lifestyle" residential blocks. Some scholars question the inevitability of metropolitan sprawl (Green 2010) and destruction of the rich social fabric of rural places in order to create so-called "inauthentic" and "placeless" suburbs dominated by a car culture and supposedly lacking any sense of community and belonging (Qvistrom 2012).

Although festivals are often regarded as places where "the community" can get together, there is an important dimension of the community to be unpacked here that has not been the subject of much research in the context of festivals and events. As has been mentioned several times in this book already, communities are not homogenous; therefore, it is important not to expect festivals to be able to bring disparate elements of a community together without explicit efforts to make this happen.

In the growth corridors on the edges of many cities, new suburbs are being created with amazing speed. These suburbs are home to a great diversity of residents, some new to the area, some new to the city or even the country, many of whom have no existing connection and no *a priori* sense of community with the place in which they now live. Existing festivals may not be constituted in a way that makes them easily accessible to new residents, particularly if the festival is celebrating a heritage or tradition that is not shared with the incoming community members. New festivals constructed to meet a particular policy aim, such as addressing diversity, may fail to strike a chord with long-term residents of an area who are keen to celebrate the nostalgic, and perhaps idealised, community they hark back to. With this in mind, we will now examine a case study of this tension, using the example of the Yakkerboo Festival, held in Victoria, Australia.

Background to case study

The Yakkerboo Festival, derived from an Aboriginal word meaning 'place of green pasture', started in the mid-1970s as a community festival. It was initially created by the local authority (then Pakenham Shire; now the Shire of Cardinia) as a way to bring members of the local community together. The impetus for the festival came from a small group of local residents who wanted to celebrate their (rural) community, and it was always intended to be a shire-wide event and not restricted to Pakenham (Pakenham Gazette September 24, 1975: 1). The local council 'wanted something for municipal recreation and something [for the community] to do,' noted one Pakenham resident who had been involved in its organisation for almost twenty-five years when interviewed in 2015.

The primary role of the festival, as noted on its website, is to bring people together.

> Yakkerboo prides itself in providing a free festival for the people, by the people, and it is the people volunteering their time in Yakkerboo, who are the heart and soul of the event. . . . *Festivals like Yakkerboo are the glue that holds communities together. The Yakkerboo Community Festival has become part of making new residents feel welcome, it is the vehicle for new residents to work and play beside established residents*, and, importantly, it brings children together; happy, laughing, celebrating and playing together . . . it is about celebrating our strong, cohesive and well-functioning community and local business and industry.
>
> (http://yakkerboo.org.au/about/, emphasis added)

When the festival started, Pakenham was a small country town, and the festival was about offering a time and place for people living in a sparsely populated area to come together and celebrate their rural lives. Now, however, the Yakkerboo Festival finds itself in a rapidly growing peri-urban area, the Casey-Cardinia growth corridor, which has quickly become an outer suburban part of Melbourne, Australia. Rapid population growth is already evident; currently in 2016, Cardinia Shire had a population of 94,492 people (ABS 2016). This is up from 19,644 in

Figure 10.1 Yakkerboo Festival, 2015 Street Parade.
Photo © Michelle Duffy.

2006, and the population is projected to increase to 175,453 by 2036 (Cardinia Shire Community Profile (2016). In terms of cultural diversity (measured by ethnicity), there has been an increase in the number of residents born overseas and speaking a language other than English, but the largest numbers of overseas arrivals are from the United Kingdom and New Zealand.

The format of the Yakkerboo Festival has not changed substantially since its inception. It has a range of components including the street parade, which is probably the best known part of the festival, as well as a street market, a funfair, fireworks, an art show and a twilight carnival. The following excerpt from Duffy and Mair (2014: 60) captures the spirit of the festival through its main character.

Mr Yakkerboo is the name given to a bunyip-like creature originally created by school children in Pakenham. These children had made individual papier maché tiles, which were then stuck onto a wire frame to form the outline of the creature, described imaginatively by one local as having a 'crazed buck-toothed grin' and that you would feel 'the earth shudder as the bilious bunyip moved his morbidly obese body' (Berwick Star April 2011). As the then festival committee's president explained, 'He is his own personality, he's not like anything' (Berwick Star March 2011). Why this particular creature is less clear. The bunyip is a mythical creature originating in Aboriginal mythology that lives in swamps, riverbeds and waterholes. Perhaps it connects to the region's terrain and local stories. The region around Pakenham, and in particular the areas in which the Casey-Cardinia growth corridor is located, lies between streams and drainage lines that channel water from the upland area just to the north of the town (Sinclair Knight Mertz 2005). Much of what was designated swamp land was reclaimed about 20 years ago, although in winter this low-lying area is prone to flooding and is often covered in mist, particularly at night. Nonetheless Mr Yakkerboo appears to be a favourite especially amongst younger children, as we found when attending the 2013 festival parade. One small girl eagerly asked us if we were also going to have some of Mr Yakkerboo's birthday cake and icecream, while a young boy excitedly waiting for the start of the parade told those around him, 'I love Mr Yakkerboo! He's my favourite!'

However, as times move on, and the nature of the local community changes, questions are being asked as to how well the Yakkerboo festival represents and is inclusive of those who are moving to the town. Support for the festival has fluctuated to such an extent that the future of Yakkerboo is now uncertain. A key concern constantly raised in local media and council strategies and policies is how to ensure a sense of community is valued and facilitated given the demographic and land use changes occurring.

Additionally, the festival organising committee has remained broadly unchanged in recent times. This naturally has benefits – the organising committee is very experienced and is very well known and connected within the community, and the festival generally runs smoothly thanks to this. However, the members of the committee are ageing, and there appears to be a lack of younger volunteers to take their place. In addition, there have been suggestions that they are perhaps a little set in their ways, finding it difficult to acknowledge within the festival the changing nature of the local area and perhaps failing to appreciate that for many of the new residents of the outer suburbs of Melbourne, a rural agricultural festival may not be representative of "their" place. This goes to the heart of the question of the role of the festival within the community – should it change with the times to become more representative of the new, suburban, multicultural residents; should it remain as it is, as a symbol of the history and heritage of this once rural place; or should it try to be all things to all men?

Yakkerboo and "the local"

In this regard, our earlier discussion on the concept of community and mobilities becomes of particular relevance. Local governments and community groups tend to focus on a geographical location; a place-based conceptualisation. This relates naturally to the mandate of local councils and authorities – to be responsible for a particular, bounded, geographical place, even if the boundaries of that place shift over time, with changes to the make-up of local authorities (Wood 2008). In this framing, however, the local is often embedded along traditional lines of an ideal community, where social relations are characterised by small-scale, personal ties, often going back many years or even generations. Local community festivals, therefore, while outwardly representing the people of a particular place, are in reality reiterating this ideal and outdated notion of community, even when the community is demonstrably culturally plural. An additional problem with the focus on place when considering community is that community is constituted in more ways than simply location. Other equally important things include communities of interest, shared values, and levels of attachment. However, local government planning for local service provision and responding to areas of deprivation is determined more readily through a focus on place (Wood 2008).

The official discourses of the Yakkerboo Festival organising committee operate to produce an "imagined" community, drawing on the agricultural traditions of Cardinia, which the festival is then planned to address. However, it has been argued (inter alia Mouffe 1996) that this official imagined community neglects the realities of our complex and contested places. Tension and debates over how community and the local are constituted play an important role in acknowledging the heterogeneity of contemporary life. Festivals, therefore, should perhaps be places where notions of place and identity are negotiated and actively questioned, rather than places where an imagined community is emphasised.

Relating these notions of local and community to Yakkerboo provides an interesting framework for considering the festival. The location and population size of Pakenham in the 1970s, when the festival began, required its residents to be relatively self-reliant. Unsurprisingly, this led to the development of a relatively conservative definition of community, one with an emphasis on locality, tradition and a sense of neighbourliness (Lavenda 1992). This has long been a defining characteristic of Yakkerboo. These rural origins are understood particularly by long-term residents as being key to maintaining connections among individuals, social groups and a particular location:

> I probably liked it better ten years ago before [Yakkerboo] got bigger. . . . I knew nearly every person, or most of the people in Pakenham. I don't know that now. I could walk up the street . . . and we wouldn't know anyone. You miss that.

As stated on the festival's webpage, the festival seeks to reconnect and recreate community – 'Yakkerboo means that for one moment people are brought together'. Given that people in general are seen to be less community minded than in the past, this is seen as a key ingredient and strength of the festival.

These traditions are, naturally, meaningful to a particular community group, and they accord with a history of particular traditions and points of view (Permezel and Duffy 2007). However, without doubt the 'official' view of how a community is represented through cultural performance differs from the 'on the ground community' view. For example, although the festival has always been intended to be representative of the broader Cardinia Shire, it is often considered to be a festival of the town of Pakenham, thereby diluting the importance of the rural settlements around the town in the conceptualisation of both the festival and the

Figure 10.2 Tractors in the street parade.
Photo © Michelle Duffy.

community. This was even acknowledged by a councillor and ex-president of the festival, who proudly shared that the focus of the festival remains deliberately on the old township of Pakenham, with very little acknowledgement of the recent changes to Pakenham or even other places within the shire. This was borne out by our observations of the street parade in 2013 (Mair and Duffy 2015). This parade appeared to be a strong reflection of the existing, older identity of the town – as well as local schools, the Country Fire Authority, State Emergency Service, and St John's Ambulance all took part. These are organisations which have played an important role in Pakenham, and Cardinia more broadly, over many years. In short, the parade reflected the identity of the traditional rural townscape (Mair and Duffy 2015). Yet, in spite of the strong presence of local community groups, it was difficult to see any major contribution from the new growth areas during the parade. The changing nature of the area, as discussed previously, can only exacerbate these divisions between the official discourse of the rural place and the actual physical reality of its busy, sometimes congested, suburban location.

Yakkerboo and encounter

The Yakkerboo Festival isn't simply about presentation or representation of community identity, although this is of course a significant component. There is also an exchange, a process by which those involved may actively acknowledge encounter, which may allow us to rethink exchange beyond economic terms.

The following extended quote from the manager of a large supermarket illustrates this:

> Look, I suppose with Yakkerboo, of course, it was all new to me too. I've been at the shire for ten months now, and when I arrived in the shire a few months later I was introduced to Yakkerboo and I went, 'Yakker what?'
>
> But when you're talking networking and really engaging with the community, I didn't know what Yakkerboo was. So I had the privilege of getting involved. I didn't get much involved in as far as organising the event, but I definitely was . . . I could tell you about that, because I obviously went to the event, and it was myself, Michael, and it was at Main Street at the time. We went to the event and we organised the barbecue. So I took care of the barbecue. And we had scotch fillet and a few other kangaroo bits, kangaroo meat. And yeah, we're really involved with the community.
>
> But I thought the event was just absolutely magnificent to really touch base with the community. You know, we always expect the community to come to our shop and shop at [major supermarket chain], which is great. That's what we want them to do. But I suppose our point was, how can we give a little bit back to the community? And when you look at Yakkerboo, it's giving something back.
>
> If you look to back when it started, it was country, yep, small. But now it seems to be getting bigger and bigger. And it was absolutely massive when we did it this year. It blew me away. Well donuts, we had a queue . . . I mean, it just goes to show how big it is.

Yakkerboo and policy

Mobility literature suggests that when festivals are used instrumentally for policy objectives, such as increasing social cohesion, there is an underlying assumption that the festival has clear and widely understood links to a bounded sense of place and community. Further, it is generally suggested that the focus is often on the resident community that is embedded in a location. What appears to be missing is a focus on how the different approaches to and understanding of mobilities can shape not only place, but also social relations that are incorporated within the festival.

Cardinia Shire Council does not have a specific events policy; rather, festivals and events are subsumed within their arts and culture policy. As Whitford (2009) notes, it is not uncommon for local authorities to include events under a range of different policy areas, including tourism, economic development and communities. This highlights a difficulty faced by small community events – having no 'home' within a council structure can sometimes lead to their falling between the cracks in terms of official council policy. The Cardinia Shire Council Arts and Culture policy specifies that the Council will 'foster and celebrate expression and appreciation of local culture and heritage, cultural diversity and the cultures of new and established communities' (Cardinia Arts and Culture Policy 2012) but doesn't explain how events may fit into this. The Yakkerboo Festival is financially supported by Cardinia Shire Council, but its relevance to the arts and culture policy appears mixed. It is clear that within this policy framework, Yakkerboo is seen as relating clearly to the resident community. It may be considered a celebration of local culture and heritage, and important in maintaining the traditions and social networks of a quickly vanishing local history, but, as noted, there are certainly questions over how well it incorporates representations of different sections of the community and has adapted to the new communities which have sprung up along the growth corridor.

However, Cardinia policies also state that the council will 'encourage, educate and increase opportunities for all sections of the community to access, participate and appreciate arts and culture' (Cardinia Arts and Culture Policy 2012). In this regard, Yakkerboo is undoubtedly successful. It is a free event, 'for the people, by the people', making it accessible to all, should they choose to attend. Additionally, the festival involves a large number of local volunteers, 'the heart and soul of the event', which again speaks to the inclusive nature of the event.

Yakkerboo and Cardinia's (changing) communities

The stakeholders of the Yakkerboo Festival are aware of the potential tensions relating to the festival, its past, its present and its future. This point is acknowledged by the event organisers, who note that the festival is in need of a revamp (*Berwick Gazette* May 2011). The organisers are taking steps to try to better engage with the new communities in the Pakenham area. For example, the organising committee has been taking Mr Yakkerboo on a tour around the local schools, including those built in new housing estates on the outskirts of the town, in order to build up the enthusiasm of the children (*Berwick Gazette* May 2011). Therefore, it may just be a matter of time before these children become part of the festival. However, it is worth noting that those people moving into new suburbs are already dealing with major changes in their daily lives (for example, settling into new homes and adjusting to new workplaces or long commutes). It could be argued that in our busy lives, becoming involved in community traditions is a low priority for new residents (Lynn and Monani 2010). Additionally, there remains a degree of resistance to change among the long-term residents of Pakenham, who feel that any alterations to "our festival" should be minimised.

Over time, it may be useful to revisit the festival, to see whether those new entrants to the Pakenham region will eventually share the notions of community and belonging that currently exist in the region. It is, of course, debatable whether the new residents will even want to be connected with this existing notion of community, given it reflects another time and arguably another place. If, as we argue, community is an ever-evolving construct, then surely the newcomers will contribute as much to any new notions of community as the existing residents. However, the current format of the event does not appear to encourage active participation by newcomers; therefore, they may not have much chance to be involved in any changes. Rather than being a site for ongoing dialogue between members of diverse communities and allowing competing narratives and ideas about what constitutes community (Permezel and Duffy 2007), Yakkerboo appears to be a representation of *one* imagined community, imposed on the festival.

The future of Yakkerboo

The sustainability of rural festivals has been linked to the event life cycle, with stages of 'foundation, growth, maturity and decline, with the possibility of revival' (Getz and Andersson 2008: 4). According to Frost and Laing (2015), this event life cycle might also affect the management structure, with people remaining on the organising committee for too long or not having fresh ideas to revive the event once it moves into the decline phase.

There is surprisingly little research on why festivals and events fail. However, according to Getz (2002), a lack of strong leadership is a key factor in event failure. This is of particular relevance to rural and community festivals. These events are often organised on a volunteer basis by local residents who have formed an organising committee. As a result, many community festivals "lack sophisticated management" (Frost and Laing 2015). In a small country town, or rural or regional area, it can be difficult to find adequate human resources with the expertise and experience needed to stage an event. This may lead to an absence of advance and strategic planning – such absence is a feature of events that do not survive for long (Frost and Laing 2015). Frost and Laing (2015) highlighted several reasons for festival failure in the rural context; namely, the level of professional assistance required to help the volunteer committee to tackle all the requirements of planning and managing an event; concerns about the representativeness of organising committees; the potential for burnout (particularly among volunteers); the lack of succession planning that is occurring; and the limited resources that are available to volunteer.

One criticism often associated with festivals, particularly long-running ones, is a lack of innovation and change. Some (e.g. Carlsen et al. 2007) suggest that change is necessary to widen the support base in the local community, as the local community itself also changes. The implication is if a festival fails to change in step with the community it was developed for, it may begin to lose its relevance to local people. A lack of broad stakeholder representation on the organising committee may contribute to this, due to committee members preferring that control of festival organisation and staging remain in the hands of a privileged few, instead of sharing it around or bringing new people into the fold, particularly new arrivals to the community (Rogers and Anastasiadou 2011).

Yakkerboo has run for 40 years, with little significant change to its format, and although stakeholders of the event recognise the need to change and better engage with the community (or more precisely, new communities) that now exists in the growth corridor, progress towards these changes has been slow. It seems that the festival has not accepted the changing demographics of the community in Pakenham. It can be argued that, for this reason, the festival is now acting almost (but not intentionally) as a space of exclusion for new community members. While Yakkerboo is still going strong at the time of writing, there are certainly question marks over its future.

Conclusion

Our findings demonstrate that although events such as Yakkerboo clearly provide opportunities for encounter, this may not always lead to the socially just and inclusive communities that the local authorities are working towards. Cardinia council authorities have policies on community building, and authorities believe that festivals and events can make an important contribution towards these policy objectives. However, there are issues with festivals which may prevent them from achieving policy objectives.

In the case of Yakkerboo, we have a representation of the idealised traditions of those people who have lived in the area for some time, who share a particular set of values rooted in the farming history of the region and who share many personal connections. Rather than inclusion, this may represent a form of unintentional exclusion of new residents. If the festival is not a true representation of the range of different cultures in the region, then it runs the risk of isolating or further excluding already marginalised sections of the community, however that may be constituted.

Further, the lack of succession planning may lead to the eventual failure of Yakkerboo, like many other small, rural festivals, and the cultural landscape of the country will be poorer for that.

References

Australian Bureau of Statistics. (2016). *Casey Region Statistics* [online]. Available at: http://stat.abs.gov.au/itt/r.jsp?RegionSummaryandregion=21610anddataset=ABS_REGIONAL_LGAandgeoconcept=REGIONanddatasetASGS=ABS_REGIONAL_ASGSanddatasetLGA=ABS_REGIONAL_LGAandregionLGA=REGIONandregionASGS=REGION [Accessed 31 March 2017].

Berwick Gazette (2011). Fresh blood for Yakkerboo. Posted 11 May [online]. Available at: http://berwick.starcommunity.com.au/gazette/2011-05-11/fresh-blood-for-yakkerboo/ [Accessed 31 March 2017].

Berwick *Gazette* (2011) Tracing birthday origins. Posted March 30 [online]. Available at: http://berwick.starcommunity.com.au/gazette/2011-03-30/tracing-birthday-origins/ [Accessed 31 March 2017].

Berwick *Star* (2011). The luck less monster. Posted April 6 [online]. Available at: http://berwick.starcommunity.com.au/gazette/2011-04-06/the-luck-less-monster/ [Accessed 31 March 2017].

Buxton, M. and Tieman, G. (2005). Patterns of urban consolidation in Melbourne: Planning policy and the growth of medium density housing. *Urban Policy and Research*, 23(2), pp. 137–157.

Cardinia Arts and Culture Policy (2012). [online]. Available at: www.cardinia.vic.gov.au/downloads/download/6/arts_and_culture_policy_2012%E2%80%9317_-_cardinia_shire_council [Accessed 31 March 2017].

Cardinia Shire Community Profile (2016). *Welcome to the Cardinia Shire Community Profile*. [online]. Available at: http://profile.id.com.au/cardinia [Accessed 31 March 2017].

Carlsen, J., Ali-Knight, J. and Robertson, M. (2007). Access – A research agenda for Edinburgh festivals. *Event Management*, 11(1–2), pp. 3–11.

Duffy, M, and Mair, J. (2014). Festivals and sense of community: an Australia case study. In: A Jepson and A Clarke (eds) *Routledge Advances in Events Research Book Series: Exploring Community Festivals and Events*. Oxon and New York: Routledge, pp. 54–65.

Frost, W. and Laing, J. (2015). Avoiding burnout: The succession planning, governance and resourcing of rural tourism festivals. *Journal of Sustainable Tourism*, 23(8–9), pp. 1298–1317.

Getz, D. (2002). Why festivals fail. *Event Management*, 7(4), pp. 209–219.

Getz, D. and Andersson, T. (2008). Sustainable festivals: On becoming an institution. *Event Management*, 12(1), pp. 1–17.

Green, S. (2010). Pushing the boundary. *The Saturday Age: Insight* 12 February, pp. 15 and 21.

Lavenda, R. H. (1992). Festivals and the creation of public culture: Whose voice(s)? In: Karp, I., Mullen Kreamer, C. and Lavine, S. (Eds.) *Museums and Communities: The Politics of Public Culture*. Washington, DC: Smithsonian Institute Press, pp. 76–104.

Lynn, M. and Monani, D. (2010). *Final Report: Building Family and Community Resilience in Cardinia Growth Corridor: A Case Study of Officer*. Windermere: Narre Warren.

Mair, J. and Duffy, M. (2015). Community events and social justice in urban growth areas. *Journal of Policy Research in Tourism, Leisure and Events*, 7(3), pp. 282–298.

Mouffe, C. (1996). On the itineraries of democracy: An interview with Chantal Mouffe. *Studies in Political Economy*, 49, pp. 131–148.

Pakenham Gazette (1975). *Festival of Culture and Art* September 24 [online]. Available at: http://caseycardinialinkstoourpast.blogspot.com.au/2016/04/yakkerboo-festival-turns-40.html [Accessed 31 March 2017].

Permezel, M. and Duffy, M. (2007). Negotiating cultural difference in local communities: The role of the body, dialogues and performative practices in local communities. *Geographical Research*, 45(4), pp. 358–375.

Qvistrlöm, M. (2012). Contested landscapes of urban sprawl: Landscape protection and regional planning in Scania, Sweden, 1932–1947. *Landscape research*, 37(4), pp. 399–415.

Rogers, P. and Anastasidou, C. (2011). Community involvement in festivals: Exploring ways of increasing local participation. *Event Management*, 15(4), pp. 387–399.

Sinclair Knight Mertz. (2005). *Melbourne 2030 Casey-Cardinia Growth Corridor, Shallow Watertable Constraints on Urban Development*. Melbourne: Department of Sustainability and Environment, Victoria.

Whitford, M. (2009). A framework for the development of event public policy: Facilitating regional development. *Tourism Management*, 30(5), pp. 674–682.

Wood, E. H. (2008). An impact evaluation framework: Local government community festivals. *Event Management*, 12(3–4), pp. 171–185.

11 Experience! The Casey Multicultural Festival

Encounter with 'the other'

Introduction

Social changes in many countries, particularly those experiencing significant inward migration such as Australia, the United States, Canada and some parts of Europe, have led to changing dynamics in the composition of communities. As discussed in Chapter 5, mobility theory and the new mobilities paradigm seek to understand how people participate in both the global and the local. We are more connected than ever before, yet this connection brings diversity to the forefront of our minds. The multicultural nature of the encounter in our towns and cities means that it is important to reflect further on this concept. In contemporary Australia, for example, the response to the economic pressures of globalisation has led the Australian nation to attempt to reposition itself as part of the Asian region (Duffy 2005). This may potentially have contentious results, if different community members perceive that the presence of diverse ethnic and cultural groups may hinder some sense of belonging at the broader community level. Divisions and tensions have, almost inevitably, resulted from these changes. A similar pattern has been repeated in many countries around the world, with European countries (particularly the UK, France and Germany) receiving significant inward migration from former colonies and the former Eastern Bloc countries and with Asian and Middle Eastern countries (such as Korea and the United Arab Emirates) receiving substantial numbers of foreign "guest workers". Additional pressure is being placed on countries around the world to accept an influx of refugees from war-torn areas of Africa and the Middle East. Governments at national, regional and local levels have engaged in efforts to ease tensions and help the dominant population to embrace diversity. They are also making efforts to ensure that the culture, heritage and traditions that migrants bring with them are not diluted or lost as a result of migration (Berry et al. 2006).

Contact theory (Allport 1954) proposes that negative attitudes and prejudices held by one group of people towards another group can be reduced by intergroup contact. The rationale of this is that the dominant resident population is most likely to anticipate positive outcomes from the relationship with a different cultural group when they perceive similarities between themselves and the minority group (Piontkowshi et al. 2000). Further, it is important that minority community members do not remain isolated within small groups from their communities of origin and that they do not feel alienated from mainstream society (Berry et al. 2006). Festivals generally are promoted as a way to shape identity and cultural difference into some form of community and so promote social cohesion and a sense of belonging (Duffy 2005). As Fincher and Iveson (2008: 176, 177) point out, festivals 'have become an established part of the repertoire of contemporary urban planning' in the hope that 'festivals will promote greater tolerance and understanding'.

Issues of diversity and difference, especially in terms of race and ethnicity, are part of attempts to 'manage public space in ways that build sociality and civic engagement out of the encounter between strangers' (Amin 2008: 6). Since active intervention is required to ensure that minority communities have access to the opportunities and facilities necessary for the maintenance of their culture, multicultural festivals have emerged in many locations as a useful instrument for promoting social harmony and integration (Lee et al. 2012a, b, c). Multicultural festivals not only encourage minorities to maintain their culture of origin, but also allow increased contact between the dominant population and minority group members, so that negative attitudes and prejudices towards each other can be reduced (Picard and Robinson 2006).

Despite the seemingly obvious nature of multicultural festivals, there are several somewhat competing definitions of what is meant by the term. For example, McClinchey (2008) emphasises the "other", with a definition based on such events being places for public celebration showcasing the ethnic culture of communities settled in a region following migration. Lee et al. (2012a), on the other hand, highlight the experience of the event visitor or attendee, proposing that a multicultural festival can be defined as a public multiculturally themed celebration at which people of different ethnicities including the dominant population have cultural experiences. However, Duffy (2005) takes a different approach, considering multicultural festivals as places for ongoing dialogue and negotiation within communities, as both individuals and groups attempt to shape meaningful concepts of identity and belonging, in addition to notions of exclusion.

Multicultural festivals often have a wide range of components but generally include traditional/folk music. Performative genres such as folk dance and ethnic music are closely linked with the presentation of ethnic culture, because traditional song and music usually have a strong sentimental value (Österlund-Pötzsch 2004). In addition, it is common for multicultural festivals to include the preparation and sharing of ethnic food and drink, which are also strongly symbolic of traditional cultures. Multicultural festivals may also include traditional dances and performance of rituals and ceremonies.

According to Lee et al. (2012a), three characteristics of multicultural festivals play a significant role in the development of successful multiculturalism. These are (1) cultural celebrations, (2) cultural identity and expression, and (3) social interactions. Lee et al. (2012a) conclude that, based on their research in Korea, multicultural festivals can help to change the attitudes and beliefs of both the dominant population and the migrant community members, through learning about traditional and new cultures, having fun and relaxing, and socialising with others.

However, as noted elsewhere in this book, festivals can have negative as well as positive outcomes. Although the intention may be to celebrate cultural diversity, or perhaps mitigate tensions (Dunn et al. 2001), too often multicultural festivals are accused of highlighting diversity, thus paradoxically encouraging community members to see differences around them. The mobilities paradigm offers us a way to understand how the idea of the 'local' can be unsettled by new ethnic and cultural connections and encounters.

This chapter uses Experience! The Casey Multicultural Festival to examine and investigate the role of multicultural festivals both in promoting tolerance of diversity and as a way to provide opportunities for migrants to maintain their culture, heritage and traditions.

Background to case study

Experience! The Casey Multicultural Festival takes place annually in Berwick, a small town in the outer south-east of Melbourne, Australia. The festival is held in part of Australia's rapidly growing peri-urban areas, the Casey-Cardinia growth corridor located in Melbourne's south-east. This once rural environment is quickly being levelled and coated in asphalt and housing slabs. Rapid population growth is already evident – in 2006, the population of the City of Casey local government area numbered 19,644, but by 2016 this number had risen to 283,000 (Australian Bureau of Statistics 2016), and the number of residents is forecast to increase to 459,000 by 2036 (City of Casey 2016). Casey is the eighth-fastest growing municipality in Australia, with the majority of this growth driven by young families moving into the region because of the affordability of housing (City of Casey 2016). Although some have suggested this growth corridor is where new and exciting urban-rural configurations can be enabled, a key concern constantly raised in local media and council policies and strategies is how to ensure a sense of community is valued and facilitated given the demographic and land use changes occurring.

Casey is an area of significant cultural diversity. More than 150 cultures are represented in the City of Casey, and over a quarter of Casey residents were born in non-English-speaking countries (City of Casey 2016). Nearly 28% of all Casey residents speak English as a second language. Naturally, this places a particular onus on the local authorities to address issues of multiculturalism and diversity in their council policies. It is clear from their policies that the councils accept that festivals and events have strong connections with community and identity and with community well-being in particular. However, unlike other local authorities, the City of Casey decided on a top-down approach in this regard, by creating, designing and staging a festival as part of their multicultural policy. The Council felt that it was important, in line with their community development objective of building community capacity, to give people a platform to identify and display their cultural identity (personal communication with Council representative 22 October 2015). The council identified a series of event objectives, and any events that are supported by the council, either financially or in-kind, must address at least one of these objectives. Of particular relevance to this case study is Objective

Figure 11.1 Experience! Casey Multicultural Festival Stalls.
Photo © Michelle Duffy.

2 – Vitality and Celebrating Diversity. The City of Casey Council notes that they will 'encourage, support and manage events that enhance the liveability and celebrate the diversity within Casey' (Casey Event Policy 2014). Experience! was clearly designed to be a key part of this policy, with the aims of the event being 'showcasing Casey's culturally diverse community and providing an opportunity for everyone to experience a variety of culture' (Experience! 2016). This is, then, an example of a festival designed to meet a specific policy objective.

Multicultural festivals and tolerance, diversity and inclusivity

Experience! The Casey Multicultural Festival was first held in 2012 as a response to the increasing diversity and changing composition of the Casey region, a result of increasing migration to Australia generally, and Victoria and Melbourne in particular. The festival is a one-day affair that includes displays of dancing, food and music from a range of cultural groups, including the Chinese, Samoan, Turkish, Romanian and Scottish communities. The festival also provides an opportunity for local service providers to meet the community – this includes multicultural service agencies, English language agencies, and community organisations, as well as Victoria Police and the State Government.

The festival space is conceived as a place to increase tolerance and understanding of community diversity, and it is hoped that the social consequences of these types of events will lead to a change in value systems as well as individual behaviour (Reid 2007). Casey Council notes that it will 'support events that bring communities together, encourage partnerships and promote participation in the community' (Casey Event Policy 2014). One way to assist in such change is to allow variety in programming to highlight cultural and ethnic diversity or to involve minority groups or otherwise marginalised groups within a community (Finkel 2006; Gorman-Murray 2009). These goals or benefits are a source of pride for organisers and can be a catalyst for community members to become involved.

Council representatives explained that the festival had been created with two aims – firstly to ensure that the celebration of cultural diversity was financially supported and secondly to send out a clear message to the community that cultural diversity is valued (personal communication with Council representative 22 October 2015). Access to the arts and to festivals is not always easy, with high entry prices or intangible cultural barriers often in place. These barriers to entry are particularly apparent when the event is seen to be a space of exclusion for certain groups or individuals within a community. The Experience! festival has no entry fee, which helps to emphasise the inclusive nature of the events.

However, accessibility relates to more than simple access. The concept of community needs to be carefully considered. Support from local government and community groups tends to focus on a geographical location – naturally enough, given their mandate to be responsible for a specific geographic location. In this framing, the local is embedded along traditional lines of an ideal community in which social relations are characterised by small-scale, personal ties, suggesting the community festival is representative of those people. Local government planning for local service provision and responding to areas of deprivation is determined more readily through a focus on place (Wood 2005); however, community is constituted in more ways than simply location (see Chapter 1 for a discussion on the concept of community). Other equally important things include communities of interest, shared values, and levels of attachment. Because there is a danger that a community festival may appear to reiterate this ideal notion of community, even when the community is recognised as culturally plural, councils must consider strengthening the community's ability to define itself and encourage self-determination. For Casey, there is a very strong focus on education and capacity building, not only in terms of event organisation (for example, insurance, risk management and road safety) but also in broader terms, relating to providing opportunities for community groups to come together and get to know each other (personal communication with Council representative 22 October 2015). Although festivals are a popular form of showcasing local government responses to culturally diverse communities, individuals and groups may feel excluded from such expressions of community belonging. Policies that support cultural diversity have been criticised because the celebration of diversity represented through what James Jupp called "spaghetti and polkas" festivals (Jupp 2002) ignores other, more practical issues of social justice, such as economic security, access and equity. In social justice terms, local government policy needs to consider the ways in which factors such as democratic struggles around gender, race, class, sexuality and the environment operate at the local scale while keeping in mind the broader regional, national and global contexts and their impacts.

Even in those instances when a festival promotes and celebrates cultural diversity, the ideals of social cohesion and community identity are emphasised and given meaning through state and local government policies on multiculturalism (Smith and Brett 1998). The official discourses of those groups controlling the festival operate to produce an official "imagined" community, which the festival is then planned to address. As a result of this, 'actions around cultural diversity tend to be framed either through discourses of inclusiveness, and celebrated as "proof" that [Australia] is a truly multicultural and tolerant nation, or criticised for the way in which these actions reinforce models of exclusivity and paternalism' (Permezel and Duffy 2007: 359).

However, it can be argued that representing the "other's" culture, although problematic, can produce new meanings in a different social and cultural setting (Duffy 2005). For Casey, an important aspect of running the multicultural festival is that it builds residents' capacity to be confident to display their cultural identity. For example, Experience! gave recent migrants from Afghanistan opportunities to talk about their home country and portray the beauty of the landscape and the richness of the culture and history, helping to dispel some of the more commonly held beliefs about Afghanistan as a war-torn and poor country. The fact that some of these migrants were female and felt confident to speak in front of an audience also demonstrates a certain level of confidence and pride in their cultural identity.

Although community festivals can generate notions of inclusivity, issues may arise because the "official" view of how a community is represented through cultural performance may differ from the "on the ground community" view, which is usually about participation in activities that are meaningful to that particular group, activities that reiterate a history of particular traditions and points of view (Permezel and Duffy 2007). Some critics go further – Hage (1998) suggests that multiculturalism and its promotion of the tolerance of difference are strategies aimed at reproducing and disguising relationships of white power, a 'form of symbolic violence in which a mode of domination is presented as a form of egalitarianism' (1998: 87). According to Hage (1998), then, multicultural festivals in Australia are not about inclusivity; rather, they are about containment and the subsequent enrichment of Anglo-Australia through a managed Anglo-Celtic appropriation of this diversity (Hage 1998).

One of the ways that Casey has tried to get around this is to include a variety of people in the performing and staging of the event. For example, in 2015, the MC was a relatively recent arrival from Somalia who, as a spoken word poet, uses his poetry as a way to relay a message about refugees generally and about his own journey as a refugee.

The role of multicultural community events in maintaining culture, heritage and traditions

Authenticity is a concept that has been applied to cultural festival research in the past (Xiao and Smith 2004). In the context of festivals that celebrate cultural plurality, concerns with authenticity correspond to concerns in maintaining an idea of an essential identity that is expressed and maintained through cultural and ethnic characteristics (Duffy 2005). Questions raised include 'whose memories are we drawing on (or denying). . . . And whose traditions are we keeping alive through the enactment of festivals and other rituals?' (Chang 2005: 248).

However, even a structured multicultural festival is not guaranteed to reflect all the diversity within a region. In the case of Experience!, it became important to understand the breadth of who was considered to be part of the local community, not simply relying on which cultural groups (e.g. Pacific Islanders or Indians) composed the largest proportion of migrants. Naturally, there is an element of pragmatism involved – for example, not all cultural groups may wish to be involved – and so the final result is always a compromise which may not accurately reflect the full diversity of the community (personal communication with Council representative 22 October 2015). The idea of "the other" as a social group in a multicultural community has interesting implications for ethnic cultural events or festivals. In her research based in Canada, McClinchey (2008) questions whether The Taste of Little Italy (a festival that aims to mimic the festivities that occur in Italian piazzas) may be a contrived spectacle so far removed from actual piazza activities that it results in an inauthentic representation of Italian culture. In other words, the collective or group memory shared by visitors at the festivals who may have never experienced authentic Italian culture may actually simply be a "myth" of culture (Bell 2003). Such commodification of culture and loss of cultural authenticity occurs through a process known as festivalisation, in which cultural artefacts are turned into commodities to be consumed by a festival audience. It can be argued that visitors create their own interpretations of what is authentic (Wang 1999; Timothy and Boyd 2006), with little regard to the "actual" authenticity of the performance.

Ethnic cultural attractions or events in a multicultural community are often characterised as pseudo-events (Boorstin 1964) and/or staged authenticity (MacCannell 1973, 1976). For Boorstin (writing about culture and heritage tourism), pseudo-events 'offer an elaborately contrived indirect experience, an artificial product to be consumed' (1964: 99). Authenticity, to MacCannell, involves some kind of 'behind the scenes' access to another culture, an unscripted encounter. Staged authenticity, on the other hand, 'lends to proceedings an aura of superficiality (MacCannell 1973: 595). Hollinshead is particularly vocal in his criticism, calling staged multicultural festivals 'inauthentic, manufactured happenings to be enjoyed in the environmental bubble of placeless-style settings' (Hollinshead 2000: 471). However, such criticisms may be somewhat unfair, particularly when considered in relation to multicultural festivals hosted by local authorities making strenuous efforts to promote the culture, heritage and traditions of the minority groups living within a community (Xiao and Smith 2004).

In the Australian context, Indigenous peoples add an additional layer of cultural diversity. In the latest census, 1,400 City of Casey residents, more than in any of the other nearby local government areas, stated they were Indigenous (ABS 2016). Some Indigenous components are usually included in all Council events and festivals, such as a welcome to country from members of the Wurundjeri

Figure 11.2 Experience! Casey Multicultural Festival Samoan Performance.
Photo © Michelle Duffy.

community; however, Experience! also included some stalls specifically manned by members of the Aboriginal community, displaying their art and doing cookery demonstrations. However, there are still opportunities for further Indigenous involvement. This serves to highlight the complexity of attempting to represent so many layers of difference in one festival and demonstrates that even the best efforts can sometimes fall short of the ideal.

Conclusion

Experience! The Casey Multicultural Festival has been very successful to date, and the City of Casey Council believes that this multicultural event can further boost tolerance and understanding of diversity. The Council aims to encourage even more residents to experience cultural diversity and find out more about particular cultures. In fact, the council is considering expanding the festival so that it takes place over a week, or even a fortnight. This would allow different sections of the community to attend a variety of events, showcasing the wealth of cultural diversity that exists in the community.

However, there are important issues relating to the implementation of top-down policies that attempt to re-shape communities. Multicultural policies generally are about the management of difference, and they often attempt to portray a simple relationship between a place and its community, as highlighted in Chapter 5. Performing within a multicultural festival can arguably position the performers as "the other" in relation to the dominant community, leading to a loss of authenticity of culture, heritage and traditions. Migrant communities are faced with a sense of belonging neither "here" nor "there", and the potential for tension and increased intolerance of diversity are amply illustrated in this case study.

Naturally, the council is aware that multicultural events alone can not solve issues of diversity. However, with its strong focus on education, capacity building and outreach, the council aims to boost the abilities of the various cultural communities within the City of Casey to be confident of their cultures and share as much as they can.

References

Allport, G. W. (1954). *The Nature of Prejudice*. Reading, MA: Addison-Wesley.

Amin, A. (2008). Collective culture and urban public space. *City*, 12(1), pp. 5–24.

Australian Bureau of Statistics (2016). *Casey Region Statistics*. [online] Available at: http://stat.abs.gov.au/itt/r.jsp?RegionSummaryandregion=21610anddataset=ABS_REGIONAL_LGAandgeoconcept=REGIONanddatasetASGS=ABS_REGIONAL_ASGSanddatasetLGA=ABS_REGIONAL_LGAandregionLGA=REGIONandregionASGS=REGION [Accessed 31 March 2017].

Bell, D. S. (2003). Mythscapes: Memory, mythology, and national identity. *The British Journal of Sociology*, 54(1), pp. 63–81.

Berry, J. W., Phinney, J. S., Sam, D. L. and Vedder, P. (2006). Immigrant youth: Acculturation, identity, and adaptation. *Applied Psychology*, 55(3), pp. 303–332.

Boorstin, D. (1964). *The Image: A Guide to Pseudo-Events in America*. New York: Harper and Row.

Casey Event Policy (2014). [online]. Available at: www.casey.vic.gov.au/council/policies-strategies/d-f/events-policy [Accessed 31 March 2017].

Chang, T. C. (2005). Place, memory and identity: Imagining 'New Asia.' *Asia Pacific Viewpoint*, 46(3), pp. 247–253.

City of Casey (2016). *Demographics*. [online]. Available at: www.casey.vic.gov.au/council/about-casey/demographics [Accessed 31 March 2017].

Duffy, M. (2005). Performing identity within a multicultural framework. *Social and Cultural Geography*, 6(5), pp. 677–692.

Dunn, K., Thompson, S., Hanna, B., Murphy, P. and Burnley, I. (2001). Multicultural policy within local government in Australia. *Urban Studies*, 38(13), pp. 2477–2494.

Experience (2016). [online]. Available at: www.casey.vic.gov.au/arts-leisure/events-activities/experience-casey [Accessed 31 March 2017].

Finkel, R. (2006). Tensions between ambition and reality in UK combined arts festival programming: Case study of the Lichfield Festival. *International Journal of Event Management Research*, 2(1), pp. 25–36.

Fincher, R. and Iveson, K. (2008). *Planning and Diversity in the City: Redistribution, Recognition and Encounter*. Hampshire, UK: Palgrave Macmillan.

Gorman-Murray, A. (2009).What's the meaning of Chillout? Rural/urban difference and the cultural significance of Australia's largest rural GLBTQ festival. *Rural Society*, 19(1), pp. 71–86.

Hage, G. (1998). *White Nation: Fantasies of White Supremacy in a Multicultural Society*. Annandale, NSW: Pluto Press.

Hollinshead, K. (2000). P Worldmaking. In: Jafari, J. (Ed.) *Encyclopedia of Tourism*. New York: Routledge. pp. 1028–1029.

Jupp, J. (2002). *From White Australia to Woomera: The Story of Australian Immigration*. New York: Cambridge University Press.

Lee, I., Arcodia, C. and Lee, T. J. (2012a). Multicultural festivals: A niche tourism product in South Korea. *Tourism Review*, 67(1), pp. 34–41.

Lee, I., Arcodia, C. and Lee, T. J. (2012b). Benefits of visiting a multicultural festival: The case of South Korea. *Tourism Management*, 33(2), pp. 334–340.

Lee, I. S., Arcodia, C. and Lee, T. J. (2012c). Key characteristics of multicultural festivals: A critical review of the literature. *Event Management*, 16(1), pp. 93–101.

MacCannell, D. (1973). Staged Authenticity: Arrangements of Social Space in Tourist Settings. *American Sociological Review* 79, pp. 589–603.

MacCannell, D (1976). *The Tourist: A New Theory of the Leisure Class*. New York: Schocken.

McClinchey, K. A. (2008). Urban ethnic festivals, neighbourhoods, and the multiple realities of marketing place. *Journal of Travel and Tourism Marketing*, 25(3), pp. 251–264.

Österlund-Pötzsch, S. (2004). Communicating ethnic heritage: Swedish-speaking Finn descendants in North America. In: Kockel, U. and Craith, M. N. (Eds.) *Communicating Cultures*. Munster: Li, pp. 14–41.

Permezel, M. and Duffy, M. (2007). Negotiating cultural difference in local communities: The role of the body, dialogues and performative practices in local communities. *Geographical Research*, 45(4), pp. 358–375.

Picard, D. and Robinson, W. P. (2006). Remaking worlds: Festivals, tourism and change. In: Picard, D. and Robinson, W. P. (Eds.) *Festivals, Tourism and Social Change: Remaking Worlds*. Clevedon, Buffalo: Channel View Publications, pp. 1–31.

Piontkowshi, U., Florack, A., Hoelker, P. and Obdrzalek, P. (2000). Prediciting acculturation attitudes of dominant and non-dominant groups. *International Journal of Intercultural Relations*, 24, pp. 1–26.

Reid, S. (2007). Identifying social consequences of rural events. *Event Management*, 11(1–2), pp. 89–98.

Smith, G. and Brett, J. (1998). Nation, authenticity and social difference in Australian popular music: Folk, country, multicultural. *Journal of Australian Studies*, 22, pp. 3–17.

Timothy, D. J. and Boyd, S. W. (2006). Heritage tourism in the 21st century: Valued traditions and new perspectives. *Journal of Heritage Tourism*, 1(1), pp. 1–16.

Wang, N. (1999). Rethinking authenticity in tourism experience. *Annals of Tourism Research*, 26(2), pp. 349–370.

Wood, E. H. (2005). Measuring the economic and social impacts of local authority events. *International Journal of Public Sector Management*, 18(1), pp. 37–53.

Xiao, H. and Smith, S. L. J. (2004). Residents' perceptions of Kitchener-Waterloo Oktoberfest: An inductive analysis. *Event Management*, 8(3), pp. 161–175.

12 The Clunes Booktown Festival
Encounters with class mobilities

Introduction

Festival and event strategies are particularly attractive for rural and regional places, as they offer a means to entice people – and potential economic gains – into a location (Felsenstein and Fleischer 2003). Such economic benefits can bring about economic, social and cultural regeneration (Sorokina 2015) allied with the promotion and enhancement of creative industries (Creative Victoria 2014) as well as encourage greater interaction and involvement in local arts industries (Smith and Richards 2013). However, as noted in Chapter 9, social capital, while the glue that holds society together (Serageldin 1996), must be constructed and maintained through investment in social networks, norms and resources. In addition, social capital has a dual nature (Johnstone 2016); 'the same ties that bind also exclude' (Narayan 1999: 8). This dual nature is particularly important in rural and regional places in which the movement of people, ideas and capital can rapidly alter the networks and relations that constitute a community. Hence the creation of social capital is intertwined with mobilities, not simply in terms of the movement of people in and out of a locality but also in terms of the movement of ideologies, class and culture that can then go on to reshape a location and challenge other, perhaps longer established networks and power relations.

While acknowledging that there are still many debates around how we conceptualise and so define rurality and regionality, "the rural" is very much part of an imagined place that stands in opposition to ideas about urban places (Woods 2011). In this rural imaginary, discussions about what a rural place is invariably focus on notions of spatial location, of inhabiting particular bounded spaces that are (perhaps) easily located on a map and at a distance from major urban and metropolitan centres. Popular imagery often focuses on the rural either as inhabited by a small population engaged in agriculture and whose lifestyle is embedded in tradition (Bonifacio 2011) or as a rural idyll that is an escape from modernity (Bunce 2003; Short 2006; Woods 2011). Particular images of the rural landscape are deeply embedded in what it means to be Australian, with 'the rural . . . often positioned on the national scale as a symbolic site for authentic national values' (Gorman-Murray et al. 2008: 43). In Australia, as in the UK and North America, such deeply held imaginaries are complicated by representations and narratives of, on the one hand, the dying country town, with those who remain struggling to make a living on the land while watching their children rapidly head for the cities and a better life (Duffy et al. 2007), with, on the other hand, images of 'idyllic vistas of ocean views or bush retreats that, even while at a far enough distance from the pace and smog of the city, nonetheless allow us to maintain the comforts of good food, wine and coffee' (Duffy and Waitt 2011: 44). Even so, these differing ways of thinking about the rural often neglect the complex ways in which a rural place is experienced, understood and constituted as not separate and bounded but intimately connected with the urban.

A specific example of such urban-rural connections is the phenomenon of amenity- or lifestyle-led migration, known in Australia as sea- or tree-change. This can be understood as part of a broader 21st-century counterurbanisation or a desire to "return" back-to-the-land (Halfacree 2007) wherein people seek a more affordable and/or better quality of life (Ruiz-Ballesteros and Cáceres-Feria 2016; Drozdzewski 2014). While a diverse group, sea- and tree-changers generally are affluent retirees seeking a 'bucolic lifestyle' of coastal or country living (Tonts and Greive 2002: 60). However, sea- and tree-changers may not necessarily live permanently in these locations, instead purchasing second homes as a means to "escape" the pressures of everyday life and work (Osbaldiston et al. 2015; Hugo and Harris 2013). These migratory flows bring to the fore a more open and complex spatial context through which different forms of social interaction emerge that are constituted out of local and non-local networks (Ruiz-Ballesteros and Cáceres-Feria 2016).

This chapter explores the role of rural in-migration in community development and planning in rural and regional places, where the festival model is used to activate opportunities for economic development or regeneration as well as enhance social connectedness through activities that often draw on local culture and history. Yet, in ways similar to the impacts of rapid urbanisation on the metropolitan fringe (see Chapter 11), such arts festivals are also potentially divisive because of the social changes wrought by in-migration populations and their associated networks. Drawing on the concept of social capital, we examine the role of class encounter through the new mobilities paradigm in order to unpack the complex networks of mobile capital and their reshaping of rural places. Our case study is the Clunes Booktown Festival that has been held annually in the Goldfields region of Victoria since 2007. In trying to address concerns about social inclusion, renewal and sustainability, the festival has raised questions around the identity of this community and who belongs.

Background to case study

Clunes is a small town located in the Shire of Hepburn, Victoria, Australia, with a population in 2011 of 1,656 (ABS 2011). It is around 20 kilometres outside the city of Ballarat and 146 kilometres north of Victoria's capital, Melbourne. Clunes was one of the first places where gold was discovered in Victoria and was at the centre of the gold rush of the late 19th century. Thanks to this, Clunes was an important town, well connected to other parts of Victoria by rail, and with significant infrastructure including banks, gold exchanges, shops, post offices, taverns and leisure and recreational facilities. Clunes was also the site of a major uprising in 1873, when the Port Phillip Mining Company brought in Chinese miners in response to miners striking to secure the eight-hour day (Heathcote 2008). At this time, the population was at its peak, numbering 6,203 – that is, approximately four times the current population (Clunes Tourism and Development Association 2017). One of the proud boasts of Clunes is that the main street was built to be wide enough to allow two carriages to turn (personal communication with a Clunes shop owner 18 August 2015). Even today, the town is recognised as one of the best preserved 19th-century towns in the Central Goldfields area (Clunes Tourism and Development Association 2017), which has made it a popular location for film and television, particularly its main street, Fraser Street, which became 'Wee Jerusalem' in *Mad Max* (1979) and transformed into 1880s versions of Euroa and Jerilderie in *Ned Kelly* (2003).

After the end of gold mining around the beginning of the 20th century, the town's importance gradually ebbed, and the town became a relative backwater, reliant on agriculture for its survival. By the early 2000s, population decline, a long drought, weakened local agriculture, high unemployment and an ageing population and a resultant struggling local economy led to what might be considered the town's lowest point (Creative Clunes 2007). However, at this time a group of local residents decided to try to do something to revitalise the town. The plan was to use books and literature to transform the economy of Clunes. From this initial idea, a complete reversal in the town's fortunes is evident. In 2016, the resident population doubled to around 2,000 (Wilson 2016), and signs of investment and growth in the town include the installation of the town's first ATM and the reopening of the railway station as a cultural hub and home for Creative Clunes and the Clunes Booktown Festival (Creative Victoria 2015). The key to this transformation has been the annual Clunes Booktown Festival. Since the event was first held in May 2007, Clunes has become a year-round destination for tourists 'looking to engage with the monthly program of talks by prominent authors, or browse their time away in one of the town's eight bookstores' (Creative Victoria 2015 online).

In light of the early success of this book festival, the organisers set up a not-for-profit incorporated organisation, Creative Clunes, which is the parent organisation behind the Clunes Book Festival and also organises book readings and meet-the-author sessions throughout the year (Clunes Booktown website). The festival regularly attracts 18,000 people, with some 50 visiting book traders bringing to the central Victorian town the largest collection of second-hand, collectable, new and small press books to be gathered in one place in Australia. For some local businesses, the festival represents over a third of their annual income, allowing them to get through the winter (traditionally a quiet time) and thus remain financially sustainable (personal communication with a Clunes bookshop owner 15 August 2015).

Clunes was accredited by the International Organization of Book Towns (IOB) in 2012. This is an international network of regional towns marketed as destinations for book lovers that includes the original booktown, Hay-on-Wye, as well as 14 other regional towns marketed as destinations for book lovers (Driscoll 2016). As Seaton (1999) and Driscoll (2016) note, the booktown model is part

Figure 12.1 Clunes Book Festival – Street Scene.
Photo © Michelle Duffy.

of an economic development strategy for peripheral towns that have experienced loss or reduction of agricultural employment. The strategy consists of converting a substantial number of commercial or unused public spaces in a rural town or a peripheral region into second-hand and antiquarian book shops, which therefore provides a critical mass of single-commodity retailing and 'allows the town or region to be packaged and marketed as a novel and unique entity – a town of books' (Seaton 1999: 390; see also Seaton 1996). Most booktowns have developed in villages of historic interest or of scenic beauty (International Book Towns 2017), and this idyllic setting serves to enhance the booktown experience. As noted in the Clunes Book Festival program:

> Visitors to Clunes throughout the year can soak up the Booktown atmosphere at a gentler pace – the many permanent second-hand book shops, cafes, giftware stores and galleries and tuning into a village culture where books and writing are part of the buzz of the kerbside conversation.

The booktown model has worked well for Clunes, with its 'sandy goldrush landscape', 'rustic architecture' and 'tightknit, friendly feel' (Wilson 2016 online), and the international links created through the IOB accreditation have increased the profile of both the festival and the town itself. Indeed, Clunes will host the 2018 International Conference of Booktowns, and the Victorian State Government has announced on-going financial support for Clunes Booktown through funding of $240,000 for 2017–2020 (Brooks 2016; Tucker 2016). This is illustrative of the overwhelming change in the atmosphere, infrastructure and ethos of this rural town. Nonetheless, although successful in terms of economic initiatives for the town, Clunes Booktown is embedded within particular frameworks of social and cultural capital that have created some tension within Clunes communities.

Revitalising rural places through social capital

Festivals are inherently about celebrating community and are understood as community-building activities. The range of people involved – organisers, performers, local government and industry representatives, audience members – all enthusiastically participate in creating and engaging with ideas of "their" community's identity. Thus, festivals are recognised as inherently about 'people celebrating themselves and their community in an "authentic" and traditional way, or at least emerging spontaneously from their homes for a community-wide expression of fellowship' (Lavenda 1992: 76). Research on festival and tourism events have drawn on Florida's (2002, 2003) creative industries hypothesis as part of regeneration strategies. Initially such programs focused on urban regeneration, recognising that cultural activities attract the so-called creative classes into economically depressed areas, which helps initiate regeneration through a cultural economy (see also Bailey et al. 2004; Evans 2005; OECD 2014; Scott 2000). More recently researchers have explored the significance of rural creativity in these sorts of redevelopment strategies (Anwar McHenry 2011; Harvey et al. 2012; Gibson 2012; Waitt and Gibson 2013). What this body of research uncovers is, perhaps unsurprisingly, diverse arrangements of networks within rural areas that interconnect with the urban but that can also operate in different and independent sorts of contexts. For example, Gibson et al. (2010) provide evidence from Darwin in the Northern Territory, Australia, that remoteness from metropolitan centres enabled distance from "faddish" urban culture and triggered new kinds of creativity specific to a particular kind of regional place. Therefore, although festivals have become a popular tool in local government policies and organisational strategies for initiating economic renewal, at their heart they are about adding social and cultural value to our everyday lives and connecting us to our daily places. This value is understood to arise out of the ways through which festivals function; they encourage community participation, enhance local creativity and foster community well-being (Gibson et al. 2009; Duffy and Mair 2014). Although local and state government play an important role in supporting such events (and indeed are necessary in many circumstances, particularly where funding is required to assist community groups establish such events), a participatory, bottom-up approach is most likely to provide successful social and economic outcomes (Johnston 2016). As Narayan (1999) explains, social capital exists with or without state support but holds its greatest public interest potential when there is state support. Even so, studies in rural Australia have demonstrated that strong government-community partnerships are important in developing strategies and programs that enhance social inclusion (Brooks 2005).

Clunes Booktown's origins lie with members of the community – all tree-changers – seeking to address what they defined as issues of social justice (personal communication with festival director 15 August 2015). As the original Clunes Booktown director explained, the severe drought affecting the region at the time 'reinforce[d] helplessness, a knowledge that the *individual* cannot act or make a difference' and that 'a willingness to dream, to imagine, and to act' in the face of this drought was what drove the group to seek to bring about social change (Brady 2012: 2, quoted in Johnston 2016: 139; emphasis added). Rather than acquiescing to ideas of permitting fast-food chains into the town as a means to renew economic and social development (personal communication with festival director 15 August 2015), the committee members of Creative Clunes proposed a rural renewal program that would instead draw on a town-focused strategy based on cultural development in general and books in particular (Kennedy 2011). The plan was that Clunes would realise 'its own place in the creative economy, through the adoption of a Booktown model and development of the town's cultural capital and built heritage assets' (Creative Clunes and Kennedy 2013: 1). This first Booktown was held in order to test the idea that books would generate tourism and was a branding exercise for Creative Clunes's broader cultural renewal objective (Kennedy 2011). Admission was free, and the crowd of around 6,000 was twice that expected (personal communication with festival director 15 August 2015). This success – although somewhat stressful for the organisers in relation to providing food, drink and even access to cash (personal communication with festival director 15 August 2015) – encouraged the staging of an annual event that was extended to two days. What is now known as the Clunes Booktown Festival is primarily an annual weekend event, with numerous second-hand bookstalls located along the main street and in public buildings throughout the town, as well as a program of writing workshops and author talks and attractions for children. This model has been so successful that this weekend event is now part of a series of book-related events (such as writing retreats) throughout the year, and, in 2014, a separate weekend festival, Clunes Booktown for Kids, was held.

As Johnston (2016: 139) points out, members of the initial group who instigated this festival were integral to the event's success because of their 'complementary core professional, governance and community skills, namely, marketing and media; government administration; community networks; logistical know-how; and writing, publishing and academic research.' However, a significant part of the success of this festival is due to the high proportion of volunteers who ensure the event runs smoothly; 'they come out of the woodwork to support it!' as the first festival director described it. Over 300 people work hundreds of volunteer hours (Creative Clunes and Kennedy 2013), which means this event has one of the highest rates of volunteering in Victoria (personal communication festival director 15 August 2015). Census data for 2011 shows that 25% of Clunes residents undertook voluntary work through an organisation or group, which is significantly higher than the average of 18% for Victoria, and is likely to be strongly related to cultural activities undertaken in the township.

Community studies researchers note that the work of volunteers plays a fundamental role in creating social capital and social connectedness (Arai 2000; Johnston 2016), as well as ensuring ongoing support for events through the establishment of mutual trust and knowledge transfer between members of the community (Ragsdale and Jepson 2014). The Clunes Booktown Festival has proved successful in its community renewal program, because in its ability to garner volunteer support it has also enhanced artistic and cultural life in the region, stimulated tourism and helped to build community capacity (Johnston 2016). In addition, as a number of business stakeholders explained in fieldwork we undertook in 2014, there is indication of change from a predominantly White, older and somewhat insular community to one that is more open and inclusive. With relatively affordable housing, there has been an increase in younger families moving into the area, as well as an influx of retirees or semi-retirees looking to downsize and spend more time in pursuits such as undertaking a PhD or becoming more involved in the arts and art practices, while some who currently use their Clunes address as a weekender hope to make the move to permanent relocation (personal communication with business owner 15 August 2015). Volunteering of both current residents and those considering relocation have opened up a means for a (re)connection with a sense of a Clunes community. As the original festival director explained, locals as well as volunteers from Melbourne and Canberra are getting more involved in the event (personal communication with first Booktown director 15 August 2015).

Class mobilities and the rural idyll

The approach taken by Creative Clunes has been successful. Instead of empty shops and a dwindling population, Clunes now has cafes, bars, bookshops and a reinvigorated sense of community. Positive changes that have taken place include an increase in tourist numbers and even a growing number of amenity migrants, that is, those who move out from Melbourne because they seek to live in what is perceived as the peace and tranquility of rural places and harmonious communities (Argent et al. 2007). Clunes has certainly been transformed, but this was achieved through creating an aesthetic appeal that capitalises on idealised images of the small rural town or village. Within the Clunes community – as in other sea- and tree-change towns – there is a complex relationship between volunteering and ideas about local connectedness. As a number of business owners pointed out, some members of the community are unhappy with the influx of people during the Booktown weekend; others have noted some tension with regard to decisions made about the festival and town direction (personal communication with business owner 15 August 2015). The place of Clunes is indeed at the centre of booktown tourism, yet whose place is this?

Mobility is important to the ways in which rural places are constructed, and, as Milbourne (2007: 382) argues, we need 'to engage more critically with discourses of mobilities, which involves them paying greater attention to the inter-connected empirical realities, representations and everyday practices of mobilities' because 'they are bound up with shifting meanings of rural places and ruralities.' The success of festivals such as Clunes Booktown has generated much interest not only

Figure 12.2 Gentrification in Clunes.
Photo © Michelle Duffy.

among industry and government stakeholders seeking to redress economic challenges in regional areas but also among academics exploring the role that rural
tourism and the creative industries can play in areas of decline. These narratives
are in many ways a continuation of an older discourse around urban-rural relations
that constructs the rural in particular ways – that is, in terms of the types of social
relations and associations that can be found in these differing locations (Sim-
mell 1903[1997]; Tönnies 1887 [1955]; Williams 1975). Although these earlier
approaches theorise the rural through a range of sociological frameworks, they
agree on the key point that urban and rural places are distinct. The work of Pahl
(1966, 1975, 2005) questioned this division through his UK-based research that
examined how middle-class commuters reinvent village life. Pahl argued that this
change was wrought by the middle classes, who were able to commute between
their places of work in major cities and their homes in rural and regional towns
and villages because the middle class has the capacity to live and work where it
wants. In his earlier work on this, Pahl stated

> The middle-class people come into rural areas in search of a meaningful
> community and by their presence help to destroy whatever community was

there. Part of the basis of the local village community was the sharing of the deprivations due to the isolation of country life and the sharing of the limited world of the families within the village. The middle class try to get the cosiness of village life, without suffering any of the deprivations, and while maintaining a whole range of contacts outside.

(Pahl 1964: 9)

Pahl (2005) himself later acknowledged some of the assumptions underlying his analysis, in particular the generational differences that are present in terms of employment, as well as wage differentials within both working- and middle-class groups that can facilitate or prevent life choices. Nevertheless, there remains today a narrative about the impact of the middle classes on rural life: this influx of people with different ideas and higher incomes leads to processes of gentrification that eventually push out the original residents by way of increased living and housing costs, increased inflation, the style of consumption in these locations and so on. In terms of the local context, middle-class people who move to rural areas – often derogatorily described as the "latté set" – are thought to not integrate with the rural communities, keeping their social and working lives located in the cities. More importantly (for those disgruntled with the movement of the middle classes into rural areas), they nonetheless come to dominate the politics and, thus, the cultural landscapes of these rural towns (Connell & McManus 2011). Complicating these relations are people who have not fully moved out of the city, people who own a second home in a rural area, which they visit on weekends or during holidays. Conflict can arise between these part-time residents and others who 'share the same spaces, but use them for different purposes' (Overvåg and Berg 2011: 419). This understanding of urban-rural relations in conflict has been critiqued by Pahl (2005) and others, who have found a more nuanced network of relationships in rural locations.

The ways in which different social groups occupy different networks in the same location are important factors in one's capacity for a mobile life. Urry (2007; see also Elliott and Urry 2010) argues that network capital – which comprises the resources that enable people to move and connect into certain sets of relations with minimal difficulty – is integral to such spatial movement. Others suggest that something about our bodily engagement, capabilities and attributes is important to this capacity to move within and across networks. Thus, what some have called 'cosmopolitan capital' (Bühlmann et al. 2013; Igarashi and Saito 2014) – that is, language skills, international experiences, and advanced education– 'make social agents better equipped to navigate the world geographically, socially and culturally' (Jansson 2016: 423). Hence, some scholars argue that these forms of social capital, rather than "colonising" the countryside, demonstrate how in-migration has often strengthened social bonds and economic health and propose that this has occurred through a re-imagining of the community (Pahl 2005). This approach seeks to examine the ways in which the urban and the rural are interdependent: connected through back-and-forth flows of people, capital and ideas. However, differing power relations remain.

Conclusion

Milbourne (2007: 385) argues that we need to be cautious of the emotive narratives often emphasised in stories of migration into rural places 'as threatening local forms of community living and the settledness of rural places.' This is not to ignore the very real inequalities that can produce uneven power relations and processes of marginalisation. Booktown festivals are, as Driscoll (2016: 11) notes, 'inextricably entwined with the status of books in contemporary society. . . . Books remain objects with significant cultural status, and interacting with books is a way for people to signal their own cultural credentials, at least to other readers. . . . That is, book-related events carry a sense of social distinction.' Nevertheless, rural festival events like Clunes Booktown are incredibly important for maintaining livelihoods as well as spaces in which residents, weekenders and tourists, with different ideas of community and belonging, coexist, albeit sometimes uneasily. As explored elsewhere (see also Duffy et al. 2007), the success of these festival events in creating a sense of community and belonging has much to do with the creation of eventful moments in which people, activities, emotions, and place come together 'charged with potential and possibilities' (McCormack 2005: 121). In the case of the Clunes region, concern about a rural town's survival led to a group of passionate volunteers 'turning a quiet village of empty shops and public buildings into a booktown' (Brady 2012: 15, quoted in Johnston 2016: 139). This model has facilitated a means for people to connect to the place of Clunes – as one of Driscoll's (2016: 9–10) interviewees who had recently moved from Melbourne to Clunes explained, participation in this festival 'was about trying to connect with our little village as well and what's around us, a sense of place I guess.'

References

ABS (2011). Clunes Population (Vic). [online]. Available at: http://clunes.localstats.com.au/population/vic/south-western-victoria/ballaratt/clunes [accessed 04/06/2017].

Anwar McHenry, J. (2011). Rural empowerment through the arts: The role of the arts in civic and social participation in the Mid West region of Western Australia. *Journal of Rural Studies*, 27(3), pp. 245–253.

Arai, S. (2000). Typology of volunteers for a changing sociopolitical context: The impact on social capital citizenship and civil society. *Loisir et Société/Society and Leisure*, 23(2), pp. 327–352.

Argent, N., Smailes, P., Griffin, T. (2007). The Amenity Complex: Towards a framework for analysing and predicting the emergence of a multifunctional countryside in Australia. *Geographical Research*. 45 (3), pp. 217–232

Bailey, C., Miles, S., Stark, P. (2004). Culture-led urban regeneration and the revitalisation of identities in Newcastle, Gateshead and the North East of England. *International Journal of Cultural Policy* 10(1), pp. 47–65.

Bonifacio, G. (2011). Introduction. In: Bonifacio, G. (Ed.) *Gender and Rural Migration*. New York, Oxon: Taylor and Francis, pp. 1–19.

Brady, T. (2012). Clunes Address. World Booktown symposium, Paju Booksori, September.

Brooks, C. (2016). Backing clunes booktown. *Victorian State Government Media Release*, September 8 [online] Available at: www.premier.vic.gov.au/wp-content/uploads/2016/09/160908-Backing-Clunes-Booktown [Accessed 31 March 2017].

Brooks, K. (2005). Re-interpreting social capital – A political hijack or useful structural concept in community regeneration?. Paper presented at the International Conference on Engaging Communities, Brisbane, Australia, August 15–17.

Bühlmann, F., David, T. and Mach, A. (2013). Cosmopolitan capital and the internationalization of the field of business elites: Evidence from the Swiss case. *Cultural Sociology*, 7(2), pp. 211–229.

Bunce, M. (2003). Reproducing rural idylls. In: Cloke, P. (Ed.) *Country Visions*. Harlow, England, New York: Pearson and Prentice Hall, pp. 14–30.

Clunes Book Town website. Available at: http://clunesbooktown.com.au/creative-clunes/

Clunes Tourism and Development Association. (2017). *Welcome to Clunes* [online]. Available at: www.clunes.org/index.php [Accessed 31 March 2017].

Connell, J., McManus, P. (Eds.) (2011). *Rural Revival? Place Marketing, Tree Change and Regional Migration in Australia*. Surrey, UK & Burlington, USA: Ashgate.

Creative Clunes. (2007). *Business plan*. Clunes: Creative Clunes Inc. [online]. www.book town.clunes.org/documents/businessplan08.pdf [Accessed 23 March 2017].

Creative Clunes and Kennedy, M. (2013). Tourism and the creative economy. *OECD Case Study of Clunes Booktown Australia*. Community Planning and Development Program, La Trobe University, assisted by the Victorian Government Department of State Development, Business and Innovation, Melbourne, Australia.

Creative Victoria. (2014). *The Arts Ripple Effect: Valuing the Arts in Communities* [Online]. Available at: http://archive.creative.vic.gov.au/Research_Resources/Resources/The_ Arts_Ripple_Effect [Accessed 24 March 2017].

Creative Victoria. (2015). *Advancing Regional Victoria and Outer Metropolitan Melbourne – Case Study: Clunes BookTown* [Online]. Available at: www.strategy.creative. vic.gov.au/news/advancing-regional-victoria-and-outer-metropolitan-melbourne-case-study. [Accessed 26 March 2017].

Driscoll, B. (2016). Local places and cultural distinction: The booktown model. *European Journal of Cultural Studies*, doi:10.1177/1367549416656856; pp. 1–17

Drozdzewski, D. (2014). 'They have no concept of what a farm is': Exploring rural change through tree change migration. In: Dufty-Jones, R. and Connell, J. (Eds.) *Rural Change in Australia: Population, Economy, Environment*. Farnham, UK, Burlington, VA: Ashgate, pp. 83–101.

Duffy, M. and Mair, J. (2014). Festivals and sense of community: An Australia case study. In: Jepson, A. and Clarke, A. (Eds.) *Routledge Advances in Events Research Book Series: Exploring Community Festivals and Events*. Oxon, New York: Routledge, pp. 54–65.

Duffy, M. and Waitt, G. (2011). Rural festivals and processes of belonging. In: Gibson, C. and Connell, J. (Eds.) *Festival Places: Revitalising Rural Australia*. Clevedon, UK: Channel View Press, pp. 44–59.

Duffy, M., Waitt, G. R. and Gibson, C. R. (2007). Get into the groove: the role of sound in generating a sense of belonging in street parades. *Altitude: A Journal of Emerging Humanities Work*, 8, pp. 1–32.

Elliott, A. and Urry, J. (2010). *Mobile Lives*. London: Routledge.

Evans, G. (2005). *Measure for Measure: Evaluating the Evidence of Culture's Contribution to Regeneration*. Urban Studies, 42 (5/ 6), pp. 959–983.

Felsenstein, D. and Fleischer, A. (2003). Local festivals and tourism promotion: The role of public assistance and visitor expenditure. *Journal of Travel Research*, 41(4), pp. 382–392.

Florida R. (2002). *The rise of the creative class: and how it's transforming work, leisure, community and everyday life*. New York: Basic Books.

Florida, R. (2003). Cities and the creative class. *City & Community*, 2(1), pp. 3–19.

Gibson, C. (Ed.). (2012). *Creativity in Peripheral Places: Redefining the Creative Industries*. London, New York: Routledge.

Gibson, C., Connell, J., Waitt, G. and Walmsley, J. (2009). *Reinventing Rural Places: The Extent and Impact of Festivals in Rural and Regional Australia*. Wollongong, NSW: University of Wollongong.

Gibson, C., Luckman, S. and Willoughby-Smith, J. (2010). Creativity without borders? Rethinking remoteness and proximity. *Australian Geographer*, 41(1), pp. 25–38.

Gorman-Murray, A., Darian-Smith, K. and Gibson, G. (2008). Scaling the rural: Reflections on rural cultural studies. *Australian Humanities Review*, 45, pp. 37–52.

Halfacree, K. (2007). Back-to-the-land in the twenty-first Century: Making connections with Rurality. *Tijdschrift voor Economische en Sociale Geografie*, 98(1), pp. 3–8.

Harvey, D. C., Hawkins, H. and Thomas, N. J. (2012). Thinking creative clusters beyond the city: People, places and networks. *Geoforum*, 43, pp. 529–539.

Heathcote, C. (2008). Clunes 1873: The uprising that wasn't. *Quadrant*, 52(12), pp. 71–81.

Hugo, G. and Harris, K. (2013). *Time and Tide: Moving Towards an Understanding of Temporal Population Changes in Coastal Australia*. Report prepared for the National Sea Change Taskforce [online]. Available at: https://stokes2013.files.wordpress.com/2014/10/report-final-april-2013.pdf [Accessed 20 March 2017].

Igarashi, H. and Saito, H. (2014). Cosmopolitanism as cultural capital: Exploring the intersection of globalization, education and stratification. *Cultural Sociology*, 8(3), pp. 222–239.

International booktowns (2017). Available at: www.booktown.net/.

Jansson, A. (2016). Mobile elites: Understanding the ambiguous lifeworlds of Sojourners. *European Journal of Cultural Studies*, 19(5), pp. 421–434.

Johnston, J. (2016). *Public Relations and the Public Interest*, Johnston, J. (Ed.) Taylor and Francis ProQuest Ebook Central. Available at: https://ebookcentral-proquest-com.ezproxy.lib.monash.edu.au/lib/monash/detail.action?docID=4406493.

Kennedy, M. (2011). Binding a sSustainable future: Book towns, themed place branding and rural renewal: A case study of clunes' back to booktown. In: Martin, J. and Budge, T. (Eds.) *The Sustainability of Australia's Country Towns: Renewal, Renaissance, Resilience*. Ballarat: VURRN Press, pp. 207–226.

Mad Max. (1979). Video. Australia: George Miller.

McCormack, D. (2005). Diagramming practice and performance. *Environment and Planning D: Society and Space*, 23(1), pp. 119–147.

Milbourne, P. (2007). Re-populating rural studies: Migrations, movements and mobilities. *Journal of Rural Studies*, 23, pp. 381–386.

Narayan, D. (1999). Bonds and bridges: social capital and poverty. World Bank, [Online]. Available at: http://info.worldbank.org/etools/docs/library/9747/narayan.pdf [Accessed 20 March 2017].

Ned Kelly. (2003). Video. Australia: Gregor Jordan.

OECD. (2014). *Tourism and the Creative Economy*. OECD Studies on Tourism. OECD Publishing. http://dx.doi.org/10.1787/9789264207875-en

Osbaldiston, N., Picken, F. and Duffy, M. (2015). Characteristics and future intentions of second homeowners: A case study from Eastern Victoria, Australia. *Journal of Policy Research in Tourism, Leisure and Events*, 7(1), pp. 62–76.

Overvåg, K. and Berg, N. G. (2011). Second homes, rurality and contested space in Eastern Norway. *Tourism Geographies*, 13, pp. 417–442.

Pahl, R. (1964). The two class village. *New Society*, 27(2), pp. 7–9.

Pahl, R. (1966). The rural-urban continuum. *Sociologia Ruralis*, 6(3–4), pp. 299–329.

Pahl, R. (1975). *Whose City?* Harmondsworth: Penguin Books.

Pahl, R. (2005). Are all communities, communities in the mind? *The Sociological Review*, 53(4), pp. 621–640.

Ragsdell, G. and Jepson, A. (2014). Knowledge sharing: Insights from Campaign for Real Ale (CAMRA) festival volunteers. *International Journal of Event and Festival Management*, 5(3), pp. 279–296.

Ruiz-Ballesteros, E. and Cáceres-Feria, R. (2016). Community-building and amenity migration in community-based tourism development: An approach from southwest Spain. *Tourism Management*, 54, pp. 513–523.

Scott, A. J. (2000). *The Cultural Economy of Cities: Essays on the Geography of Image-producing Industries*. London: Sage.

Seaton, A. V. (1996). Hay on Wye, the mouse that roared: Book towns and rural tourism. *Tourism Management*, 17(5), pp. 379–382.

Seaton, A. V. (1999). Book towns as tourism developments in peripheral areas. *The International Journal of Tourism Research*, 1(5), pp. 389–399.

Serageldin, I. (1996). Sustainability as opportunity and the problem of social capital. *The Brown Journal of World Affairs*, 3(2), pp. 187–203.

Short, B. (2006). Idyllic ruralities. In: Cloke, P., Marsden, T. and Mooney, P. (Eds.) *Handbook of Rural Studies*. London: Sage, pp. 133–148.

Simmel, G. (2001) [1903]. The metropolis and mental life. In: Spillman, L. (Ed.). *Cultural Sociology*. New York: Wiley-Blackwell, pp. 11–19.

Simmel, G. (1903[1997]). The Metropolis and Mental Life. In: M. Featherstone and D. Frisby (eds.), *Simmel on Culture*, Sage Publications, London, pp. 174–186.

Smith, M. and Richards, G. (2013). *Routledge Handbook of Cultural Tourism*. London: Routledge.

Sorokina, N. (2015). Sustainable event management: A practical guide. *Tourism Management*, 47, pp. 77–78.

Tönnies, F. (1887 [1955]). *Gemeinschaft und Gesellschaft*. London: Routledge and Kegan Paul.

Tont, M., Grieve, S. (2002). Commodification and Creative Destruction in the Australian Rural Landscape: The Case of Bridgetown, Western Australia. *Australian Geographical Studies*, 40(1), pp. 58–70.

Tucker, A. (2016). Funding to benefit Booktown /*Maryborough Advertiser*/ 9 September. [Online]. Available at: www.maryboroughadvertiser.com.au/2016/09/funding-benefit-booktown/ [Accessed 29 March 2017].

Urry, J. (2007). *Mobilities*. Cambridge: Polity.

Waitt, G. and Gibson, C. (2013). The spiral gallery: Non-market creativity and belonging in an Australian country town. *Journal of Rural Studies*, 30, pp. 75–85.

Williams, R. (1975). *The Country and the City*. New York: Oxford University Press.

Wilson, A. (2016). Clunes Booktown is history in the making. *The Courier* 9 April. [Online]. Available at: www.thecourier.com.au/story/3839740/clunesbooktownishistoryinthemaking/, [Accessed 26 March 2017].

Wood, M. (2007). Engaging the global countryside: globalization, hybridity and the reconstitution of rural place. *Progress in Human Geography*. 31 (4), pp. 485–507.

Woods, M. (2011). *Rural*. London, New York: Routledge.

13 The Noosa Jazz Festival

Encounter with the senses

Introduction

A close study of such representational characteristics of festivals – that is, that ideas of identity are expressed through certain cultural features – can tell us much about the construction of communal identities and specific forms of allegiance that these may activate. Yet this approach is less helpful when attempting to understand and assess how events can contribute to *feelings* of connectedness and belonging, or, conversely, alienation and exclusion. The transitory nature of the event – the brief encounters and exchanges that occur within the festival space – may produce different and often conflicting configurations of identity, place, and belonging. In addition, festivals are not solely focused on the actual locality; rather, various forms of engagement and participation configure residents and non-residents in terms of community and collective identity (Connell and Gibson 2003; Curtis 2010; Whiteley et al. 2004). Festivals are, therefore, complex sites for localness and belonging, celebrating diversity and connections beyond that of the locally defined community. The difficulty lies in how we might conceptualise and capture these various ways of participating in events and connecting to a festival community.

One way to approach this is exemplified in the work of researchers who have examined motivations for event participation (Crompton and McKay 1997; Nicholson and Pearce 2000), as well as in the psychological frameworks that have provided a particular understanding of motivation in terms of needs, consumer behaviour and marketing (Filep et al. 2015; Getz and Andersson 2010; Getz and McConnell 2011; Nyaupane and Poudel 2012; Pearce and Pabel 2015). These approaches can tell us much, for, as some scholars working in media and cultural studies argue, consumption plays a significant part in generating social bonds because of the ways in which a subcultural style is constructed through elements such as dress, music preferences, lifestyle choices, and what is purchased (Hebdidge 1979; see also Hall and Jefferson 1975/1991). More recent work in tourism and leisure industries points to the growing centrality of experience to a range of tourism activities (Cohen 2010; Cohen 1979; Morgan et al. 2010; Pine and Gilmore 1999). This 'experience economy' is important to the ability of markets, particularly in the developed world, to maintain a competitive advantage (Morgan et al. 2010). Nevertheless, such frameworks of consumption practices have some resonance with the origins of festivals in religious celebrations and public cultural practices, not least because of participants' search for a sense of "authenticity" and (re)connection to community.

Many festivals incorporate specific traditions, and activities such as rituals and associated symbolic practices are used as a means to identify group members (Ahmed 1992; Diaz-Barriga 2003; Nolan and Nolan 1992; Ruback et al. 2008). Scholars drawing on the work of Durkheim (1912/1976) and Turner (1969) explore how events encourage opportunities for enacting a collective conscious-ness through the generation of strong, often spontaneous feelings of connected-ness (refer to Chapter 4 of this book). This body of literature does understand such community events within a ritual framework – that is, as something set apart from the everyday (Durkheim 1912/1976); however, it also notes the importance of the senses in creating a heightened state of feeling and emotion within and between participants (Howes 2006; Low 2012). Durkheim understood this as integral to the binding of individuals together that then encourages opportunities for enact-ing a collective consciousness (Eade and Sallnow 2000; Falassi 1987; Handelman 1990; Sepp 2014). This conceptualisation is useful in addressing music festivals, which are explored in this chapter, because the music genres performed – the song lyrics, instrumentation, melodic structures or performance styles – are understood as constructions of identity associated with specific cultural groups or lifestyles. This approach can tell us much about place-based belonging – cultural practices such as music do help forge place-based identifications. Nonetheless, it does not help us understand and articulate the experiential processes involved, the ways in which participation in music activities has an impact on our bodies and our feel-ings, and what this may mean in terms of processes of subjectivity, identity and, hence, notions of community building and belonging (Ehrenreich 2007, Thrift 2008). As Waitt and Duffy (2010: 458) argue, 'festival spaces may create an affec-tive ambience that encourages an openness to others, and sustain a social iden-tification through the intangible feeling that encompasses an emotional space of belonging together.' However, the generation of certain feelings may instead close down processes of connectedness and social identification (see also Ansdell 2004; Benzon 2001; Ehrenreich 2007).

Bodies and the senses

As discussed in detail in Chapter 6 on non-representation theory, researchers have turned to a range of sensory approaches to better understand festivals, bodies, emotions and affect. In relation to the senses, these include sound, listening and hearing (Boyd and Duffy 2012; Waitt and Duffy 2010; Wood et al. 2007), smell (Classen 1993; Dann 2003; Law 2001; Low 2005; Pennycook and Otsuji 2015), emotion and affect (Anderson 2009; Bondi et al. 2005; Duffy 2016; Chalip 2006) and bodily movement (Bull 2000, 2004; Gallagher 2015; Waitt et al. 2015), to note a few. However, in this range of work it is important to acknowledge that our senses are not simply identified as unmediated physiological responses to the world and therefore pre-cultural in their formation (Classen 1993). As Sim-mell (1997 [1903]: 109) suggested, our sensory perceptions underpin human interaction, and our sensory impressions constitute 'the meanings that mutual sensory perception and influencing have for the social life of human beings, their coexistence, co-operation and opposition.' The meaning we attribute to certain registers of the senses arises out of cultural constructions that reveal 'society's aspirations and preoccupations, its divisions, hierarchies, and interrelationships' and that the senses therefore have a 'role in *framing* perceptual experience in accordance with socially prescribed norms' (Classen 1997: 402; italics in original). We may not recognise this as a process of socialisation because, as Edensor and Falconer (2012: 75) suggest, the

> immersive qualities of the multi-sensual apprehension of space [may] blind us to the ways in which senses are learned in particular spatial and cultural contexts and grounded in iterative practices that make them habitual.

This framing also means that, although we can focus on individual senses and explore how each addresses differing ways of engaging with and being in the world, such an approach ignores the interconnectedness of the senses in human perception (Pink and Howes 2010). Pink (2009: 2) suggests that by turning to the senses we can expand our understanding of everyday life beyond the conventional parameters of analysis, for the very reason that the senses are 'interconnected and interrelated'. This echoes the work of Rodaway (1994), who argued that we need to critically examine the role of the senses because such an approach contributes to 'the fullness of a living world or everyday life as a multisensual and multidimensional situatedness in space and in relationship to places' (1994: 4). As perceptual psychology and neurobiology have found, the differing senses 'reinforce one another, giving us a unified picture of everyday reality taken from multiple perspectives' (Cytowic 2010: 46). The meanings we give to the totality of sights, sounds, odours, tastes and tactilities are 'essential clues to the ways by which a society fashions and embodies a meaningful world' (Classen 1997: 405). This means that our bodily encounters in and with the world are 'not simply perceptual, but always involve emotional, cognitive and imaginative engagement; they are always relational' (Ansdell 2004: 200). Hence, we need to consider the validity of separating out the different senses, because our perceptions of the world around us are multisensory (Pink 2009; see also Grasseni 2007). Sensual and bodily engagement is, therefore, a political act, because our various bodily, emotional and affective responses mark us as belonging or not belonging to the festival community. In order to examine how this works, we need to draw on approaches that best capture these fleeting, hard to verbalise and often non-conscious ways that we participate in the world.

Music festivals, emotions and affect

It may seem a contradiction to focus on a music festival so as to explore our sensory engagement within festival events, given the emphasis is more usually on a festival's sounds and music. A significant body of research explores through the lens of representation the relationships among (a) music, (b) festival participation and engagement, and (c) place and community (Cohen 1993, Connell and Gibson 2003, Kong 1996; Kong and Yeoh 1997; Quinn 2003). In this approach, the music genres performed – the song lyrics, instrumentation, melodic structures or performance styles – are understood as constructions of identity associated with specific cultural groups, places or lifestyles (Bowen and Daniels 2005; Gibson and Connell 2005; Curtis 2010; Goulding and Saren 2009). Nonetheless, as many scholars working in musicology, sound art and cultural geography have pointed out, there is no simple relationship between music and meaning (Cox 2009; Duffy 2016; Duffy and Waitt 2011; Ingham et al. 1999; Lipsitz 1994; Mitchell 1996; Holman Jones 1998; de Nora 2000; Waitt et al. 2015). Rather, the interactions between musician, listener and the cultural context in which music is performed result in complex and multifarious sets of meanings that are constantly formulated and reinscribed. This means that the relationship between music and identity is always ambiguous and contextualised.

However, it is not the sounds of a music festival alone that conjure up an identity, place or community. A festival's sights, sounds, smells and movement and the emotions aroused are integral to generating the particularities of a festival's ambience and constituting feelings of belonging or exclusion in the community or perhaps the location in which the event is held. One important way in which music operates is that it taps into our affective, emotional and intuitive selves, and this opens up a means through which to examine how feelings influence social interactions (DeNora 2000; Duffy 2014; Juslin and Sloboda 2001; Smith 2000). As Steven Feld, in conversation with Charles Keil (1994: 167), explains it:

> music does this in directly feelingful ways. It's the physicality of being in the groove together that brings out a lot of this emotional co-presence and co-construction. James Brown's point is great, that we are hearing it before we are seeing it, and that physically the sense of seeing is something apart, out there, whereas you feel the resonance of your voice inside your head and chest. The sense of touch, the sense of feel, the sense of sound are so deeply and thoroughly integrated in our physical mechanism.

Feld here reminds us that we experience sound around, in and through our bodies, which can remind us how place and people are very intertwined (Duffy and Waitt 2011; Kahn 1999; Wood et al. 2007). Therefore, it is not simply that music represents subjectivity and identity; rather, it is that subjectivities are constituted within the very unfolding of the sonic event in ways that may enhance feelings of belonging, connection, exclusion or alienation (Duffy and Waitt 2011; Waitt and Duffy 2010). An important aspect to the sonic event is raised by political economist Jacques Attali, who argues in his seminal text *Noise: The Political Economy of Music* (1992) that the ways in which sound is defined as music or noise is an expression of power. He goes on to explain that the appropriation and control of sound reflects and affirms the sociopolitical structures of a community. Therefore, music is not an aesthetic experience alone but a medium through which the social world is made and remade through social relations. How we respond is significant to these socialising processes.

Given the sensual, emotive and physiological ways we engage with sound and music, we can explore how music makes us feel through two broadly different categories: emotion and affect. Often these two terms are used interchangeably, yet emotion most often refers to psychological states (e.g. anger, disappointment, resentment, joy) of which we are consciously aware, if only partially. Even so, an emotion is not simply something felt within an individualised body; rather, it is produced within networks of relations, both human and non-human (Bondi et al. 2005). The scholarly exploration of affect has produced a body of literature with no one definitive meaning that is further complicated through its association and interchange with terms such as emotion, feeling and sensation (Shouse 2005). Yet, in very broad terms that originate in the work of 17th-century philosopher Baruch Spinoza, affect is understood as the bodily capacity to act and being acted upon (Brennan 2004; Massumi 2002; Probyn 2005). Affect is therefore understood as relational and as integral to an 'emergent and transforming experience' (Thrift 2008: 176). Although we may not conceptualise emotion and affect as entirely discrete things – and some have argued that making distinctions between them sets up 'unhelpful dualisms' (Bondi 2005: 445) – there are differing conceptuali-sations that are important to the ways in which music moves us. Some argue that we need to make 'an analytic distinction between the corporeality inherent in a notion of affect and the more mindful conception of emotion' (Watkins 2011: 137) in order to understand the complex relations between these states of being. Others argue that separating affect and emotion remains unresolved (Kenway and Youdell 2011). Nonetheless, both frameworks draw on phenomenology and the body as the initiator of knowledge. Where they differ lies in the linking (or not) to cognition and thought.

In the section that follows, we focus our discussion on a specific music festival – the Noosa Jazz Festival, held in Noosa Heads, on the Sunshine Coast in Queens-land, Australia. We will critically explore the ways in which music arouses certain emotions and bodily affects that 'tap into our hearts and minds' and thus bring about the 'building [of] a sense of community or belonging within a particular music style' (Curtis 2010: 101). Yet, as will be discussed, these responses are not simply moments of perhaps joyous engagement with a particular arts practice; they are very much embedded within the social, cultural and economic networks that come together in the location of Noosa Heads.

Background to the case study

Noosa Heads, where the Noosa Jazz Festival is held each year, is around 90 min-utes' drive from the Queensland state capital, Brisbane. Located in the broader Shire of Noosa region of the Sunshine Coast, this is a place with significant natu-ral assets, awarded recognition as a UNESCO biosphere reserve (Mullens 2010). Its amenable lifestyle associated with the combination of national park, small villages in proximity to beaches, and a pristine estuarine river system, as well as restricted low-level development (Richins 2009), have made this region attractive to tourists and residents wanting an idyllic coastal lifestyle. Noosa Heads, with a population of around 4,000, is a small pocket of advantage within the Noosa region, with above-average income and a significant proportion of second homes and retirees (AEC Group 2015; EMDA 2006; Richins 2009). As described in the Lifestyle section of *The New York Times*, this

> is a sophisticated beach resort whose hub is leafy, boutique-lined Hastings Street. Low-rise designer condos, with whirlpools on almost every balcony, have replaced the simple holiday units. Alfresco cafés overlook the grassy slopes behind Main Beach. The campground at the end of Hastings Street is gone, replaced by native bush. . . . Hastings Street has developed into a classy shopping street shaded with wispy poinciana trees. The boutiques are full of stylish casual clothes and Aussie swimsuits and surfing gear. There are plenty of ice cream parlours but not a fastfood chain or tacky souvenir shop in sight; those are reserved for nearby Noosa Junction.
>
> (Henley 2002: 10)

These cosmopolitan lifestyle factors are important to Noosa as a resort destination, and they contributed to its brand development of 'genuine, natural, a unique style, relaxed, and sophisticated' (Uhlhorn 2002: 13; Noosa Tourism 2007). However, given its popularity with tourists, Noosa residents sought to preserve its distinctive features through a sustainable tourism strategy with a focus on the local community as well as appropriate tourism (NCTB 2001; Richins 2009). Event tourism can play a significant part in such regional development, and not only in terms of economic improvement (Whitford 2004). Rather, festivals are increasingly understood as enabling interrelated social *and* economic returns, especially in small towns (Gibson and Connell 2012). Recent work in this area explores how these events can improve social and community health and well-being through increased opportunities for interaction and sociality. For Noosa, the jazz festival has come to capture not just the image of 'a sophisticated beach resort' as described in the *New York Times* article, but also how this cultural landscape can be experienced through bodily and sensory engagement with the genre of jazz music.

The Noosa Jazz Festival began in 1991, initiated by Frank Johnson, a pioneer of the traditional jazz scene in Australia after World War II, who, after moving to Noosa in the late 1980s, wanted to establish an avenue for nationally and internationally acclaimed Australian jazz musicians (Rickard 2015). This first festival was held over a weekend in September and was located in the restaurants of Hastings Street as part of a deliberate strategy to boost Noosa's off-peak tourism economy (personal communication with festival director 25 November 2015). The event included a small parade along Hastings Street, a jazz ball at the Sheraton and a jazz mass in Noosa Woods with music composed by local musician Ken Evans. It ended with a concert in Noosa Woods that Sunday evening (Rickard 2015). The festival has evolved over the years, and, in 2015, when we conducted fieldwork interviews, the event was run by a small company directed by Vickii Cotter. An integral part of the festival under Cotter's leadership was to ensure community participation and engagement, including a commitment to building community capacity (personal communication with festival director 25 November 2015).

Figure 13.1 Preparations Begin for the Noosa Jazz Festival.
Photo © Michelle Duffy.

This is exemplified by two broad initiatives; first, in terms of jazz performance, the festival program included youth orchestras and performers, as well as workshops and panels; second, undergraduate tourism and event management students from the Universities of Queensland and the Sunshine Coast were part of the volunteer cohort setting up festival venues and activities (personal communication with festival director 25 November 2015). Such strategies are important to enacting social justice aims and increasing regional participation and its social and economic benefits. However, we also wanted to explore how this festival may provide a space of encounter between a relatively small and affluent population concentrated in Noosa Heads living alongside a larger group of people who are relatively older and with lower household and personal income levels than even South East Queensland and broader Queensland region socio-economic indicators (AEC 2015). We perceived that the key opportunity for this was during Tastings on Hastings and the parade that officially opens the Noosa Jazz Festival.

The Tastings on Hastings event, highly anticipated by members of the 'Noosa glitterati', is sold-out well before the festival, even at a cost just under AU$90 per seat. It is particularly popular with local residents (personal communication with festival director 25 November 2015). During this event, Hastings Street, the main street in Noosa Heads, is closed to traffic, while a range of local restaurants set up tables and chairs along the entire length, albeit only one side, of Hastings Street.

On offer is a set menu of gourmet cuisine – such as Italian, Japanese, French and Australian seafood – drinks and plenty of jazz music. Although the event is targeted primarily at paying lunch guests, those who simply wish to wander up and down the street observing and enjoying the atmosphere have opportunities to do so. As a post on the Visit Noosa website explains:

> The opening parade is a fun and vibrant event down Hastings Street on Friday from noon, right before the legendary Tastings on Hastings which transforms the famous shopping street into a massive outdoor restaurant with some of Hastings Street's best restaurants serving up.
>
> (Mikkelsen 2015)

In examining this particular event, we consider the role of the senses in generating feelings of attachment to a space that may be characterised by advantage yet facilitates feelings of inclusion that are achieved through what could be considered a heightened sensory experience of Noosa's everyday 'international resort glamour . . .[,] pristine beaches, national park and lush hinterland' (Australian Tourism website; www.australia.com/en/places/qld/qld-noosa.html, accessed 17 February 2017). The significance of the everyday is important to establishing ways of acknowledging and celebrating ideas of community, yet what might seem the mundane habits, practices and experiences of daily life often go unnoticed,

Figure 13.2 Tastings on Hastings, Noosa Jazz Festival.
Photo © Michelle Duffy.

even though recent arguments in social and cultural theory propose that such things matter profoundly (Horton and Kraftl 2006; Lorimer 2008).

An important discussion that arises out of the sensual geographies literature questions how best to capture and communicate the ways in which we are entangled in and through the places and communities in which we live. It highlights that we are embodied beings who encounter and interact through the senses with our everyday world. We include an example from ethnographic notes taken at the 2015 Tastings on Hastings event in order to capture how different bodies felt in the period immediately prior to the parade and lunch – ours as researchers as well as the bodies of those around us. This allows us to critically consider the ways in which the senses shape and influence the expectations of the festival event. In doing so, we follow the methodological approach offered by Longhurst et al. (2008: 215), who recommend that researchers use their bodies as 'instruments of research' by drawing on the embodied experiences. This close observation and awareness of bodily responses, we argue, can provide insight into differing forms of sensual encounters that may offer opportunities for collective involvement.

A multisensory engagement can tell us much more about how festival activities may lure us in and arouse emotions that have the potential to encourage us to be more, or less, open with others. As Thibaud (2011: 204) suggests, our multisensory engagement with the spaces we inhabit gives rise to 'an ambiance [that] expresses an "affective tonality"' . . . ambiance gives access to the various moods and emotional tones of urban life.' The experiential qualities of festival events are therefore significant to how we may respond to what is going on around us. The ethnographic note attempts to capture the various bodily attitudes of those on Hastings Street during the time leading up to the parade and lunch events. For many attendees –both those who had taken up prime viewing positions earlier that morning and those who had bought their tickets months ago and could afford to wait until shortly before the parade was expected to start – there was a sense of anticipation.

Ethnographic note: Waiting for the parade

The Tastings on Hastings event involves local restaurants providing lunch for up to 650 diners seated outdoors along the entire length of Hastings Street. This morning, those lucky enough to get tickets are already gathering, greeting friends and looking around for a possible early drink. Hospitality staff are busily setting up tables along the southern side of this road's divide; smoothing table cloths, carefully placing cutlery, ensuring white wine has been placed in buckets of ice. We can hear the sizzle of barbecue at some restaurants, and the aroma of what is cooking makes our mouths water. Somewhere ahead of us we can hear the clink of glasses. Young waitresses stand in the shade of the pandanus trees that line this street, chatting while they wait for the lunch guests to be seated. Unlike the more languid movement of shoppers yesterday, there was a definite buzz around us. Some, possibly knowing how difficult it will be to even get a cup of coffee until well after the event has finished, are happily seated at the Rococo Noosa, a restaurant whose style of seating arrangement encourages its clientele to people-watch. A waiter glides out carrying a tray of coffee cups, and he deftly hands out the latté, mocha and flat white to the correct customers. Others hurry into the shopping mall, perhaps trying to get last-minute groceries before the midday crowds make it hard to get around. Those who are young, and perhaps more interested in getting down to the beach for the day, take little notice of the bustle around them, unaware as those organising the street closure call out to them to mind where they are walking. We finally manage to find ourselves a bench to sit on that will allow us to observe both the parade and those having lunch.

We hear the sound of 'Waltzing Matilda' coming towards us. Those of us sitting along the footpath dash out to stand along the barriers running down the centre of the road, cameras at the ready, waiting for a glimpse of the band. Leading the parade are three young women holding banners proclaiming the Noosa Jazz Festival, closely followed by a tall, slightly self-conscious young man wearing a cap and holding a banner for the James Nash State High School, which is located in Gympie. Until now, 'Waltzing Matilda' was played in a fairly straightforward manner, but as the jazz band marches by us we can hear much more of a jazz inflection in the melody and the syncopated rhythm of the trumpet. While many of us watching decide to remain in the shade of the pandanus trees, people who look to be the grandparents of those in the band stay out in the sun, taking photos or videos on their phones, and waving to those they recognise among the performers. A white, open car drives into view, and seated on the back seat are the jazz festival 'monarchs', smiling and waving. Members of the Brisbane Jazz Club, carrying parasols, smile and giggle at something one of the members has said. A couple display their skills at swing dancing, although the music of the marching band is now hard to hear, and at one point they miss catching hands as they turn. She laughs, and they move on. Two women who twirl hoops around their arms and torso while wearing high-heeled ankle boots come into view. They keep smiling, but you do get the feeling that it is hot and hard work. Around us are the sounds of people talking, laughing and the occasional clink of glasses. Eventually a group of ukulele players moves towards us, all of them wearing brightly coloured shirts and hats, most wearing sunglasses against the sun's glare. Although we can see them strumming and singing, it is very difficult to make out what the song is. Behind them a unicycle rider in tartan pants, cap and full beard weaves around a stilt walker, who swirls around in her costume of red and yellow. It's a surprising jumble of performers! The final two entrants – a motorbike hauling a two-seater that holds a banjo and guitar duo, and then a surfing mascot for the Noosa lifeguards in a beach buggy – and the parade is over. Behind us, someone claps along with the banjo and guitar duo. Glad to get out of the sun, we decide to try and find a café for a cool drink.

Field notes, 4 September 2015, Noosa Jazz Festival

In the ethnographic examples presented here, it can be seen that the lunch and parade are embedded and structured within the public space of Hastings Street but that this facilitates varying levels of participation – some people are fully involved, but not all can be. The smells of different foods, the sounds of cooking, the preparation for the parade, and the excitement of those settling in to eat – all create an ambience that invites others in. Yet, with the high ticket prices and early ticket sell-out, not all can gain admission. So, an examination of the bodily, affective and emotive experiences can help us to understand the different ways participation can be enabled.

Probyn's (2000) exploration of 'gut reactions' offers a means to reveal how such experiences unfold. This expression refers to a process that draws attention to moods, emotions and bodily sensations. Such bodily responses (that may be felt and named, for example, as comfort, guilt, shame or pride) allow us insight into how an individual experiences a particular context. This insight, in turn, facilitates an understanding of the affective relations that arise out of participation and engagement in the festival. Naturally, this is not something that can be examined or inspected objectively – we cannot fully know how people feel simply through observation, or even through interview and discussion. Nonetheless, psychologists argue that we do possess a communicative capacity that helps decode emotions that elicit certain responses in others (Oatley and Johnson-Laird 2011). This has ramifications for the organisers of festivals, as they need to be aware that the emotions and affect generated have 'the potential to reconfigure listeners' relationships to place, to open up new modes of attention and movement, and in so doing to rework places' (Gallagher 2015: 468).

Conclusion

Community events are often staged by local authorities as a way to boost the local economy, improve social cohesion and foster a sense of belonging. Although it is arguably comparatively straightforward to conceptualise how events may contribute in terms of economic impact, it is much more difficult to understand and assess how events can contribute to feelings of connectedness and belonging.

To date, event studies have focused strongly on what people think of events – their motivations for attending, their satisfaction levels, their self-reported experience and their likelihood of returning. With the example presented here, we draw attention rather to what embodied people do and how this may provide clues as to how they feel in terms of engagement. Our observation and analysis suggests the embodied nature of Noosa Jazz Festival participants contributes towards the creation of feelings of inclusion. It is likely that this is related to their sensual engagement in the event, which captures their attention and draws them into the event. It is possible that these feelings remain long after the festival is over and that they help to create a sense of belonging (Cohen 1997; Connell and Gibson 2003; Kong 1996).

Our observations suggest three key themes of particular relevance in this case. In relation to sound, paying guests at the lunch did not enjoy a better experience than non-paying visitors – in fact, the paying visitors were fixed in their ticketed locations and were less able to walk up and down the street listening to the variety of music on offer at different cafes and bars. This provides evidence that the festival is encouraging wider participation from all sectors of the community, one of the aims of this particular festival. With reference to the visual spectacle of the festival, all visitors (paying guests and passers-by) were able to watch the street parade which took place just prior to the lunch being served. This ensured that inclusion in the event did not require possession of any particular resources, such as money to buy a ticket. Finally, in relation to ambience, the street parade and lunch creates an ambience that sets up expectations about Hastings Street that extend beyond the day. The bodily experiences aroused by walking around Hastings Street, and the emotions and affects this generated, are integral to establishing community social relations, as well as expectations that this event will continue into the future as a way to re-affirm these feelings of community. This relates back to the notion of festivalisation (discussed in Chapter 4), in which the influences and effects of a festival event spill out beyond its temporal and spatial boundaries. In summary, the Noosa Jazz Festival is helping to build an inclusive community embedded within the sensual geographies of Noosa Heads and its environs, and it enables people to engage and participate at a number of levels.

References

AEC Group (2015). Community Profile: Noosa Shire Council, Final Report, [online]. Available at: www.noosa.qld.gov.au/documents/40217326/40227843/AEC%20-%20 Noosa%20Community%20Profile.pdf [Accessed 31 March 2017].

Ahmed, Z. U. (1992). Islamic pilgrimage (Hajj) to Ka'aba in Makkah (Saudi Arabia): an important international tourism activity. *Journal of Tourism Studies,* 3(1), pp 35–43.

Anderson, B. (2009). Affective atmospheres. *Emotion, Space and Society*, 2(2), pp. 77–81.

Ansdell, G. (2004). Rethinking music and community: Theoretical perspectives in support of community music therapy. In: Pavlicevic, M. and Ansell, G. (Eds.) *Community Music Therapy*. London, Philadelphia: Jessica Kingsley Publishers, pp. 91–113.

Attali, J. (1992). *Noise: The Political Economy of Music*. Minneapolis: University of Minneapolis Press.

Benzon, W. (2001). *Beethoven's Anvil: Music in Mind and Culture*. New York: Basic Books.

Berger, H. (1999). *Metal, Rock, and Jazz: Perception and the Phenomenology of Musical Experience*. Hanover, NH: University Press of New England.

Bondi, L. (2005). Making connections and thinking through emotions: between geography and psychotherapy. *Transactions, Institute of British Geographers. 30*, pp. 433–448.

Bondi, L., Smith, M. and Davidson, J. (Eds.). (2005). *Emotional Geographies*. London: Ashgate.

Bowen, H. E and Daniels, M. J. (2005). Does the music matter? Motivations for attending a music festival. *Event Management*, 9(3), pp. 155–164.

Boyd, C. and Duffy, M. (2012). Sonic geographies of shifting bodies. *Interference: A Journal of Audio Culture*. [online]. Available at: www.interferencejournal.com/articles/a-sonic-geography/sonic-geographies-of-shifting-bodies [Accessed 31 March 2017].

Brennan, T. (2004). *The Transmission of Affect*. Ithaca: Cornell University Press

Bull, M. (2000). *Sounding Out the City, Personal Stereos and the Management of Everyday Life*. Oxford: Berg.

Bull, M. (2004). Automobility and the power of sound. *Theory Culture and Society*, 2(4–5), pp. 243–259.

Chalip, L. (2006). *The Buzz of Big Events: Is It Worth Bottling? Kenneth Myer Lecture in Arts and Entertainment Management*. Geelong: Deakin University.

Clarke, G. (1981/1990). Defending skijumpers: A critique of theories of youth subcultures. In: Frith, S. and Goodwin, A. (Eds.) *On Record: Rock, Pop and the Written Word*. London: Routledge, pp. 175–180.

Classen, C. (1993). *Worlds of Sense: Exploring the Senses in History and Across Cultures*. London: Routledge.

Classen, C. (1997). Foundations for an anthropology of the senses. *International Social Sciences Journal.* 49 (153), pp. 401–412.

Classen, C., Howes, D. and Synnott, A. (1994). *Aroma: The Cultural History of Smell.* London: Routledge.

Cohen, E. (1979). A phenomenology of tourist experiences. *Sociology*, 13(2), pp. 179–201.

Cohen, S. (1993). Ethnography and popular music studies. *Popular Music*, 12(2), pp. 123–138.

Cohen, S. (1997) Liverpool and the Beatles: Exploring relations between music and place, text and context. In: Schwarz, D., Kassabian, A., and Siegel, L. (Eds.) *Keeping Score: Music, Disciplinarity, Culture.* Charlottesville: University Press of Virginia, pp. 90–106.

Cohen, S. (2010). Searching for escape, authenticity and identity: Experiences of 'lifestyle travellers'. In: Morgan, M., Lugosi, P. and Ritchie, J. R. B. (Eds.) *The Tourism and Leisure Experience: Consumer and Managerial Perspectives.* Bristol, Buffalo, Toronto: Channel View Publications, pp. 27–42.

Connell, J. and Gibson, C. (2003). *Sound Tracks: Popular Music, Identity and Place.* Milton Park: Routledge.

Cox, C. (2009). Sound art and the sonic unconscious. *Organised Sound*, 14(1), pp. 19–26.

Crompton, J. L. and McKay, S. L. (1997). Motives of visitors attending festival events. *Annals of Tourism Research*, 24(2), pp. 425–439.

Curtis, R. A. (2010). Australia's capital of Jazz? The (re) creation of place, music and community at the Wangaratta Jazz Festival. *Australian Geographer*, 41(1), pp. 101–116.

Cytowic, R. (2010). Extraordinary secrets of our linked-up senses. *New Scientist.* [online]. https://www.newscientist.com/blogs/culturelab/2010/04/extraordinary-secrets-of-our-linked-up-senses.html. Accessed 14 March 2017.

Dann, G. (2003). Tourism smellscapes. *Tourism Geographies*, 5(1), pp. 3–25.

de Nora, T. (2000). *Music in Everyday Life.* Cambridge, Cambridge University Press.

Díaz-Barriga, M. (2003), Materialism and Sensuality: Visualizing the Devil in the Festival of Our Lady of Urkupiña. *Visual Anthropology*, 16(2–3), pp. 245–261.

Duffy, M. (2014). The emotional ecologies of festivals. In: Bennett, A., Woodward, I. and Taylor, J. (Eds.) *Festivalisation of Culture: Identity, Culture and Politics.* Farnham: Ashgate, pp. 229–250.

Duffy, M. (2016). Re-sounding place and mapping the affects of sound. In: Leppänen, T., Moisala, P., Tiainen, M. and Väätäinen, H. (Eds.) *Becoming With Music and Sound: Musicking Deleuze and Guattari.* London, Oxford, New York: Bloomsbury, pp. 189–203.

Duffy, M. and Waitt, G. (2011). Rural festivals and processes of belonging. In: Gibson, C. and Connell, J. (Eds.) *Festival Places: Revitalising Rural Australia.* Clevedon, UK: Channel View Press, pp. 44–59.

Durkheim, E. (1912/ 1976). *The Elementary Forms of the Religious Life.* Trans. J. Swain. London: Allen and Unwin.

Eade, J. and Sallnow, M. J. (2000). *Contesting the Sacred: The Anthropology of Christian Pilgrimage.* Urbana, Chicago: University of Illinois.

Edensor, T. and Falconer, E. (2012). Sensuous geographies of tourism. In: Wilson, J. (Ed.) *The Routledge Handbook of Tourism Geographies.* Oxon: Routledge, pp. 74–81.

Ehrenreich, B. (2007). *Dancing in the Streets: A History of Collective Joy.* London: Granta Books.

EMDA. (2006). *Noosa Tourism Monitor.* Noosa, QLD: Economic and Market Development Advisers.

Falassi, A. (1987). *Time out of Time: Essays on the Festival.* Albuquerque:University of New Mexico Press.

Filep, S., Hughes, M., Mostafanezhad, M., and Wheller, F. (2015). Generation Tourism: towards a common identity. *Current Issues in Tourism*. 18(6), pp. 511–523.

Gallagher, M. (2015). Sounding Ruins: Reflections on the production of an "Audio drift." *Cultural Geographies*, 2(3), pp. 467–485.

Getz, D. and Andersson, T. (2008). Sustainable festivals: On becoming an institution. *Event Management*, 12(1), pp. 1–17

Getz, D., and McConnell, A. (2011). Serious sport tourism and event travel careers. *Journal of Sport Management*, *25*, pp. 326–338.

Gibson, C. and Connell, J. (2005). *Music and Tourism: On the Road Again*. Clevedon: Channel View Publications.

Gibson, C., and J. Connell (2012) *Music Festivals and Regional Development in Australia*. Farnham: Ashgate.

Goulding, C. and Saren, M. (2009). Performing identity: An analysis of gender expressions at the Whitby goth festival. *Consumption, Markets and Culture*, 12(1), pp. 27–46.

Grasseni, C. (2007). Communities of practice and forms of life: Towards rehabilitation of vision. In: Harris, M. (Ed.) *Ways of Knowing: New Approaches in the Anthropology of Evidence and Learning*. Oxford: Berghahn, pp. 203–221.

Hall, S. and Jefferson, T. (1975/1991). *Resistance Through Rituals: Youth Subcultures in Post-War Britain*. London: HarperCollins Academic.

Handelman, D. (1990). *Models and Mirrors: Towards an Anthropology of Public Events*, Cambridge: Cambridge University Press.

Hayes-Conroy, J. and Hayes-Conroy, A. (2010). Visceral geographies: Mattering, relating, and defying. *Geography Compass*, 4(9), pp. 1273–1283.

Hebdige, D. (1979). *Subculture: The Meaning of Style*. London, New York: Methuen.

Henly, S. G. (2002). Noosa: Surf with a side of latte; flanked by two national parks, a Queensland resort balances development and preservation. *The New York Times*, 151.52053 (March 10): Lifestyle: pTR10

Holman Jones, S. (1998). *Kaleidoscope Notes: Writing Women's Music and Organisational Culture*. Walnut Creek, AltaMira (SAGE publications).

Horton, J. and Kraftl, P. (2006). Not just growing up, but going on: Materials, spacings, bodies, situations. *Children's Geographies*, 4(3), pp. 259–276.

Howes, D. (2006). Charting the sensorial revolution. *Senses and Society*, 1(1), pp. 113–128.

Ingham, J., Purvis, M. and Clarke, D. B. (1999). Hearing places, making spaces: Sonorous geographies, ephemeral rhythms, and the Blackburn warehouse parties. *Environment and Planning D: Society and Space*, 17, pp. 283–305.

Juslin, P., and Sloboda, J. (2001). *Music and Emotion: Theory and Research*. Oxford: Oxford University Press.

Kahn, D. (1999). *Noise Water Meat: A History of Sound in the Arts*. Cambridge, MA: MIT Press.

Keil, C., Feld. S. (1994). *Music Grooves*. Chicago: University of Chicago Press.

Kenway, J. and Youdell, D. (2011). The emotional geographies of education: Beginning a conversation. *Emotion, Space and Society*, 4(3), pp. 131–136.

Kong, L. (1996). Popular music in Singapore: Exploring local cultures, global resources and regional identities. *Environment and Planning D: Society and Space*, 14, pp. 273–292.

Kong, L. and Yeoh, B. S. (1997).The construction of national identity through the production of ritual and spectacle: An analysis of National Day parades in Singapore. *Political Geography*, 16(3), pp. 213–239.

Law, L. (2001). Home cooking: Filipino women and geographies of the senses in Hong Kong/. *Ecumene*, 8(3), pp. 264–283.

Lipsitz, G. (1997). *Dangerous Crossroads: Popular Music, Postmodernism and the Poetics of Place*. London, Verso.

Longhurst, R., Ho, E. and Johnston, L. (2008). Using 'The Body' as an 'Instrument of Research': kimch'i and pavlova. *Area*, 40(2), pp. 208–217.

Lorimer, H. (2005). Cultural geography: The busyness of being "More-Than-Representational." *Progress in Human Geography*, 29, pp. 83–94.

Lorimer, H. (2008). Cultural geography: Non-representational conditions and concerns. *Progress in Human Geography*, 32(4), 551–559.

Low, K. (2005). Ruminations on smell as a socio-cultural phenomenon. *Current Sociology*, 53(3), pp. 397–417.

Low, K. (2012). The social life of the senses: Charting directions. *Sociology Compass*, 6(3), pp. 271–282.

Martin, P. (1995). *Sounds and Society: Themes in the Sociology of Music*. Manchester, UK: Manchester University Press.

Massumi, B (2002). *Parables of the Virtual: Movement, Affect, Sensation*. Durham & London: Duke University Press

Middleton, R. (1990). *Studying Popular Music*. Milton Keynes and Philadelphia, PA: Open University Press.

Mikkelsen, S. (2015). Hot music and cool vibes at Noosa Jazz Festival *Noosa: What's On* [online]. Available at: www.visitnoosa.com.au/blog/hot-music-and-cool-vibes-at-noosa-jazz-festival [Accessed 31 March 2017].

Mitchell, T. (1996). *Popular Music and Local Identity: Rock, Pop and Rap in Europe and Oceania*. London, Leicester University Press.

Morgan, M., Lugosi, P. and Ritchie, J. R. B. (2010). Introduction. In: Morgan, M., Lugosi, P. and Ritchie, J. R. B. (Eds) *The Tourism and Leisure Experience: Consumer and Managerial Perspectives*. Bristol, Buffalo, Toronto: Channel View Publications, pp. xv–xxii.

Mullens, M. (2010). The Noosa biosphere. *Ecos,* 155(June/July), pp. 31–39.

Nyaupane, G., and Poudel, S. (2015). Application of appreciative inquiry in tourism research in rural communities. *Tourism Management*, 33 (4), pp. 978–987.

NCTB. (2001). *Noosa Tourism Action Plan 2011*. Noosa, QLD: Noosa Collaborative Tourism Board.

Nicholson, R. and Pearce, D. G. (2000). Who goes to events: A comparative analysis of the profile characteristics of visitors to four South Island events in New Zealand. *Journal of Vacation Marketing,* 6(3), pp. 236–253.

Nolan, M. L. and Nolan, S. (1992). Religious sites as tourism attractions in Europe. *Annals of Tourism Research,* 19(1), pp. 68–78.

Oatley, K. & Johnson-Laird, P. (2011). Basic Emotions in Social Relationships, Reasoning, and Psychological Illnesses, *Emotion Review*, 3(4), pp. 424–433.

Pearce, P., and Pabel, A. (2015). *Tourism and humour*. Bristol, UK: Channel View.

Pennycook, A. and Otsuji, E. (2015). Making scents of the landscape. *Linguistic Landscape*, 1(3), pp. 191–212.

Pine, B. and Gilmore, J. (1999). *The Experience Economy: Work Is Theatre and Every Business Is a Stage*. Boston, MA: Harvard Business School Press.

Pink, S. (2009). *Doing Sensory Ethnography*. Los Angeles, London, New Delhi, Singapore, Washington, DC: Sage.

Pink, S. and Howes, D. (2010). Debate section: The future of sensory anthropology/ the anthropology of the senses. *Social Anthropology/ Anthropologie Sociale*, 18(3), pp. 331–340.

Probyn, E. (2000). *Carnal Appetites: Foodsexidentities*. Routledge: London

Probyn, E. (2005). *Blush: Faces of shame.* UNSW Press: Sydney

Quinn, B. (2003). Symbols, practices and myth-making: Cultural perspectives on the Wexford festival Opera. *Tourism Geographies,* 5(3), pp. 329–349.

Richins, H. (2009). Environmental, cultural, economic and socio-community sustainability: A framework for sustainable tourism in resort destinations. *Environment, Development and Sustainability,* 11, pp. 785–800.

Rickard, A. (2015). Music and all that jazz. *Noosa News* (28 August), pp. 16–17.

Rodaway, P. (1994). *Sensuous Geographies: Body, Sense, and Place.* London: Routledge.

Ruback, R. B., Pandey, J. and Kohli, N. (2008). Evaluations of a sacred place: Role and religious belief at the Magh Mela. *Journal of Environmental Psychology,* 28(2), pp. 174–184.

Sepp, T. (2014). Pilgrimage and Pilgrim Hierarchies in Vernacular Discourse: Comparative Notes from the Camino de Santiago and Glastonbury. *Journal of Ethnology and Folkloristics,* 8(1), pp. 23–52.

Shouse, E. (2005). Feeling, emotion, affect. *M/C Journal,* 8(6). [online]. Available at: http://journal.media-culture.org.au/0512/03-shouse.php [Accessed 31 March 2017].

Simmel, G. (1903[1997]). The Metropolis and Mental Life. In: M. Featherstone and D. Frisby (eds.), *Simmel on Culture,* Sage Publications, London, pp. 174–186

Smith, S. (2000) Performing the (sound)world. *Environment and Planning D: Society and Space.* 18(5): 615–637.

Thibaud, J-P. (2011). Sensory design: The sensory Fabric of urban ambiances. *Senses and Society,* 6(2), pp. 203–215.

Thrift, N. (2008). *Non-Representational Theory: Space/ Politics/ Affect.* London, New York: Routledge.

Tourism Noosa. (2007). *Local Government Reform Submission.* Noosa, QLD: Tourism Noosa.

Turner, V. (1969). *The Ritual Process: Structure and Anti-Structure.* Chicago: Aldine Press.

Uhlhorn, B. (2002). *Noosa the Brand.* Brisbane, Australia: George Patterson Bates.

Urry, J. (1990). *The Tourist Gaze.* London: Sage.

Waitt, G. and Duffy, M. (2010). Listening and tourism studies. *Annals of Tourism Research,* 37(2), pp. 457–477.

Waitt, G., Harada, T. and Duffy, M. (2015). 'Let's have some music': A visceral approach to automobility. *Mobilities,* doi:10.1080/17450101.2015.1076628

Watkins, M. (2011). Teachers' tears and the affective geography of the classroom. *Emotion, Space and Society,* 4(3), pp. 137–143.

Whiteley, S., Bennett, A. and Hawkins, S. (2004). *Music, Space and Place: Popular Music and Cultural Identity.* Aldershot: Ashgate Publishing.

Whitford, M. (2004). Regional development through domestic and tourist event policies: Gold Coast and Brisbane, 1974–2003. *UNLV Journal of Hospitality, Tourism and Leisure Science,* 1, pp. 1–24.

Wood, N., Duffy, M. and Smith, S. J. (2007). The art of doing (geographies of) music. *Environment and Planning D: Society and Space,* 25(5), pp. 867–889.

14 Conclusions

This book has shown, if any further proof were needed, that festivals are an important part of our communities. Our modern lives make us more globalised than ever, but, at the same time, this highlights the importance of the local, and of our communities, however they might be defined.

As we have demonstrated, festivals can be staged for a number of different reasons and may wax and wane, but all have significance for the communities that host them. In some cases, festivals celebrate traditions, rites and rituals that have been around for centuries or more. And this is important because, as we have demonstrated, various facets of festivals contribute to community well-being, such as the opportunities for residents and participants to socialise and have fun, the celebration of achievement and the relevance of the event to the local community. Some festivals are staged expressly for instrumental policy reasons. Such policy imperatives include economic development, boosting tourism, showcasing diversity and creating social cohesion. Given that these festivals have specific desired outcomes (variously expressed as social cohesion, community pride, sense of belonging and in other terms), this book examines how such festivals may be planned and managed with a better understanding of the processes that contribute to these positive outcomes and how, perhaps, to address those times when the goals of the festival are not achieved.

Our underpinning framework for this book has been the notion of the encounter. Festivals, as public spaces, can be seen as a site for facilitating social relationships, public discourses and political expression. Festivals offer a space for encounter, in all its various forms, but simply bringing people together is not enough to result in the positive social cohesion outcomes that policymakers seek, or simply to make people aware of possible tensions within communities. Rather, festivals may need to more carefully engage with *meaningful* encounter, with a focus is on purposeful and organised activities that can help participants break out of traditional or fixed ways of relating to each other. This then offers a space not just for the act of encounter, but also for exchange, in which participants acknowledge the complexities and contradictions that can arise through encounter and can then use these occasions to build upon processes that inform community making.

An issue of great significance for generating positive social outcomes of festivals is the notion of inclusion/exclusion. Festivals can act as spaces of inclusion, in which positive social relations are formed. These positive social relations can have lasting benefits, including the development of social capital – particularly bonding, bridging and linking social capital. Festivals can offer practical opportunities for enacting community through activities such as volunteering, which can help residents develop skills for community capacity-building, and providing economic livelihoods. However, festivals can also act as spaces of exclusion, in which there is a clear demarcation between "us" and "them"; between who belongs and who does not; between those who can afford to participate and those who can't; between those who want to be involved and those who do not. This can be particularly visible in our expanding, diverse and mobile society. Yet, it is important to remember that a certain amount of discussion and debate about how a community is constituted should not be considered as something negative; rather, it is a reflection of the processes inherent in the constitution of a community that necessarily arises out of ongoing dialogue and, thus, the representation and the participation of many voices.

Following on from this debate about inclusion and exclusion is the question of how, and if, festivals are successful in contributing to the social justice aims of those funding and staging them. In social justice terms, local government policy needs to consider the ways in which factors such as democratic struggles around gender, race, class, sexuality, and the environment operate at the local scale while keeping in mind the broader regional, national and global contexts and their impacts. Festivals appear to have a rather mixed track record in this regard. In pragmatic terms, festivals can improve access to paid employment and income opportunities by giving local people opportunities to extend their administration, organisational and leadership skills. Other festivals work diligently to improve accessibility for all. However, some festivals appear to reiterate an ideal notion of community, rather than reflect how the community is actually constituted. Others produce (through their official discourses) an "imagined" community that may or may not correspond to the lives of those in that location. Such outcomes are arguably unlikely to increase mutual respect, to encourage increased civic and political participation, or to achieve any other positive social outcomes sought.

As well as trying to understand the social relationships that are facilitated by festivals, this book has turned to the senses, and to the individual located within the community and the festival event, as a way to gain deeper insight into the way that bodies can help us to consider the complex processes inherent in social cohesion. A focus on the ways in which bodily experiences constitute bonds of social connectedness is a fundamental part of the emotional, affective and sensual dimensions of festivals. Non-representation theory, the so-called geography of what happens, is presented as a loose framework for investigating festival participants' embodied experiences. As discussed, the generation of strong, often spontaneous feelings of connectedness arise out of the participants' responses to the sensual elements of an event. These responses are a significant part of the process of sociality, producing *communitas*. Importantly, these intense feelings of belonging can operate across social structures such as class, ethnicity and gender, serving to re-affirm group identity and belonging. We drew on the notion of 'affective political terrains' to highlight the emotive and affective politics embedded in the festival encounter and how these can be harnessed to understand our multiple networks of community belonging.

The four case studies presented in the book demonstrate the various aspects of the festival encounter, and they show how local authorities and other stakeholders have sought to use festivals to address particular objectives.

The Yakkerboo Festival in Pakenham, Victoria, is an example of a relatively long-running festival that was created with community-building objectives, yet it has arguably failed to remain in step with the changes to the community occasioned by our growing mobility. The community, formerly a close-knit country town, is now part of Melbourne's urban sprawl, yet the festival remains firmly a representation of the area's agricultural past. This naturally raises questions as to whether the Yakkerboo Festival still represents the community/communities that live in the place or whether organisers are vainly trying to maintain a community tradition that is no longer representative of many of those who live there.

Also part of Melbourne's encroaching urban sprawl, the City of Casey is home to a rapidly increasing and highly diverse community. The local authority, in trying to address policy objectives of improving social cohesion and promoting tolerance of the diversity of their community, set up the Experience! Casey Multicultural Festival. This festival has been running for only a few years, but it has a very strong ethic of inclusion. The festival offers opportunities for various community groups (ethnic, cultural and religious) to showcase their traditions such as singing, dancing, food and drinks. Yet, creating and showcasing a multicultural festival to promote diversity may, at the same time, be highlighting the difference that surrounds us, highlighting this difference as 'other', and emphasising divisions between us and them.

In Clunes, Victoria, a group of interested locals created a book festival to try to revive a dying agricultural community, with a great deal of success. Clunes is now an International Book Town, has improved amenities and facilities and is enjoying economic improvements. However, our case study draws attention to the ways that the success of the book festival has changed the make-up of the local community, drawing the 'sea-' and 'tree-changing' class to create their version of the rural idyll and potentially excluding the existing agricultural community from their visions for the future of the town.

Finally, the Noosa Jazz Festival has been running for more than 20 years, providing fun and entertainment, as well as a boost to tourist numbers, for the town of Noosa. Noosa is a very affluent town, with high property prices, elegant buildings and a beautiful beach. This suggests that the community is exclusive, with the usual financial barriers to access. However, an examination of the Noosa Jazz Festival, using the notion of embodiment and drawing on sensual geographies, allows us to understand how well the music at this particular event permits participation even by those who cannot afford to pay high prices for ticketed entry. Emotion and affect – listening, watching, feeling – permit the inclusion of all in an apparently exclusive event. This highlights the importance of taking an alternative viewpoint to examine the issue of inclusion/exclusion.

This book has highlighted some of the key points of our research to date, but the one thing that stands out to us is just how much more research is needed before we can truly say that we understand festivals and the encounters that they facilitate.

Index

-rural interface105–6, 119, 159; -rural relations 47, 127–8, 131, 134–5
Urry, John 52

Vannini, Phillip 65
volunteer/volunteering: issues for 16, 89, 108, 113; and social capital 100, 101, 132–3, 158; and social inclusion 86–7, 91, 106, 112, 136

Waitt, Gordon 63, 67, 68, 142
White: Australia 48; community 133; non- 65; power 6, 122
Wilks, Linda 100–1

Yakkerboo Festival 7, 78, 106–14, 159

Žižek, Slavoj 55

Printed in the United States
by Baker & Taylor Publisher Services